D1710250

Alien Imaginations

Alien Imaginations

Science Fiction and Tales of Transnationalism

Edited by Ulrike Küchler, Silja Maehl, and
Graeme Stout

Foreword by Dame Gillian Beer

Bloomsbury Academy
An Imprint of Bloomsbury Publishing Inc

B L O O M S B U R Y
NEW YORK · LONDON · NEW DELHI · SYDNEY

Bloomsbury Academic

An imprint of Bloomsbury Publishing Inc

1385 Broadway	50 Bedford Square
New York	London
NY 10018	WC1B 3DP
USA	UK

www.bloomsbury.com

BLOOMSBURY and the Diana logo are trademarks of Bloomsbury Publishing Plc

First published 2015

Library of Congress Cataloging-in-Publication Data
Alien imaginations : science fiction and tales of transnationalism / [edited by] Graeme Stout, Ulrike Küchler, Silja Maehl.
pages cm
Includes bibliographical references and index.
ISBN 978-1-62892-115-1 (hardback)
1. Science fiction films—History and criticism.   2. Science fiction, American—History and criticism.   3. Science fiction, English—History and criticism.   4. Alienation (Social psychology) in motion pictures.   5. Alienation (Social psychology) in literature.
I. Stout, Graeme A., editor.   II. Küchler, Ulrike, editor.   III. Maehl, Silja.
PN1995.9.S26A43 2015
809.3'8762–dc23
2014029816

ISBN: HB: 978-1-6289-2115-1
ePUB: 978-1-6289-2116-8
ePDF: 978-1-6289-2117-5

Typeset by RefineCatch Limited, Bungay, Suffolk
Printed and bound in the United States of America

Contents

Notes on Contributors

Dame Gillian Beer was educated at St Anne's College, Oxford. A Fellow at Girton College, Cambridge, between 1965 and 1994, Gillian Beer began lecturing at Cambridge in 1966 and became Reader in Literature and Narrative in 1971. She was made Professor of English in 1989 and in 1994 became King Edward VII Professor of English Literature and President of Clare Hall at Cambridge. She is a Fellow of the British Academy and of the Royal Society of Literature, and a Foreign Honorary Member of the American Academy of Arts and Sciences and of the American Philosophical Society. Her books include *Darwin's Plots: Evolutionary Narrative in Darwin, George Eliot and Nineteenth-Century Fiction* (1983), *Virginia Woolf: the Common Ground* (1996), and *Open Fields: Science in Cultural Encounter* (1999). Exploring the relationship between the worlds of literature and science in nineteenth century writing as well as the relations between literature, science, and psychoanalysis, Gillian Beer has made major contributions to the theory and practice of interdisciplinary studies.

Andrew M. Butler is a senior lecturer at Canterbury Christ Church University and the author of *Solar Flares: Science Fiction in the 1970s*, as well as books on Philip K. Dick, cyberpunk, Terry Pratchett, Postmodernism, and film studies. He has edited books on Ken MacLeod, Terry Pratchett, and Christopher Priest and was the co-editor of *The Routledge Companion to Science Fiction* and *Fifty Key Figures in Science Fiction*, as well as the journal *Extrapolation*. His article, "Thirteen Ways of Looking at the British Boom," won the Pioneer Award. He is the non-voting Chair of Judges for the Arthur C. Clarke Award. Currently, he is researching the cognitive uncanny.

Jen Caruso earned a PhD in Comparative Literature with a specialization in critical theory and modernist literature from the State University of New York at Buffalo and an MA in Theory and Criticism from the Center for the Study of Theory and Criticism at the University of Western Ontario. She is Assistant Professor of Liberal Arts at the Minneapolis College of Art and Design and the University of Minnesota. Her research interests include future-present science fiction, cultural responses to ecological crisis, and fashion in literature and film.

Matthew Goodwin, PhD, is a Lecturer in Comparative Literature at the University of Massachusetts Amherst. His research and teaching interests are centered on migration as represented in multiethnic and world literature, with an emphasis on Latino/a literature. Other areas of interest include food and immigration, digital culture, science fiction, critical theory, and aesthetics. His current book project explores US Latino/a science fiction and digital culture.

Célia Guimarães Helene, MA, is an independent scholar and was an adjunct professor of English Literature and Technical and Literary Translation at Mackenzie Presbyterian University, São Paulo, Brazil until 2012. Prior to this, she had been the coordinator of the language and translation courses at Mackenzie Presbyterian University, São Paulo. Her research interests include American, British, Irish, South African, and Australian literature.

Joela Jacobs is currently completing her PhD in Germanic Studies at the University of Chicago. Her dissertation examines a persistent engagement with the ambiguity of the human and non-human in literary grotesques of German modernism from Oskar Panizza to Franz Kafka. Joela's main areas of research within nineteenth- to twenty-first-century literature and German film are animal studies, the history of science, posthumanism, the history of sexuality, biopolitics, classification systems and hybridity, theories of the monstrous, censorship, Jewish identity, and multilingualism.

Ulrike Küchler is currently completing her PhD in Comparative Literature at Freie Universität Berlin, Germany. She worked as a lecturer at Freie Universität Berlin, Eberhard Karls Universität Tübingen, Germany, and Brown University, USA, and was a visiting scholar at the University of Cambridge, UK. Her teaching and research focuses on art and artificial life in science fiction and on the relation between aesthetics and new media. She has published on cultural history, science fiction, and media aesthetics. Her current projects examine the aesthetics of old and new media and explore themes, modes, and forms of digital storytelling.

Silja Maehl is currently completing her PhD in German Studies at Brown University. Her dissertation examines the role of bilingualism and translation in the works of Georges-Arthur Goldschmidt and Yoko Tawada. She has published on Yoko Tawada in the collection *New Perspectives on German Women Writers and the Spatial Turn* (forthcoming with De Gruyter). Her main areas of interest are literary multilingualism, transnational writing, translation, psychoanalysis, and twentieth- and twenty-first-century literature.

Emilie McCabe, MA, is an independent scholar who lives and works in Toronto. Through the lens of Michel Foucault's theories of "technologies of power" and "technologies of the self," her research centers on the role that science fiction plays in the current understanding of human subjectivity. Due to the speculative nature of the genre, science fiction is uniquely able to lay bare the dominant discourses—such as gender, technology, and language—that inform subjectivity while simultaneously proposing new and different ways of understanding what it means to be human.

John Mowitt holds the Leadership Chair in the Critical Humanities at the University of Leeds. He was formerly professor in the department of Cultural Studies and Comparative Literature at the University of Minnesota. His publications range widely over the fields of culture, politics, and theory. In 2008 he collaborated with the composer Jarrod Fowler to transfigure his book, *Percussion: Drumming, Beating, Striking*, from a printed to a sonic text/performance, "'Percussion' as Percussion." His *Radio: Essays in Bad Reception* appeared in 2011 from the University of California Press, and his current book, *Sounds*, is also forthcoming from California. In addition, he is a senior co-editor of the journal *Cultural Critique*.

Andrew Opitz is an assistant professor of English at Hawaii Pacific University. His research interests include transatlantic literature, transpacific media studies, and representations of utopian/dystopian communities in fantasy and science fiction. He has written for journals such as *Comparative Literature, Cultural Politics, Cultural Critique, Darkmatter*, and *African American Review*, and has recently started a research project examining former plantation economies and debates about sustainability and food security in both Hawaii and the Caribbean.

Gerrit K. Rößler received his PhD in German literature and culture from the University of Virginia in 2013 and is the director of the German Academic International Network (GAIN) at the German Academic Exchange Service (DAAD) in New York City. He worked as assistant adjunct professor at Queens College, CUNY from 2011 to 2012. Currently, he is working on a book on utopian imaginaries in radio drama. He has published a chapter on religious fundamentalism in American popular culture in *The Politics of Post-9/11 Music: Sound,*

Trauma, and the Music Industry in the Time of Terror (2011) and on horror in science fiction in *Dawn of an Evil Millennium: Horror und Kultur im neuen Jahrtausend* (2011).

Graeme Stout is Senior Lecturer and Film Studies Coordinator in the Department of Cultural Studies and Comparative Literature at the University of Minnesota. Prior to this, he was a visiting scholar at the Minneapolis College of Art and Design. His teaching and research focus on the nature, deployment, and transformation of power in the modern age, and the relationship of aesthetic form to social consciousness. He has published articles on Italian cinema, American television, and the visual arts. His current book project studies the cultural legacy of terrorism in Italy and Germany from the late 1960s to the present day.

Bianca Westermann, PhD, received her doctoral degree in Media Studies in 2010. She is a research and teaching assistant (Wissenschaftliche Mitarbeiterin) in the Department of Media Studies at Ruhr-Universität Bochum. Her current research interests include robots, cyborgs, and prostheses as well as postmodern identity in digital media.

Foreword

Dame Gillian Beer
King Edward VII Professor Emeritus
at the University of Cambridge, UK

This collection of essays probes two contradictory incentives, common to all organisms: the urge to migrate and the urge to stay put, protecting territory. The pressure created by these irreconcilable impulses fuels the energy of much literature, and particularly of science fiction. Life is always on the move. Migration is the natural condition, from the passages of cells, to migrating birds, to plants finding fresh environments, to laborers on foreign projects, to war- and famine-displaced people, and all those organisms, human and other kinds, seeking opportunities elsewhere. It is not a privileged condition; rather, one necessary for survival. And those who arrive seemingly powerless may prove to be the drivers of change quite as often as those who arrive as invaders and conquerors. In *The Mara Crossing*, Ruth Padel brilliantly demonstrates through poetry and prose writing how all things, including hosts and parasites, evolve together through movement and change. "Parasites drove evolution. When their hosts evolved ways of protecting themselves, parasites adapted to evade the policing and the host had to adapt further to protect itself [. . .]. Today parasites make up most life on earth and outnumber other living species by four to one" (2012: 19f.). These proliferating incomers are by no means easily welcomed by the biota already established in a place. And that incursion and resistance forms one of the major topics of the essays gathered here, which trace boundary transgression, border control, and alien anxiety.

Colonizing, invasion, and war are the forms of arrival that involve killing, enslaving, even extirpating those who are there already and mounting a new culture over their remains. Science fiction has in the past, and still in cinema, offered many examples of that kind of violent take-over, or heroic resistance to that attempted take-over. A theme that has developed out of that violence is the invasive power of market forces that disrupt an originary and usually islanded community, as in *Avatar* (2009) where the main character switches to side with the indigenous people in a way that brings to light the uneasy relationship between empathy and treachery. Bianca Westermann's essay here, for example, uses this and other films to probe the twenty-first-century search for "unambiguousness" after postmodern reliance on the ambiguous. Andrew Opitz examines the "interplanetary logic of late capitalism" through Philip K. Dick's *The Three Stigmata of Palmer Eldritch* (1965), which, he argues, sheds light, albeit unwittingly, on our current global predicament "in which capital crosses borders while most of the population remains trapped on islands of poverty and ice caps melt and sea levels rise."

One of globalization's most striking effects is to turn us all into foreigners: there is no longer an enclosed homeland within which to dwell. Globalization has certainly created new psychological and social troubles that can be explored intensely in science fiction. The stress on the universal breeds a compensatory counter-emphasis on the constrained, on small-time nationalism, on claimed autochthony. Instead of the ideal of nomadism, developed by Rosi Braidotti in the 1990s (see Braidotti 2011), there is a current turn to idealizing the local, the particular, the ethnically "pure." Despite the leveling effects of an imagined global community, each of us has also to learn that we are the alien, however much "the others" may appear monstrous. In the emphasis on "the other" we may avoid learning that each of us—*and* that communal "we"—is other too. Age, class, color, money, all curtail access to parts familiar to others: and that applies to the old, the young, women, men, the poor, the rich, the black, the white: not equally, in all places, but pressingly in the places where you don't feel "at home." This unease is what science fiction thrives on and compels us to pay attention to.

Science fiction takes on the task of alienation. It helps us to learn how to be foreigners. That task was central to travel literature in the nineteenth and early twentieth centuries, and the two genres lie close alongside each other. In travel literature marvels are expected and skepticism is allowed. The *science* in science fiction demands a different kind of belief. In science fiction we learn to look at the world as a foreign place. We must dwell on the threshold between our known order and the different compulsions of these imagined orders. We experience multiple identifications: with incomers, with blended beings such as cyborgs, and with stalwart native inhabitants.

These reversed, swerved, and reluctant indwellings make us see what's strange in current organizations of experience. Margaret Atwood's work is particularly adept at forcing a tendency to its possible extreme and taking us into a culture entirely clustered along that trajectory. She does it with gender and patriarchal oppression in *The Handmaid's Tale* (1985) and with post-apocalypse survival in her violent and compassionate trilogy, which also delves into the longing to reach back to a primitive communal innocence through the movement, God's Gardeners.[1] In the present collection, essays on "migrants and the dystopian state" and "abjection and the construction of race and gender" explore other such works that radically disturb our current assumptions of what constitutes natural order and thus force our attention back onto how we live now.

Travel literature thrives on remoteness and so does much science fiction. But another powerful strain in science fiction is that of the controlled experiment in which just one feature of our current organization is shifted so that we can mark more precisely the ensuing and mounting deviations. Here, John Mowitt offers an intricate account of the slippages within language and within the reproductive capacities of the present order in "Was of the Worlds" and Jen Caruso examines the embodied symptoms of globalization in shifts between two of William Gibson's novels.

But there is another aspect to what is scientific in science fiction, and that is learning how to observe, which can only be fully achieved through a mixture of conscious alienation and empathy at once. That fusion can be one of the most telling achievements of science fiction as a form of thought experiment. It issues particularly strongly out of the tradition of the scientific travel writer. The scientific traveler differs from the hero of many travel tales in that he (she) is presented as a reliable narrator, writing in pursuance of fact, knowledge, and revelation. These principles can be reached only by coming to acknowledge that the self and the home country are not normative.

I give, as an extended example of observation, misconstrual, and alienation, Darwin's early land voyages during his five-year journey round the world on HMS *Beagle* in the 1830s. Such writing lies behind science fiction's tonic inquiry into how we can manage transnational living now. Darwin learnt to become a fabulous observer: untiring, committed, open-minded, and intimately attentive to all the phenomena that concerned him, whether climbing plants, fossil trees, ants, worms, barnacles, dogs, orchids, or people from multiple cultures.

In the course of five years Darwin observed creatures, plants, fossils, and mountains—and he observed and interacted with a great variety of indigenous peoples whom he met in the course of his journeying by sea and land. These people were in the main at home, in their own country. The young Darwin was the foreign observer. But, like many of us, he found that idea hard to stomach and showed a certain incredulity when *he* was treated as the alien. He had to learn to be foreign. There's a nice example when he is traveling in Chile. Indeed, the episode is instructive in relation to the questions "What is it to be foreign?" and "Who is the foreigner?" since it involves several degrees of foreignness.

"A German collector in natural history" has a conversation with "an old Spanish lawyer," a Chilean, which the German then, somewhat mischievously, repeats to Darwin: this is how Darwin describes the episode in *The Voyage of the Beagle*:

> One day, a German collector in natural history, of the name of Renous, called, and nearly at the same time an old Spanish lawyer. I was amused at being told the conversation which took place between them. Renous speaks Spanish so well, that the old lawyer mistook him for a Chilean. Renous, alluding to me, asked him what he thought of the King of England sending out a collector to their country, to pick up lizards and beetles, and to break stones? The old gentleman thought seriously for some time, and then said, "It is not well—*hay un gato encerrado aqui* (there's a cat shut up here). No man is so rich as to send out people to pick up such rubbish. I do not like it: if one of us were to go and do such things in England, do not you think the King of England would very soon send us out of his country?"
>
> Darwin 2001: 239–40

Notice that the lawyer imagines the German collector to be "one of us," a native of the country, so well does he speak Spanish. Therefore he does not figure *him* as a foreigner. Effectively, the German naturalist acts as double agent, speaking English in private to Darwin and Spanish to his local friends (language is one of the tests of affinity and assimilation in many science fictions). Darwin is amused by the reported conversation, he claims. But he doesn't quite get its full implication. Darwin reports the Spanish saying that "there's a cat shut up here," but it is not at all clear that he understands that the lawyer thinks him a spy—or at least as involved in some covert dealings since his overt occupation is so manifestly absurd: picking up lizards and beetles and breaking stones. Darwin caps the story with a self-righteous comment implying how ill-educated even the most educated here must be: "And this old gentleman, from his profession, belongs to the better informed and more intelligent classes!" (240). Who is the foreigner in this tale? And who has failed to understand the clues so manifest to local people, or to particular professions—and so obscure to others? Both the Spanish lawyer and the British Darwin. Only the German collector operates freely across the various zones. The German collector is professionally at home with Darwin in their shared natural history preoccupations and their European background, and he is at home with the Chilean Spanish lawyer so excellent is his Spanish and so habituated is he to the society.

But he is not always exempt from the dangers of foreignness—as Darwin reveals with perhaps some slight satisfaction in the next anecdote.

> Renous himself, two or three years before, left in a house in San Fernando some caterpillars, under charge of a girl to feed, that they might turn into butterflies. This was rumoured through the town, and at last the padres and Governor consulted together, and agreed it must be some heresy. Accordingly, when Renous returned, he was arrested.
>
> Darwin 2001: 240

Here is another kind of exclusion and understanding of what it is to be foreign: heresy perverts proper local belief and authority (which believes itself to be universal, so calls in religious sanctions). Spanish Catholicism is particularly emblematic of the foreign to Darwin, who is still at this time considering becoming an Anglican clergyman. The Hispanic presence in South America is often associated with a violent colonialism and slave culture in Darwin's descriptions, even while at other times he enjoys its stately hospitality. Much later in the journey, in Van Dieman's Land (Tasmania), he at last cannot avoid recognizing what his own countrymen have done in colonial subjugation.

The idea of heresy has to do with what's considered important in a community: how could a grown man pay money to have trivial creatures like caterpillars looked after? Caterpillars turn into butterflies: that's the order of things and unremarkable. Only foreigners would make a fuss about it. Foreigners disturb the social order by paying attention to what we take for granted. That is one of their most disconcerting propensities. They are thus readily seen as spies or heretics. Scientific observers may come under similar suspicion. That strain from scientific travel writing enters science fiction and its paranoid under-song.

Alien encounter is one of the staples of science fiction. It often takes the form of a solitary traveler meeting a being or society inconceivably other, yet one that gradually becomes more and more intimately known and identified with the narrator, often through experiences of the arts. That trope is drawn from travel literature too (Samuel Butler's *Erewhon*, 1872, with its musical statues and Handellian harmonies is poised on the threshold between travel literature and science fiction in this way). This rich ground is studied here in essays by Ulrike Küchler and by Emilie McCabe, who considers the re-imagining of gender through the exchange of cultural objects. The collection as a whole succeeds in demonstrating new ways of understanding the importance of science fiction, particularly as a tool of cultural investigation.

Note

1   *Oryx and Crake* (2003), *The Year of the Flood* (2009), *MaddAdam* (2013).

References

Braidotti, R. (2011), *Nomadic Subjects*, New York: Columbia University Press.
Darwin, C. ([1839] 2001), *Voyage of the Beagle*, New York: Modern Library.
Padel, R. (2012), *The Mara Crossing*, London: Chatto and Windus.

Acknowledgments

Such a volume does not come together without the help and support of many people who work tirelessly behind the scenes. Special thanks are due to Mary Al-Sayed, Katie Gallof, and Laura Murray from Bloomsbury, who each provided an infinite reserve of help, encouragement, and patience as we moved through the process, from proposal to press. Our many authors showed a great deal of professionalism and enthusiasm in greeting the challenges of developing such a project. They have our thanks. Additional thanks go to Mark Bould and Chris Love whose early support helped move this project ahead. We are indebted to Dame Gillian Beer for her assistance and willingness to provide an excellent foreword to the collection as well as to Sherryl Vint, William Stephenson, and John Namjun Kim for the invaluable feedback and advice on earlier versions of the project.

The first iteration of this book project started at the American Comparative Literature Association meeting in Vancouver in 2011. Over the years the project has grown and the cast of participants and writers has similarly developed. We are certain, however, that without the opportunity that the three-day seminar afforded us and the ideas and conversations that emerged from the presentations, the overall project would never have evolved as it did.

Introduction

Ulrike Küchler, Silja Maehl, and Graeme Stout

In his essay "The Stranger," originally published in 1908 as an excursus to a book chapter on the sociology of space, Georg Simmel describes the stranger as the exemplary liminal figure: he is at once near and far, a member of a group but moving at its periphery. In order to distinguish the stranger from the alien, Simmel extends his argument into outer space: "The inhabitants of Sirius are not really strangers to us, at least not in any social logically relevant sense: they do not exist for us at all; they are beyond far and near" (1971: 143–4). Thus separating the alien categorically from the stranger, Simmel does not take seriously the imaginative power that "other worlds" have exercised upon the minds of science fiction writers, theorists, and enthusiasts alike. The appeal of science fiction, which can be the most creative and wondrous mode of writing available to us today, is that its visions hold the potential to reveal a good deal about the societies in which they are conceived. One premise of this collection, therefore, is that the most alien may be furthest removed from us spatially or temporally, but it also lies at the heart of modern and postmodern consciousness. The absences or gaps of knowledge we have concerning the alien are filled by our imagination as to the nature of this foreignness. Consequently, that which appears the most alien resides within rather than outside of us.

As the essays in this volume demonstrate, a joint discussion of strangers and extraterrestrials extends the critical scope that Simmel saw for the stranger by pointing to the hypothetical encounter with the extraterrestrial as a means of working through terrestrial encounters between peoples. In order to emphasize the critical potential of science fiction and to move beyond the confines of genre—boundaries that are especially limiting and even undesirable to maintain in the case of science fiction—this book offers a perspective on the alien that connects to recent experiences and scholarship on transnationalism, immigration, and border policing, building on the dialectical interaction between its imaginations and material realities of the flows of people and capital.

Imagining the alien

While the alien is first and foremost a universal other or another (lat. *alius*), the English word more specifically designates a foreigner: someone who is not a naturalized citizen of his country of residence. For most, however, the word "alien" conjures up images of extraterrestrials. In either use of the term, we find someone or something that is out of place and which confronts us with its alterity. Fictions of travel, migration, and transnationalism as well as science fiction deal with varying degrees of otherness: whereas science fiction imagines a complete other along with a possible future world, the foreigners on Earth are temporary strangers (e.g. guests and tourists), precarious peoples (e.g. refugees or settlers), or permanent outsiders on the inside (e.g. resident aliens), they seek acceptance and integration or demand their otherness to be recognized as such. As the undocumented immigrant or refugee, the alien has challenged the nation-state and our universal, inalienable rights; as the creature from outer space, the alien allows us to imagine something that is truly foreign and, through its eyes, to look at ourselves as if from the outside. As an overarching concept, the alien is a powerful interdisciplinary one that encourages us to rethink antinomies of inside and outside, self and other.

This volume seeks to understand the speculative draw of the alien, as our social and cultural imagination relies heavily, if not entirely, on that which is outside of it as a means of self-conscious understanding through dissociation. The title, *Alien Imaginations*, can thus be read in three ways: it refers to the way we as humans imagine the alien, whether the foreigner or the creature from outer space. It could also refer to the way the alien imagines *us*, how the alien looks back upon us "as through a glass darkly." Finally, alien serves as an adjective that, like Freud's *uncanny*, points to a quality that slips between the known and the unknown, the certain and the uncertain. While the alien as the stranger or foreigner enables us to distinguish between what is known and what is unknown, what is familiar and what is not, it is important to remember how the alien is not a figure that can be separated from the society and the discourse that has created it and into which it enters as a critical reflection. In fact, the alien is not a figure at all, in an ontological sense, but instead a representation within our cultural imagination. As Sara Ahmed rightly points out, "it is the processes of expelling *or* welcoming the one who is recognized as a stranger that produce the figure of the stranger in the first place" (2000: 4). Representing the danger of the unknown as such, the same is true, to a greater extent, of the alien: "the alien stranger is hence not beyond human, but a mechanism *for allowing us to face that which we have already designated as the beyond*" (3, emphasis in the original).

Drawing on, among others, Benedict Anderson's examination of the creation of nations as *Imagined Communities*, Arjun Appadurai in *Modernities at Large* characterizes our contemporary world as a complex postnational construction of "imaginary landscapes" (1996: 31). He posits the imagination as "the key component of the new global order," defining it as a "social fact":

> No longer mere fantasy (opium for the masses whose real work is elsewhere), no longer simple escape (from a world defined principally by more concrete purposes and structures), no longer elite pastime (thus not relevant to the lives of ordinary people), and no longer mere contemplation (irrelevant for new forms of desire and subjectivity), the imagination has become an organized field of social practices, a form of work (in the sense of both labor and culturally organized practice), and a form of negotiation between sites of agency (individuals) and globally defined fields of possibility.
>
> Appadurai 1996: 31

Appadurai's reading of imagination resonates in the title of our collection, in which alien imaginations are not read as escapist fantasies, a "criticism" that science fiction often undeservingly receives, but as a material force in the world. From a Marxist perspective, such a reading of imagination takes ideology to be not simply an illusion, but an active and transformative force within the social world, one that can change history.

At the height of modernity, before the twentieth century marked itself as one of the bloodiest in human history, Simmel's evocation of the stranger and the alien looks both backwards and forwards. At the end of European colonial expansion, the figure of the stranger speaks to larger histories of "first contact" between different cultures, societies, and world views. Simmel's stranger also looks ahead to a century that, according to Hannah Arendt, would be defined by the refugee, the stateless masses "who, unlike their happier predecessors in the religious wars, were welcomed nowhere and could be assimilated nowhere" (1973: 267). The alien stands for the dispossessed who cannot be reconciled within the normal state of political life. It is an exception that undermines the rule. As such it has a self-critical force that functions on a collective as well as an individual level. Bernhard Waldenfels sees the alien as a chaotic concept that undermines ontological certainty:

> If we take the alien [...] as something that cannot be pinned down, if we take it as something that seeks us out in our own home (German *heimsuchen*) by disturbing, enticing, or terrifying us, by surpassing our expectations and eluding our grasp, then this means that *the* alien always affects our own experience and thus turns into a *becoming-alien of experience*. Alienness is self-referential, and it is contagious.
>
> 2011: 3, emphases in the original

Shifting registers, we can think of Waldenfels' reading of the alien as a reading of the figure of the alien in literature and film. If Waldenfels offers a particular hypothetical, phenomenological approach to the study of the alien, the essays in *Alien Imaginations* seek to build on such theoretical models while connecting them to the political and cultural histories of the twentieth and twenty-first centuries, centuries defined by national and ideological conflicts.

"Alien studies"

As many critics have noted, science fiction's encounters with alien others are inspired by ethnographical accounts and the history of imperialism and colonialism (see Dame Gillian Beer's foreword to this collection). Other lands and travel narratives have always exerted an immense influence on the human imagination as they offer the chance to think and dream, as both are social acts, in ways that escape and even confront the ordinary. Early European science fiction has been modeled on European travel narratives and thought-experiments about other worlds—from Montaigne and Fontenelle to Swift and Voltaire. In Fontenelle's *Entretiens sur la pluralité des mondes* (*Conversations on the Plurality of Worlds*, 1686), for instance, we witness how the idea of an expansive universe and the possibility of extraterrestrial life helps the natural philosopher to appreciate the joys of discovery while, at the same time, serving as a thinly veiled metaphor for European encounters with the peoples of the "New World." By the end of the nineteenth century with the emergence of invasion literature, the alien was transformed into a threat to national, linguistic, and racial boundaries and identities (e.g. Wells, Lovecraft, Heinlein).

Works such as Ray Bradbury's short story "Dark They Were, and Golden-Eyed" (1949) or Philip K. Dick's *The Three Stigmata of Palmer Eldritch* (1965), address real-life issues of racism, colonialism, and citizenship. By the late twentieth century, the threatening figure of the alien (both the extraterrestrial and the refugee) was frequently replaced by a sympathetic one (e.g. Le Guin, Miéville, Arnason) that allowed us to interrogate our own post-national existence.

We conceive of our collection of essays as part of a larger discussion that has emerged within science fiction studies of the past decade. Academic studies of the literature and cinema of science fiction have, most often, been housed within English departments and have had, for obvious reasons, a particularly Anglophone orientation. Recently, studies of science fiction have engaged quite productively with issues surrounding both science fiction and post-colonial studies. Two monographs that develop both fields while arguing for their essential relationships are John Rieder's *Colonialism and Emergence of Science Fiction* (2008) and Jessica Langer's *Postcolonialism and Science Fiction* (2012). Two collections of essays that continue and expand upon the ideas and interests of these books are Hoagland and Sarwal's *Science Fiction, Imperialism and the Third World* (2010) and Ashraf Raja et al.'s *The Postnational Fantasy* (2011). The breadth of the essays and the literary and cinematic works they analyze point to the robust nature of the intersection of science fiction and postcolonial studies.

Building on thinkers such as Arjun Appadurai, Zygmunt Bauman, Seyla Benhabib, and Saskia Sassen and their analyses of the global order, a 2012 issue of *Science Fiction Studies* undertook to examine what a globalized version of science fiction studies would be and how it would help to develop both the fields of science fiction and globalization studies. Building on the analysis of John Rieder and others, Roger Luckhurst notes that, with nineteenth- and early twentieth-century colonial expansion, world's fairs and exhibitions became fertile ground for science fictional thinking as "early laboratories for immersive capitalist dreamworlds" (2012: 397). Following in a similar theoretical trajectory, Eric D. Smith's *Globalization, Utopia and Postcolonial Science Fiction: New Maps of Hope* (2012) offers an innovative and even optimistic investigation of utopian and speculative fiction from around the world. Together, these works speak to a larger shift in studies of science fiction to expand its generic and cultural horizons as well as a trend in postcolonial and globalization studies to look to utopian venues for a new understanding of the cultural transformations of our current age. *Alien Imaginations* places itself within this larger dialogue between science fiction and critical studies of the global age.

Border experiences

In his introduction to a recent issue of *Science Fiction Studies,* David Higgins
notes how science fiction not only records "the imprint of globalization on
artistic and cultural productions," but how speculative literature can also "theo-
rize globalization" by providing insights into the practices and implications of
global interconnectivity. The guiding question emerging out of this two-way
relation is: how does science fiction reflect upon and challenge global regimes of
social, economic, and political power? The literature and films under discussion
in this volume engage with this question. While most of these works are European
and North American in origin, their critical intent and potential undermine
many of the central notions of Western hegemonic discourses: key amongst
these is that of the nation.

A unifying theme among the essays in our collection is the transgressive
force of travel and the concomitant crossing of geographical, cultural, or
linguistic borders. As Sandro Mezzadra and Brett Neilson argue in their recent
Border As Method, Or the Multiplication of Labor, the border has inscribed
itself at the center of our contemporary experience as material and symbolic
boundaries "overlap, connect, and disconnect in often unpredictable ways,
contributing to shaping new forms of domination and exploitation" (2013: vii).
What ensues from this movement, be it between and across material or symbolic
borders, is, on the one hand, the both liberating and frightening awareness that
some clear-cut divisions, which have previously been validated, become increasingly impossible to maintain: state boundaries and the rules and regulations of
capital and work forces are, in many ways, rendered "invisible." On the other
hand, we might become aware of the existence of previously unregistered
boundaries within a world taken for granted: the self and that which we presumed
to be "ours" is now perceived as always already traversed by the alien. This collection traces boundary transgression and migration, border flow and control, as
well as alien anxiety and "stranger danger" (Sara Ahmed) as some of the unifying
themes of science fiction and tales of transnationalism—that is, narratives
conceived outside of a national setting and canon—arguing that stories of aliens,
cyborgs, and other liminal beings have much in common with the fates of
(im)migrants.

The essays in the collection are deliberately not divided along generic,
regional, linguistic, or chronological lines. Rather, they are arranged according to

the similarities of their approaches and themes. In this way, they can enter into a cross-cultural and interdisciplinary dialogue with one another without being confined to the very categories that this volume attempts to transgress. Although many of the authors' approaches and texts are anchored within national literatures and cultures, all speak to a desire to "alienate" in order to critique one's own cultural preconceptions and limitations.

Part 1, **Alien Language**, starts the collection with four essays that examine issues of translation, multilingualism, the philosophy of language, and psychoanalysis through a discussion of works both classic and contemporary. As the cradle of all fiction, imaginative power is especially essential to science fiction, a mode of writing that relies heavily on literary experimentation, linguistic play and innovation, as well as creative premonition. Many of the works under analysis in this volume's essays exemplify this facet (e.g. Kubin, Zamyatin, Gibson, and Arnason). John Mowitt's deconstructive reading of H. G. Wells' *The War of the Worlds* offers an analysis of the unconscious motivations and tensions that subtend this seminal work of science fiction. In particular, the theme of invasion is given a novel import through the ultimate threat that the aliens manifest to the sociobiological foundation of the Western world. In her discussion of "Alien Art," Ulrike Küchler examines literary works of European modernity: H. G. Wells' *The Time Machine*, Alfred Kubin's *The Other Side*, and Yevgeny Zamyatin's *We*. Her essay traces a shift of the function of art—from convention via communication to cognition—in the encounter with the alien other that employs various sorts of "interart" references. Joela Jacobs unpacks the complicated relationship of ethnic identity in late Wilhelmine and early Weimar Germany through an analysis of two works: Oskar Panizza's *The Operated Jew* and Salomo Friedlaender's *The Operated Goy*. Both texts play with notions of ethnic identity and the caricatures built around Jews and Germans, by parodying the pseudo-scientific discourses of race and health through a series of physical and linguistic transformations. Silja Maehl's essay provides a close reading of selected early German texts from the collection "Talisman" by Yoko Tawada, an author living in Germany while producing two distinct bodies of work in Japanese and German. While Tawada's work is more overtly relatable to questions of multilingualism, transnationalism, and postcolonialism, her literary estrangement techniques are also similar to science fiction as a mode of writing, a reading that is supported by the central role assumed by themes of alienation, travel, and virtuality.

Part 2, **Alien Anxieties**, takes up two "contact scenarios" in science fiction: one in which aliens seek humans out on Earth—the topic of classic invasion literature—and the other in which humans explore and invade alien worlds, which is, rather euphemistically, associated with discovery and exploration. Here, however, our authors emphasize alien encounters as more than sources of fear and conflict. The four authors in this section think of anxiety in terms of the larger twentieth-century fears that still plague us and that we have yet to overcome. Key amongst these are ethnic and national conflict, racism, and environmental degradation. Andrew M. Butler's discussion of Neill Blomkamp's *District 9* questions the ways in which this film has been interpreted as a cinematic allegorization of apartheid in South Africa. Butler also discusses how the multi-layered representations of race and political violence are much more complicated and problematic than many others have argued. Through a discussion of abjection, he argues that the visceral nature of the film and its images of bodily transformation speak to larger fears associated with race and miscegenation. Similarly, Andrew Opitz's reading of Philip K. Dick's novel, *The Three Stigmata of Palmer Eldritch*, asserts that the novel has a prophetic and potentially psychotic character that critiques commodity culture and the pharmacological society of both Dick's age and our own. By reading Dick's novel alongside Blomkamp's most recent film, *Elysium*, Opitz contends that the technologically enabled transformation of the body found in literature and cinema speaks to larger social, economic, and environmental issues at work in our world. Matthew Goodwin's study of José Luis Alverdi's short story "Sugar on the Lips" ("Azúcar en los Labios"), Gabriel Trujillo Muñoz's short story "Cajunia," and Cherrie Moraga's play *The Hungry Woman: A Mexican Medea*, illuminates the ways in which the Mexico-United States border serves as a rich source for the construction of fictional dystopian states. Furthermore, his discussion points to the ways that utopian thinking is held up as a potential field of creativity and resistance. Bianca Westermann's analysis of *District 9* and *Avatar*—placed in dialogue with *The Fly* and *Dances with Wolves*—argues that the changing face of ambiguity in popular film speaks to larger transformations in postmodern culture. By comparing these films as two groups of two, Westermann makes a case for a general shift in the cultural value and import of ambiguity at the beginning of the twenty-first century.

Part 3, **Alien Identities**, uses the figure of the alien to question how identity is reshaped in the twenty-first century, both as a series of conceptual inquiries and as the reality of social life in a global age. The five essays in this section investigate new formulations of identity—both individual and collective—through investigations of gender, ethnicity, labor, migration, and cyberspace. Emilie McCabe explores the alien as an ambiguous concept where cultural discourse and sexual discourse overlap. Her essay on Eleanor Arnason's *Ring of Swords* discusses how the linkage between the migration of works of art and the migration of individuals in the novel allows for an alien encounter that, unexpectedly, leads to a peaceful understanding between two alien societies. Célia Guimarães Helene's analyses of Ray Bradbury's "Dark They Were, and Golden-Eyed" along with Archie Weller's "Going Home" focuses on the ways that two very different genres—science fiction and psychological realism—both provide us with a critical understanding of what it means for someone to live between two cultures while being accepted and understood by neither. In "Case Histories: Alienated Labor in William Gibson's *Pattern Recognition* and *Zero History*," Jen Caruso explores the role of labor and gender in the novels of William Gibson, tracing the image of the "cool hunter" as an allegorical representation of immaterial labor and commodity fetishism. Graeme Stout's essay provides a reflection on two key modes of transportation—the shipping container and the commercial jetliner—within two films by Michael Winterbottom: *In This World* and *Code 46*. Although these films differ in their generic qualities—docudrama and science fiction respectively—they share a common goal in critiquing, in both didactic and allegorical modes, the changing nature of labor, migration, and power in a transnational age. Gerrit K. Rößler's rereading " 'This is I, Hamlet the Dane!' " centers around the metamorphoses of one of the most famous figures in literary history: from I, Hamlet to iHamlet. In his essay, the migrant meets the avatar and performs the multifaceted transition between the medieval and the modern stage in a theater that employs structures and functionalities of cyberspace.

The thirteen essays collected in this volume approach the alien as an aesthetic and ontological concept that sheds light on the transition between discourses of the alien other and their fictionalization in media and arts. As individual essays they offer unique and challenging interpretations of literary and cinematic works both classical and contemporary and are marked by a diversity of texts and methodological approaches and concerns. In their various readings, the authors employ a multitude of theoretical perspectives that expand upon the previous studies of the texts they cover. This openness allows for a number of productive comparisons and associations between the essays, ideas, and texts within the volume. As a whole, *Alien Imaginations* continues to open a field of studies that brings together science fiction and transnational studies in order to present new venues for research and, above all, imagination.

References

Ahmed, S. (2000), *Strange Encounters. Embodied Others in Post-Coloniality*, London and
New York: Routledge.

Appadurai, A. (1996), *Modernity at Large. Cultural Dimensions of Globalization*,
Minneapolis, MN and London: University of Minnesota Press.

Arendt, H. (1973), *The Origins of Totalitarianism*, New York: Harcourt Brace Jovanovich.

Higgins, D. (2012), "Introduction," *Science Fiction Studies*, D. Higgins and R. Latham
(eds), 118, www.depauw.edu/sfs/abstracts/a118.html#higgins, accessed 11 July 2014.

Hoagland, E. and Sarwal, R. (2010), *Science Fiction, Imperialism and the Third World:
Essays on Postcolonial Literature and Film*, Jefferson, NC: McFarland.

Langer, J. (2011), *Postcolonialism and Science Fiction*, New York: Palgrave Macmillan.

Luckhurst, R. (2012), "Laboratories for Global Space-Time: Science-Fictionality and the
World's Fairs, 1851–1939," *Science Fiction Studies*, 118: 385–400.

Mezzadra, S. and Neilson, B. (2013), *Border as Method, Or, the Multiplication of Labor*,
Durham, NC: Duke University Press.

Raja, A. *et al.* (2011), *The Postnational Fantasy: Essays on Postcolonialism, Cosmopolitics
and Science Fiction*, Jefferson, McFarland & Co.

Rieder, J. (2008), *Colonialism and the Emergence of Science Fiction*, Middletown, CT:
Wesleyan University Press.

Simmel, G. (1971), *On Individuality and Social Forms*, Chicago and London: University
of Chicago Press.

Smith, E. D. (2012), *Globalization, Utopia, and Postcolonial Science Fiction: New Maps of
Hope*, Basingstoke: Palgrave Macmillan.

Waldenfels, B. (2011), *Phenomenology of the Alien: Basic Concepts*, A. Kozin and
T. Stähler (trans), Evanston, IL: Northwestern University Press.

Part One

Alien Language

1

"Was of the Worlds"

John Mowitt
Leeds University, UK

Linguistricks

By his own count Derrida only ever read four words of Joyce. These words, gathered in two pairs, are "he, war," and "say, yes." Doubtless, "read" means something unusual here. Be that as it may, it is the first of these pairs that will concern me here: "he, war." Although my immediate attention turns to the "war" part of the pair, in the course of my remarks the significance of the masculine pronoun, especially as it factors in the problem of the gendered reproductive dynamics of the family romance put in crisis by alien invasions of all sorts, will also emerge. Derrida reads these words, teases them out of *Finnegan's Wake*, in a set of improvised remarks given at the Centre Pompidou in 1982.[1] Although there would be a great deal to say about the entirety of Derrida's brief intervention, what I want to draw the reader's attention to is the puzzle that attracts Derrida's own. Namely, how do we read, that is, secure the sense of, a phrase that, in ceaselessly flickering between English and German makes *war* (in German) mean, in English, both war (taken as a homonym) and was (when translated)? As Derrida notes in passing he is thinking, among other things, about Freud's formula: "*Wo Es war, soll Ich werden*" (an impossible sentence that I will render as, "where the It was/*war*, the I will take its place"). But he is also thinking about Joyce's preoccupation with the Old Testament, about the violence and violation of an "I am" when displaced from the present to the past, and from first person to third. It is partly this violence that Derrida hears (and his improvisation concerns itself repeatedly with hearing) in the war that was. But he is also concerned to develop the theme of violence in relation to the unruly Babel that is figured in the audible but illegible (*war*/war) flicker between German and English, proposing that translation is impossibly fraught because, no matter how expert, a translation fails in principle to render the multiplicity of language(s) that motivates it. Indeed, beyond suggesting that every war that ever was, was one because those who made it were haunted by some was, some past, Derrida asks us to hear in the trans-lingual homonym that war is always necessarily sparked and fanned by an irreducible alienation of the sort with which translation wrestles. For him, as if all friends were *faux amis* (in French, deceptive cognates), every utterance is overrun, overturned, by the expressive potential that enables it. Here, our relation to war and was is the same (they say the same thing) without being identical (they say it differently). This is a perplexing thought and in an effort to grapple with its suggestive implications, I want to turn to a reading of H. G. Wells' oft-reiterated "scientific romance," *The War of the Worlds* (1898).[2]

The particular angle of my reading, however, is captured, in effect crystallized, in the opening sequence of Barry Sonnenfeld's *Men in Black* (retronymically now referred to as MIB1 in light of the franchise tentatively brought to completion in the summer of 2011 with MIB3). Tommy Lee Jones, who appears in the scene and stars (along with Will Smith) in the film, has claimed authorship of the segment, characterizing it as a "joke" in the Special Features commentary that accompanies the DVD of the film. Although there is no evidence that Jones is conversant with Freud's study of *Witz*, the scene suggests that his unconscious is.

Its opening shot effects a decisive transition between the cinematic and the filmic, that is, it moves us from the title sequence (common to the cinematic mode of production) to the first piece of the diegesis, to the first step in the plot of *this* film. The shot, massively dependent on CGI effects, tracks an insect as it smashes into a windshield. As Thierry Kuntzel might have insisted (1980: 8–25), we have just seen the entire film: a creature descending from the sky has been reduced to goo on an utterly ordinary avatar of the cinema, a windshield. Be that as it may, this windshield belongs to a truck smuggling Mexicans across the Mexico-US border at night. As if anticipating the current impasses of the debate over immigration reform in the United States, the truck is almost immediately intercepted by the border patrol. As the patrol begins to search the truck, their work is interrupted by the arrival of a second car, this one containing two "men in black," one of whom is Sonnenfeld in a cameo walk-on. The other is Tommy Lee Jones, who orders the border patrol to back off, which they do, deferring to his authority. In reasonably fluent Spanish, Jones orders the Mexicans huddled into the back of the truck out into a lineup where an interrogation begins. Quickly, he isolates one figure in the lineup—someone revealed by the shibboleth of the Spanish language—then, to the consternation of the border patrol, he instructs the others simply to "*váyanse*," to "go" in the imperative.

This begins the second segment of the sequence where the figure isolated is soon revealed to be Mikey, an extraterrestrial, hidden beneath the sartorial markers of "Mexicanness." Jones violently slits through the costume exposing, as he puts it when later recounting the "joke," the illegal alien inside the *illegal alien*. Predictably, it is at this moment that the patience of the border patrol thins to breaking point. One of them approaches from the rear, Mikey sees him and rushes to destroy him. After some plot enabling fumbling, Jones draws a weapon and reduces Mikey to goo, saving the border patrol officer while simultaneously motivating the use of a "neurolyzer," a device that wipes the memories of those exposed to it without the characteristic sunglasses of the "men in black." In the dialogue, the neurolyzer is significantly presented as an explanatory device and a memory bomb. If Freud's formula cited above can also be rendered as "consciousness rises instead of a memory-trace" (Freud 2001: 25), then the neurolyzer is also an instance of the war/*war* overlap that interested him.

While the scene achieves many effects (for example, reminding us that borders are policed as much by knowledge as by patrols or fences) and commits many blunders (for example, accepting the characterization of undocumented Mexican workers as illegal aliens), it is its haunting presentation of the overlap between immigrants and extraterrestrials that holds our attention and invites elaboration. My interest here is not in the mere linguistic fact that *alien* functions as a heteronym in English, but in the social fantasy that allows immigrants to provide extraterrestrials with ubiquity, and extraterrestrials to provide immigrants with menace.[3]

Alienations

Doubtless, one is hard-pressed to say much if anything new about a text as well-combed as *The War of the Worlds*.[4] It has been attached to Wells' biography, the British Fabians, the Copernican revolution effected by Darwin, the British empire in the late nineteenth century, the discovery of aluminum, and on and on. Surprisingly, in David Lodge's novel effort to rethink Wells' sexuality—see *A Man of Parts* (2011)—he has little if anything to say about the figure of the wife that haunts this text, and this despite the fact that he discusses Wells' wives and mistresses in relation to the corpus with a deliciously scandalized abandon. Although stressing this may suggest that my reading will center on the wife, my point will be different. Instead, I want simply to acknowledge the insurmountable challenge of saying something new, and insist upon the value of restating the familiar, differently. So in addition to the wife, I want to dwell on the figure of the Jew, and the figure of the Tasmanian in relation to "the Martians," especially as these, or more specifically their impossibly sudden arrival, figure as an instance of *scriptura interruptus*.

The figure of the Jew appears in the chapter titled "Exodus from London" (note the particular Biblical reference made). The caricature is unmistakable ("bearded," "eagle-faced") as are the behaviors (flinging himself on his "heap of coins"). In Bryan Cheyette's comprehensive *Constructions of "the Jew" in English Literature and Society* (1995), he underscores the many anti-Semitic clichés at work in this passage and Leon Stover, the editor of the critical edition of the text published by McFarland (Wells 2001), draws emphatic attention to the importance and apparent originality of Cheyette's reading. I will confess that this last strikes me as a bit odd, because this scene is painstakingly re-created (if updated and relocated) in the 1953 film by Byron Haskin and George Pal. Clearly *somebody* recognized the scene for what it was, indeed it stands out even more starkly in a plot that zooms in on Cold War Christianity for the finale. Of course, one might argue that this particular plot twist is present in the original (God in "his" wisdom did, after all, place bacteria on the Earth), but in the end too much emphasis on this dimension of the text's anti-Semitism misses something more fundamental. This has to do with the articulation of immigrants and extra-terrestrials, or more particularly with Jews and Martians.

Among the many touchstones in Cheyette's study is the Alien Act of 1905. In summarizing the impact of what was also referred to as simply the "Immigration Act," Cheyette writes: "The Immigration Act both incorporated elements of the urban working class into a racial-Imperial 'Englishness,' and, at the same time, excluded 'undesirable' Jewish 'aliens' from the shores of Britain and, thereby, severely narrowed the liberal 'idea of the Nation'" (1995: 159).

I will return to the theme of empire, but here it suffices to draw attention to the notion that the tensions of class, race, and ethnicity were active and in play during the decade prior to the parliamentary decision that took shape in the Alien Act, that is, during the gestation of *The War of the Worlds*. And, because it bears stating emphatically, the English word "alien" is here deployed by a sovereign state as a synonym for an immigrant community: the Jews.

The importance of this period has been spelled out in considerable detail by Bernard Gainer in *The Alien Invasion* (1972) where, among other things, he draws attention to the emigration of Russian Jews to England as a result of Czarist housing policies, policies obliging Jews to live outside the Pale of Settlement on the Polish border. Beyond the pale, indeed. This emphasis on the Russian provenance of Jews emigrating to England—they were not, in effect, English speakers—is coupled in Gainer's analysis with an attentive reading of the formation of the British Brothers League and the popular press in which the public reception in Britain of this immigrant community is recorded. Here, I will suggest, we can tease out not so much the figure of the Jew in Wells, but the trace of anti-Semitism in the menace of his monsters.

Noting that the League's excited motto was: "Britain should not become the dumping ground for the scum of Europe" (1972: 50), Gainer goes on to demonstrate that the organization insisted upon the foreignness of Jews. They were said to raise rents while also being willing to accept and occupy substandard housing. Self-serving paradox personified. Gainer also combs the newspapers, drawing attention to stories about the filth, the smell, and the noise of the Jewish neighborhoods in East London. In particular, "all night hammering in backyard workshops" (50) was decried.

With this in mind, consider the passage that occurs early in Wells' text as our narrator is describing the scene at the pit created by the first Martian cylinder: "All night long the Martians were hammering and stirring, sleepless, indefatigable, at work upon the machines they were making ready, and ever and again a puff of greenish-white smoke whirled up into the starlit sky" (2001: 92). Unlike the passage from "The Exodus from London," there is no telltale evocation of *the Jew*. Rather, what we have is a scene given meaning by a journalistic discourse in which there is a substitution, a metaphor, where instead of Jews hammering all night in their filthy, substandard housing, we have Martians acting, as it were, not like Jews, but *as* Jews. Important here is not Wells' ingenuity as a writer, but his ability to effect a substitution based on a discursively maintained anxiety about foreigners, not simply as strangers, but as presences known to be present, but somehow differently. Menacingly. Beyond garden-variety xenophobia what one has here is a figure in which the ubiquity of foreignness transfers from the all-too-possible to the impossible, as if the transfer were itself the event of invasion. Whence the *frisson* of Wells' otherwise clumsily narrated plot. The fact that Wells' text first appeared serialized in the popular press (*Pearsons* magazine) is important, perhaps even decisive, given that it places its metaphors in the same discursive register that circulated them among his initial readers.[5]

A version of this point has been made by Judith Halberstam in *Skin Shows* from 1990. Although she does not discuss *The War of the Worlds*, she is keen, through the concept of the "technologies of monstrosity,"[6] to show how the figurative systems of gothic novels are caught up in a process of othering, a process that in Bram Stoker's *Dracula* allows one to recognize the presence of the Jew in the character of the vampire. This matters to Wells' text because, as Stover points out, the Martians are repeatedly figured as vampiric. Their cylinders are compared to "poisoned darts," and the "red slime" that spreads everywhere seems directly tied to their draining of human blood, a motif given hysterical resonance in the artilleryman character as played by Tim Robbins in Spielberg's post-9/11 *War of the Worlds* (2005). Again, through the figure of the vampire (useful, one will recall, even to Marx in *Capital*), Wells gives shape to the presence of the Jewish foreigner and uses this shape, the shape of the immigrant, to bring the impossible, the monstrous, near. While this feels right to me, I also want to suggest that this nearness has not yet attained the essential insidiousness of the ordinary. Both the vampire and the Martian are extraordinary in ways that things thematized by the British Brothers League and the popular press are not: smells, sounds, behaviors. These, especially sounds, have access to us in a way that establish that the invasion, the end of the world, is always already happening. It always was.

Having invoked psychoanalysis, it is important to note that in his own pass over such matters—I am thinking here of *Civilization and its Discontents*—Freud tied what I have called a structural anxiety to *Schuld*, guilt, or as Nietzsche always insisted guilt/debt (see the second essay of *On the Genealogy of Morality*). It is with this in mind that I urge us to retrieve the thread of empire.

In the passage cited from Cheyette's discussion of the Alien Act of 1905, he stresses that one of its goals was to displace a displacement, that is, to displace a class tension with an ethnic tension and do so in the context of precisely the sort of imperialist nationalism that was in play during the Boer War (1899–1902). Englishness, which had excluded the working class (and this despite the Reform Act of 1832), could now fold together both Jews and the Dutch settlers in South Africa as threats: both in certain ways challenges to empire— one from the Europe within, the other from diasporic Europe. Thoroughly unacknowledged here, perhaps even in principle, is the enabling prior displacement of the tribal formations of South Africa. Here Cheyette succumbs to the critique

of anti-Semitism that often loses its moral compass in the thickets of exceptionalism. More important, however, is that one also risks losing the constituent
elements of the structural anxiety sustaining a technology of monstrosity in
which immigrants and extraterrestrials bolster one another.

More to the point, however, is that precisely such matters figure decisively
in Wells' text, suggesting that its canonical status in the genre of scientific
romance is tangled up with the wars of the was, wars that, as Renan memorably
said of the nation, we cling to through the never-ending labor of forgetting (see
Renan 1990).

As readers will recall, Wells' text is dedicated to his brother Frank who, if one
rashly collapses the narrator and the author, even serves as a walk-on narrator.
Frank meets the swashbuckling Miss Elphinstone and observes the exodus from
London. While it has been established that Miss Elphinstone deliberately shares
her name with Mount Stuart Elphinstone who served under the British Raj and
would thereby invite us to tie Frank to empire, I want to stress a different point
about the fraternal narrator. In their copious correspondence it is recounted that
Frank, while out on a walk with Herbert George, urged his brother to speculate
on whether an alien invasion of the Earth would be perceived by humans in the
same way as the arrival of Europeans (notably, according to Stover, the Dutch
and the British) in Tasmania was perceived by the Tasmanians. Significantly, this
kernel displays a slightly different shell in Wells' text where the pertinent passage
reads as follows:

> And before we judge of them [the Martians] too harshly, we must remember
> what ruthless and utter destruction our species has wrought, not only upon
> animals such as the vanished bison or dodo, but upon its own inferior races.
> The Tasmanians, in spite of their human likeness, were entirely wiped out of
> existence in a war of extermination waged by European immigrants, in the space
> of 50 years. Are we such apostles of mercy as to complain if the Martians warred
> in the same spirit?
>
> Wells 2001: 55

Many have deplored in print the way this rhetoric bespeaks some of the most
odious aspects of both Wells' socialism and his Darwinism, but it behooves
us to first note that this "navel" of the text (I am thinking here of Freud's figure
of the "navel of the dream"), the point at which it stages its own genesis, involves
a subtle displacement. Whereas Frank's triggering observation concerned itself
with the possibility of an invasion and the character of its reception, his brother
deploys the story to entertain both the implicit cause of the invasion and its

moral defensibility. In effect, this passage (and this is not the only example wherein the extinction of the dodo is given melodramatic force) asks us to recognize as the cause of the alien invasion the very logic of what the French called *la mission civilisatrice*.[7] But more important than the matter of the moral relativism thereby authorized, and hence my recourse to the motif of displacement, is the matter of the guilt/debt here understood to play a causal role in the invasion. Somehow, it speaks to an extimate need to expel by overcoming, a recursive ensnarement with the other. To frame the matter in terms of a once resonant political slogan: they are here, because we went there. We was there.

The textual detail that warrants my characterization of this as a displacement belonging to an indefinite series of like displacements is the fact that when Wells places himself in the scene, when he semantically cashes out the "we," he refers to the Dutch and British imperialists as "European immigrants." Here then we have the telling parallel: immigrants like extraterrestrials are exterminators. What is more, immigrants are here, everywhere, always already ending someone's way of life, and inevitably because we ourselves are immigrants in this precise sense. We "war" and are indebted to the "*war*" that always was. To be clear: Wells is not here indulging in a form of guilt-driven hand-wringing. Rather, he is giving textual shape to an indebtedness that morality is incapable of either thinking or countering. Or, to put the point in terms more typical of Wells criticism, at issue here is not the moral implications of natural (or sexual) selection, and this despite the text's effort to motivate the invasion by proposing that extraterrestrials (and thus *all* life) are driven by the need to survive. Instead, or at the very least in addition, Wells invites us to wonder whether Martians share with earthlings what I have here been calling a structural anxiety, a guilt/debt, the very genealogical motor of morality. And, *mutatis mutandis*, whether Jews and wives do as well.

Married to the Blob

Wives? As note 7 suggests, the wife joins the Jew-Tasmanians series via the motif of "the strange." Were one to read this text by listening to it, one would surely note its repeated recourse to the grammatical inflection strange, stranger, strangest, including at the very end the embellished superlative: "strangest of all." For example, as I have noted, the early emphasis on the "strangeness of the object" (referring to the first cylinder); or, even closer to home, the narrator's "strangest sense of detachment" (alien-ation?) from both himself and the world (Wells 2001: 85); or, even more emphatically, the narrator's assertion, "now comes the strangest part of my story" (244), a not altogether strange strangeness that amounts to a three-day lapse into unconsciousness, a blackout; all of which culminates in the grammatical cascade that brings the epilogue to closure: "And strangest of all is to hold my wife's hand again, and to think that I have counted her, and that she counted me, among the dead" (254). Of all the strange things— and there have been many including the anxiously anticipated event of "first contact," and the narrator's act of murder—the strangest of all, in fact, a strangeness worthy of being added to the text as its exclamation point (the epilogue was not part of the serialized text), is the perfectly ordinary event of holding the wife's hand. To be sure, we are dealing with a romance (whether scientific or not) and there is thus generic pressure being brought to bear here, but this strikes me as a rather thin account of the insistent narrative staging, the *mise-en-scène*, of the nameless wife. If Kristeva was willing to entertain the notion that "women" were the first strangers (see *Strangers to Ourselves*, 1991), perhaps Wells invites us to consider that the wife is the quintessential immigrant and therefore extraterrestrial.[8]

But surely that is an overstatement. What can it actually mean? Isn't the wife presumably British, Gentile, and an object of Martian menace? To sort the matter it is useful to plot what I have called the staging of the wife. To begin with she shares the narrator's home. She is present at the "last civilized meal," indeed she has prepared it. When it is clear that a war of the worlds is underway, the need to reassure her, to bring color back into her whitened face, helps calm the narrator. In an act of desperate gallantry Wells contrives to have her transported, by dogcart, to her cousin's house in Leatherhead where the narrator leaves her. This separation haunts the narrator and, in effect, prepares us for the final scene (in the original series) where she swoons into the narrator's arms upon their reunion. This Homeric trajectory however is punctuated by an important, and I will propose, decisive scene. Holed up in the house on Putney Hill, the narrator reports that while trying to rest, "three things struggled for possession of my mind: the killing of the Curate, the whereabouts of the Martians and the possible fate of my wife" (Wells 2001: 220). He continues:

> And suddenly that night became terrible. I found myself sitting up in bed staring at the dark. I found myself praying that the Heat-Ray [one of the Martians' more lethal weapons] may have suddenly and painlessly struck her out of being. Since the night of my return from Leatherhead I had not prayed. I had uttered

prayers, fetich [*sic*] prayers, had prayed as heathens mutter charms when I was in extremity; but now I prayed indeed, pleading steadfastly and sanely face to face with the darkness of God. Strange night, strangest in this that so soon as dawn had come, I, who had talked with God, crept out of the house like a rat leaving its hiding place—a creature scarcely larger, an inferior animal, a thing that for any passing whim of our masters might be hunted and killed.

Wells 2001: 221

Inexplicably, Stover—who footnotes the passage—observes only that the prayer is insincere, passing over in silence the intricate death wish given expression here. The narrator is imagining the death of his wife, and is doing so while fretting about his own actual murder of the Curate. Moreover, at the now predictable turnstile of "the strange and the strangest" he is imagining himself— via the inferior animal of the rat—in the position of the wife, that is, as someone subject, willy-nilly, to the death drive of a master. Even if we are inclined to grant him the nobility of sparing his wife a more vicious and painful death by wishing her a sudden and painless one, the displacement that follows interferes, and interferes deeply, with such a motivation. In short, the narrator is presented in a way consistent with the twisted Wellsian theme of the eugenically necessary and thus even desirable invasion from Mars, only here this necessity is indexed to a strangeness that attaches him—ultimately figured in clasped hands but here figured as prayer—to the character only ever named "my wife." It is in this sense that perfectly ordinary handholding becomes "the strangest of all": he comes to hold hands with the person he has wished dead in this scene.

Amplifying the echo between these two stagings of the wife is the not uninteresting textual fact that, like the "Epilogue," "The Man on Putney Hill" (Book II, Chapter vii) was not in the serialized publication of the text. Both were added when *The War of the Worlds* was later published as a novel. With the supplement of the epilogue in particular what results is a reiteration in which the swoon that answers to the narrator's three-day blackout, recurs as handholding between two phantoms: one simply feared dead, the other wished dead. Commentators have noted this awkwardness, even in some cases complaining about the inadequacy of the swoon, but without puzzling over the apparent attraction or even the necessity of the reiteration itself. Why stage the present absence of the wife twice?

I would like to suggest that here we are dealing with more than the motif of "overwhelming joy," but to get at it recourse to both David Lodge and Foucault is indispensable. In the first and last volume of the latter's history of sexuality, two discussions converge. In volume one, *The Will to Know*, Foucault, while listing four figures put in play by the apparatus of sexuality and its deployment, includes among them something he calls "the Malthusian couple." Little is said here about Thomas Robert Malthus as such, but it is clear that this couple is invested by the apparatus of sexuality to assure the existence of population. In effect, figured in the Malthusian couple is a sexuality defined by heterosexual monogamy and the evolutionary responsibility of reproduction. Although he does not use the term himself these figures are crystallizations of the dynamic of problematization, that is, absent causes of the very deployment of sexuality.

In volume three, *The Care of the Self*, notably in the part devoted to "the Wife," Foucault readily deploys the concept of problematization, but in keeping with the general drift of volumes two and three, he dials back the apparatus of sexuality not precisely to detach it from the eighteenth century, but to trace the lines of convergence that knotted in that period back to the pre-Christian era. In the discussion of the wife, he is at pains to show that while she is in important respects conceived of in Malthusian terms—as consigned to the task of sexual reproduction—this occurs within the context of a different problematization, namely, the urgent question of trying to figure out how men should "care for themselves." Thus, the focus becomes issues such as should a man (perhaps especially a philosopher) marry, and if so why and with what responsibilities to himself and others? Having children is only one of several such goals. As if anticipating my turn to his text, Foucault also refers us here to Pliny the Younger's letter on a man's responsibilities to his relationship when separated from his wife.[9]

Reading forward, one might propose that the Malthusian couple also became an answer to the question of how to care for the self, and one that sought to reduce that care to the anxious matter of population, in effect, copulation control. Here Lodge's "disclosures" assume a different significance. While *A Man of Parts* appears to justify itself by detailing what he calls "the fugitive impulse," (Lodge 2011: 91) in Wells (his numerous infidelities and remarriages), it resists the effort to place any of the novels in relation to something like the apparatus of sexuality, preferring instead to sniff happily about in the realm of biography. Were one, however cautiously, *not* to do this, a figure like the wife in *The War of the Worlds*, especially a wife whose present absence is twice narrated, invites attention.

So as not to belabor the obvious: in a text where euthanasia is eugenically inflected, and inflected on an interplanetary scale, its association with the figure of the wife in the Malthusian couple invites one to recognize in her the problematization of population. The apparatus of sexuality tells us, somewhat independently of race and class, that the wife is where generation and degeneration are co-possible. Or, if generation always risks assimilation, it is degeneration. Famously, Wells argued against Zionism because it would keep Jews from assimilating. Like Franz Boas, Wells opposed anti-Semitism by urging Jews to miscegenate and thus succumb to slow, evolutionary annihilation (see "People of the Abyss"), in effect, to join a humanity in the process of cleansing itself of, to use the Artilleryman's colorful term, "skeedaddlers." In a sense, the narrator's relation to the wife bespeaks the anxiety, not of exterminating but of reproducing one's kind to death. Never mind the Heat-Ray, his death wish aims more directly at her as a locus of generation, a generation that might always produce monstrosity either in the form of the eugenically suspect, or in the form of a generation simply folded into itself one more time. While this might suggest that the narrator is fantasizing himself as the Martian, it seems more to the point that the Martian thus fantasized is a figure for the anxiously invested current flowing between the two poles of the Malthusian couple. Sexual reproduction must take place, but in its very taking place one's way of life is exposed, risked. In this sense the ordinary, the ubiquitous encounter with the immigrant—one that might always become a "path to citizenship"—feels like, shares the unsettling affect-tone, of the impossible encounter with what ends the world as we know it, the extraterrestrial.

Wells says this without knowing it. In fact, he repeats it. However, this form of textual repetition does not stop there. Or, put differently, it assumes precisely the form of what earlier I called *scriptura interruptus*, a detail that ties in a rather startling way the motif of copulation control to the very medium of printed prose. One of the more striking features of *The War of the Worlds* is its organization of the plot/story relation and the attendant distribution of narrative voice. If one, in following the formalist school, distinguishes between the plot and the story by characterizing the former as the sequence of diegetic events as related versus that sequence as lived, then one is struck by how Wells' text is plotted such that it is narrated after the fact. The narration of the war always places it in the time of the was. We know the outcome of the story almost immediately—a fact structurally repeated in the very existence of an epilogue—and Wells' achievement is to produce an enabling amnesia that sustains what suspense the story is capable of generating. Crucial to this effect is the introduction within the story of the scene of writing that is interrupted by the unfolding of the plot. As our narrator tells us late in the text upon re-entering his home and immediately prior to the wife's return and swoon, he was working on an essay titled "On the Probable Development of Moral Ideas" (Wells 2001: 247). Precisely because "moral ideas" surface repeatedly in the text (consider the conversations with the Curate and the Artilleryman), the reader is given the impression that *this text*, the novel, occurs as an elaboration or development of the other text, the "Moral Ideas" essay. And yet, this relation is rather conspicuously turned inside out in that the plot situates the lived event of the essay *within* the narration of *The War of the Worlds*. This inversion, or as Derrida might urge, "invagination," (see his "The Law of Genre" or "Living On") is figured in the motif of "interruption." Whereas the narrator and the wife are able to finish their civilized meal, the scene of writing is a scene interrupted.

But what does this have to do with copulation control? If *coitus interruptus* is, among other things, a form (however unreliable) of birth control, then the interrupted relation between the two texts as rendered in the organization of the plot/story relation—especially as this is reiterated through the device of the epilogue where the strangest of all apparitions, the phantasmatic hand-holding with the wife-wished-dead, is staged—this relation is presented as broken off by the appearance of the Martian who, like the Jew, the Tasmanian, the immigrant, happens right where it is most expected, literally at the site of reproduction. This site, in the context of the problematization of the Malthusian couple, assumes a powerful textual shape that puts the relation between magazines and books (where the wife's return is epilogically restaged) in the service of the apparatus of sexuality. In this, copulation and distribution converge, and textual selection assumes, or at the very least replicates, a certain biological function.

I am here suggesting—indeed I am arguing—that "was" and "war" likewise converge. The scene of writing that was interrupted by the war of the worlds structurally superimposes the was and the war, rendering here the flicker that so intrigued Derrida in Joyce's text. The alien invasion is not something one anxiously awaits, hallucinates (alien abduction is almost always about sexual reproduction) or prepares for. It, and the war it provokes, by virtue of the logic of debt/guilt, always was. Moreover, as Derrida insisted, this menacing flicker grips language itself, a fact anticipated by Wells when his narrator says:

> In spite of Oglvy [an acquaintance of the narrator and early victim of the Martians], I still believed that there were men in Mars. My mind ran fancifully on the possibilities of its [the first cylinder] containing manuscripts, on the

difficulties in translation that might arise, whether we should find coins and models in it, and so forth.

Wells 2001: 69

Here, through the age-old "plurality of worlds" chestnut (are there other humans or other beings on other worlds?), the narrator not only preemptively aligns the Martians and the Jews through the motif of the coins, but through the "difficulties in translation" he both underscores the Russian (non-Anglophone) provenance of the Jews, while also linking the aliens to the multiplicity of languages, the very medium of the was/war flicker in Joyce. Although the resonance is faint, the anticipated encounter among languages is also presented through the device of manuscripts, as if the scene of writing that was interrupted by the war that was, was so by virtue of the arrival of another text from another world. But which text and which world?

If it makes sense to refer to the possibility of this interrupted encounter as itself war, perhaps this is because it always was one for straight white men trying to care for themselves in the midst of the problem they themselves have become, in a world on the wane. *The War of the Worlds* thus demands to be read as an intricately coded signal transmitted to Earth as if from survivors of the deliberate catastrophe of kinship, a catastrophe made unimaginable by the simple fact that it always already was.

Notes

1   Derrida's remarks at the Centre Pompidou, "Two Words for Joyce," have been translated into English by Derek Attridge and collected in *Post-Structuralist Joyce: Essays from the French* (Derrida 1984: 145–59). His second reading of Joyce, "Ulysses Gramophone: Hear Say Yes in Joyce," from two years later appears in *Acts of Literature* (Derrida 1992: 253–309). See here as well the volume *Derrida and Joyce: Texts and Contexts* (Mitchell and Slote. 2013) for a thorough combing of these materials. Obviously, I am drawing attention to the exaggerated brevity of Derrida's endless encounter with Joyce so as to repeat differently his own feint. Litotes have both tone and content.

2   I am thinking here of the fact that Wells' text has become a radio play, two films (not counting "covers" like Roland Emmerich's *Independence Day*), and a short-lived television series. There is something here that the West cannot let go of and my remarks seek to amplify, render audible, some of the sources of this tenacity.

3   Katarzyna Marciniak in *Alienhood: Citizenship, Exile and the Logic of Difference* (2006) draws attention not only to this scene, but also to some of the Chicano parodies of the scene that appeared in response. She is keen to make sense of her own "alienhood," and draws attention to a host of themes that have come to resonate in international feminism; themes such as bodily integrity, boundary violation, viscosity, and solidity. These are pertinent to aspects of Wells' text, but establishing this particular connection does not interest her.

4   For those unfamiliar with the text, the following synopsis may prove useful. In its novel form (the text first appeared as magazine installments), it opens with narratorial musings about Earth and its attraction for survivors of a dying world, turning quickly to astronomically noted anomalies that become spaceships launched from Mars. The first of these ships lands outside London where it is soon discovered that it is "manned" by beings with both hostile intent and advanced weaponry. The invasion begins once the war machines stowed in these spaceships are assembled, an event witnessed by the narrator who then sets about trying to save his wife and warn others. Although the British armed forces are mobilized, the Martians make steady, if not entirely unimpeded, progress toward London. After various encounters with both Martians and men, the narrator, who has decided that extinction is imminent, is stunned to realize that the Martians are defeating themselves. Specifically, they succumb to bacteria put on Earth by God. With the Martians routed, the narrator returns home to be reunited with his wife whom he had feared dead.

5   Psychoanalytic theory has routinely drawn attention to the logic of what I have here called a substitution, or metaphor, noting that a structural anxiety, a built in relation to, in Kristeva's terms, "the strangeness within," is what propels everything from scapegoating (Girard) to racism and ethnic cleansing (Žižek). It is precisely because we are already extimately (the intimate exterior) exposed to the other, that we thrash about trying to contain and extradite its representatives, its "away team." If we are to believe a film like *District 9*, this is not unique to the so-called West or North, but perhaps it is also worth acknowledging that psychoanalysis itself belongs deeply to this logic (cf. Andrew M. Butler's essay, Ch. 5 in this volume). It is not for nothing that early analysts were called "alienists." Doubtless this is why Lacan insisted that "the way out, is the way in." Getting inside someone's head (an unfortunate, but pervasive, metonymy) has always already taken place. Indeed, if analysis works, this is why.

6   Cf. Chapter 4 in *Skin Shows*.

7   As if predicting Norbert Elias' articulation of the civilizing process and table manners, Wells' narrator adumbrates the encounter with the invaders by saying: "I did not know it, but that was the last civilized meal I was to eat for many strange

and terrible days" (88). As this passage also puts in play the decisive association between strangeness and the narrator's wife, it calls for and will receive further elaboration.

8   Bonnie Honig has developed Kristeva's discussion of the "Story of Ruth" so as to explore the relationship between the immigrant/wife/refugee and the foreigner. Although her discussion tends toward the schematic—she wants to develop a politically charged contrast between the foreigner who comes and goes, versus the foreigner who stays—her concept of the foreign forges an important link between the wife (even as an anthropological "gift") and the immigrant. See her *Democracy and the Foreigner* (2003).

9   See in particular the discussion of the man's responsibilities to the wife that occurs between pages 160 and 161 (Foucault 1988).

References

Cheyette, B. (1995), *Constructions of "the Jew" in English Literature and Society*, Cambridge, MA: Cambridge University Press.

Derrida, J. (1984), "Two Words for Joyce," in D. Attridge and D. Ferrer (eds), *Post-Structuralist Joyce: Essays from the French*, Cambridge, MA: Cambridge University Press.

Derrida, J. (1992), "Ulysses Gramophone: Hear Say Yes in Joyce," in D. Attridge (ed.), *Acts of Literature*, New York: Routledge.

Foucault, M. (1978), *The History of Sexuality, Volume One: An Introduction*, R. Hurley (trans.), New York: Vintage Books.

Foucault, M. (1988), *The Care of the Self: History of Sexuality Volume Three*, R. Hurley (trans.), New York: Vintage.

Freud, S. (2001), *The Standard Edition of the Complete Psychological Works of Sigmund Freud*, vol. 18, J. Strachey (ed.), London: Vintage.

Gainer, B. (1972), *The Alien Invasion: The Origins of the Alien Act of 1905*, London: Heinemann.

Honig, B. (2003), *Democracy and the Foreigner*, Princeton, NJ: Princeton University Press.

Kristeva, J. (1991), *Strangers to Ourselves*, L. Roudiez (trans.), New York: Columbia University Press.

Kuntzel, T. (1980), "Film-Work, 2," *Camera Obscura* 2 (spring): 6–70.

Lodge, D. (2011), *A Man of Parts: A Novel*, New York: Viking.

Marciniak, K. (2006), *Alienhood: Citizenship, Exile and the Logic of Difference*, Minneapolis, MN: University of Minnesota Press.

Mitchell, A. J. and Slote, S. (eds) (2013), *Derrida and Joyce: Texts and Contexts*, Albany, NY: State University of New York Press.

Renan, E. (1990), "What is a Nation?" in H. Bhabha (ed.), *Nation and Narration*, New York: Routledge.

Wells, H. G. ([1898] 2001), *The War of the Worlds: A Critical Text of the 1898 London First Edition with an Introduction, Illustration and Appendices*, L. Stover (ed.), Jefferson, NC: McFarland Books.

2

Alien Art: Encounters with Otherworldly Places and Inter-medial Spaces

Ulrike Küchler

Freie Universität Berlin, Germany

What shapes the imagination of the alien? This volume's title alludes to two promising ambiguities: the tension between the alien's imagination and our imagination of the alien,[1] and between these alien imaginations and their images, that is representations.[2] In science fiction and tales of transnationalism these tensions are manifest as translation problems resulting from the diverse matters and modes of expression and interaction of the self and the alien other, and of their representations. They cause recurring conflicts and changes of perspective for both protagonists and recipients. It is hence the "dialogue [...] with the real world" (Delany 1980: 185)[3] *and* "its explicit intertextuality" (Jameson 2005: 2), including, by extension, inter-art references, that not only apply to science fiction—"few other literary forms have so brazenly affirmed themselves as argument and counterargument" (Jameson 2005: 2). In fact, this dialogical and dialectical structure marks an important intersection between both genres.

Lost in translation: Alien other and alien art

The protagonists in (and recipients of) both genres are travelers who explore alternative places and thus comprehend familiar spaces. In the beginning, however, many of them are in one way or another literally lost in translation, as is already the case in one of the early milestones of science fiction writing, H. G. Wells' *The Time Machine* (1895).[4] In his encounter with the alien other, a future species named Eloi descended from the turn-of-the-century upper class, the time-traveling narrator faces a language barrier that sets him back to the use of basic sign language in an attempt to close the linguistic gap:[5] silence and refusal of communication is what dominates the initial interaction with the alien other and what defines the "canvas" for the story's further development.[6] Others, such as the narrator in Alfred Kubin's only novel *Die andere Seite* (*The Other Side* 1909), who is, like Kubin, both an author and a painter, desperately try to overcome the difference between the reality of the alien other and its representation—only to realize that both are constructions. His travels begin with the painting and story of a former friend and future fiend ruling an allegedly utopian Eurasian Dream State whose totalitarian reality does not concur with the picture he imagined.

This essay is particularly interested in such works of literary fiction that assume an aesthetic perspective on the problem of transition and translation. Their protagonists are artists or aesthetic theorists whose journeys are initiated, mediated, or accompanied by encounters with various objects of art and different artistic "languages." This is the case with the first-person narrators in Kubin's novel *The Other Side* (1909), Frigyes Karinthy's story "Utazás Faremidóba" 1916 ("Voyage to Faremido"), and Evgenij Zamyatin's novel *Мы* (*We*, 1921). All three of them link the figure of the alien other to the problem of alien art. Their travelers and first-person narrators enter foreign countries and cultures while engaging with foreign forms of art, discussing painting as language in Kubin, language as music in Karinthy, and music as art in Zamyatin. The stories re-read the characteristic science fiction dialogue between two worlds that illuminates the "historical present" (Jameson 2005: 345) as a dialogue between two artistic worlds in order to reflect on the current "aesthetic present." Employing various narrative techniques ranging from inner-diegetic aesthetic discussions to *mise-en-abyme* and various forms of inter-mediality,[7] the stories thus stage an "aesthetic estrangement," to borrow from Darko Suvin's re-reading of Bertold Brecht's *Verfremdungseffekt*.[8] They not only challenge the definition of the self in its relation to the alien other but (re-)define traditional concepts of mediality and art in general and established differences between the written word and other artistic languages in particular. Also, the three works show a shift in and development of the notion of art that is characteristic for the modern era: Kubin's apocalyptic novel reads as a morbid analysis of the contemporary "state of the art" that centers around convention and the idealization of the past, Karinthy rehabilitates art as a, if not *the*, means of communication in the present thus unveiling new aesthetic potentials, while Zamyatin's novel enhances art's potential by presenting it as a means of cognition in the future.

Art as convention

Alfred Kubin's only novel *The Other Side* (1909) links the painter and author's personal "crisis of representation" with modernism's more general one (Jameson 2005: 183).[9] Kubin drew on language at a point in his artistic career where he did not find in painting the possibilities of expression he was looking for (see Assmann 1999: 90f.): "*The Other Side* is actually [...] a work of fiction whose author put pictures into words which [...] he was unable to draw" (Lippuner 1977: 78, my translation).[10] For Kubin, this artistic language offered a new form of artistic involvement: "While the fascination in writing usually lies not in the description but in the discovery of feeling, it lies for Kubin in those hidden instances of ekphrasis" (van Zon 1991: 58f.). Transferring those inner pictures into language, however, is only one dimension of his novel, which is accompanied by fifty-two black and white illustrations that, reversely, put the story's words into pictures. For his reader, this dialogue between the narrative's linear language and immediate illustrations also combines two types of aesthetic engagement: "Kubin narrates or rather: lets his viewer poeticize in reading his pictures. While we draw an inner picture in reading a text by Kubin, we fabulate in viewing his paintings" (Schwanberg 1999: 116, my translation).

Both perspectives intertwine and add to the novel's complexity when considering its narrative perspective: the story is told from the point of view of a first-person painter-narrator whose "initiation" throughout the story is, time and again, ironically commented upon by another, implicit authorial voice. The protagonist's development extends the function of the first-person narrator to a first-person illustrator: akin to an author and illustrator like Kubin, the narrator serves as a twofold counter-picture. Together with his wife, the narrator decides to flee the artistic and economic pressures of the present in favor of the promises of the past held by the Dream Realm: an allegedly utopian yet museal state that idealizes the middle of the previous century[11] from its everyday-life to aesthetics (with a particular inclination for seventeenth-century Dutch painters) and institutionalizes a refusal of the modern present. In retrospect, his story follows a dialectic tripartite: it develops the tension between the image(ination), the experience, and the apocalypse of the Dream Realm. The dialogue between the story's words and illustrations mirrors and breaks this development. The illustrations are thus characterized by a tension between authorial and personal perspective that reflects that of the narrative voice; almost none of the illustrations, for instance, show the narrator himself but many capture his personal views and (inner) pictures.[12] The narrative perspective thus challenges and expands the problem of authorship to a genre—book art and illustration—that is traditionally thought of as being authorial by definition, either as embellishing decoration or reflexive interpretation.[13] It redefines the (utopian) book as a space where word and picture enter a dialogue: "as *synthesis of the arts*, where the visual elements neither only refer to the content of the text nor serve just as an ornament, but function as equal elements of a text-image-entirety in the format of a book" (Neugebauer 1996: 10, my translation, emphasis in the original).

The progressive perspective on the interplay of words and pictures suggested by the dialogue between the novel's narrative framework and languages is even more emphasized by the contrasting, reactionary setting of the Dream Realm against which the novel poses its aesthetic questions. To put it differently: while for Kubin and the story's ironic authorial voice, the encounter with an alien art form (literary language) implies an engagement with new artistic languages in order to reach aesthetic advancement, for his narrator the alien art he is looking for in the Dream Realm is not so alien after all but promises, as a sort of aesthetic "safety net," a confirmation of traditional and familiar artistic conventions: he would rather hold on to familiar modes of artistic production than develop new ones.

A short look at the Dream Realm shall illuminate the setting. A fictional Eurasian and Europeanized state, the Dream Realm was founded by the narrator's childhood friend Patera. Twelve years ago he began with the colonization of a region in central Asia. Quickly, the place turned into an escapist parallel world that explores and challenges utopian/dystopian story-telling techniques and illustrates wonderfully Michel Foucault's notion of "discourse":[14] separated from the rest of the world by a high wall, this "state of the future" (Kubin 1909: 4) is actually a "museum" (84) where time has stopped before industrialization and where scientific progress is taboo, making it "a sanctuary for all those who are unhappy with modern civilisation" (4). Meanwhile, the main purpose of the state's administration[15] is to install ridiculous rituals including the "Great Clock Spell," whose only function it is to perpetuate the state's bureaucratic structure, and to implement a "strict selection process" determining who is to enter this exclusive society. Cultivating a utilitarist understanding of art, the people in the Dream Realm "don't have special museum buildings or art galleries" with all works of art being "shared out, 'in use,' so to speak" (16). Patera is the state's absolute ruler and chief collector. He carefully selects and combines

historical objects older than the 1860s—from houses to interior decoration
to art—from all over the world to furnish the Dream Realm. And he invites
all sorts of "historicizing subjects"—backward-looking people sharing his
passion for the past—to live with him. They create a mosaic of decontextualized
artifacts and biographies that have lost their meaning and net of references.
Their only remaining function is discursive preservation and ideologization,
thus turning the Dream Realm into a state that is a space of the past without
being a historical place. Of the former population only a blue-eyed clan stayed,
while the new inhabitants of the Dream Realm, and its newly founded capital,
Perle, are mainly Germans. From the beginning in the flashback on the state's
cultural imperialist history, its further totalitarian development and ultimate
apocalypse—revealingly initiated by Patera's conflict with a stereotypical
American—thus establishes the narrative as a critical reading of the early
twentieth-century's present and even sketches a frighteningly accurate picture
of its future.[16]

A short look at the story's development illustrates how the narrative links
the encounter with the alien other and alien art to assume a critical perspective
on aesthetic concerns in general and those of the modern era in particular.
In the novel's first part the narrator's initial encounter with the alien other
serves to unfold the interplay between the construction of histories and stories.
At a time of economic depression, when he can only make a poor living as
an artist and illustrator, the narrator is paid a visit by one of Patera's agents,
Franz Gautsch. He is not only a traveler between the modern world and the
alien world of the Dream Realm but also an accomplished storyteller and
"advertiser" of the state as a promised land. In fact, he composes and presents
the narrator's invitation along with the Dream Realm's history as an exclusive[17]
"multi-media" narrative that reads like a commentary on storytelling techniques:
in the beginning, he delivers a formal invitation, supported by some dry statistics
and facts about the state and its citizens. He literally adds life to his story with
a painted portrait of Patera along with some biographical details. Finally, he
wraps up his story with a second, handwritten invitation by Patera with just
five words, "*If you want to, come*" (Kubin 1990: 11, emphasis in the original),
accompanied by a colorful summary of the Dream Realm's and Patera's (hi)story.
In the course of this "dream story" (6), we virtually follow the narrator's mind to
"the other side": first, he listens with a skeptical and distanced attitude to
the words of the "lunatic" but each new story element leads him to "a mood of
optimism and curiosity" (8), triggering a "dreamlike shimmer of an image from

a long-forgotten past" (11) and colorful visions of "a rich artistic harvest" (19) for the future. It is ultimately Patera's painting and handwriting, the image and the written sign, that testify to the Dream Realm's veracity—a development that not only signifies the alien state as a set of constructed alien (hi)stories but also reveals a certain ironic twist, considering that later on the narrator realizes that no one in the Dream Realm ever actually *sees* Patera in person.[18] The novel's first part thus establishes the dialogue between the alien other—the Dream Realm as opposed to the modern world—and alien art—painting as opposed to writing—as a poetic strategy.

Against this backdrop, the second part of the story has a different emphasis. The narrator's everyday life in the capital Perle serves as a case study to challenge the role of art and, in particular, the relationship between content and form at the turn of the century. On that account, the novel sketches the interplay between three perspectives: it links matters of production aesthetics to the media discourse, work aesthetics to the social discourse, and reception aesthetics to a critical reflection on the aesthetic discourse. What links these discourses in the Dream Realm is a claim of artistic form for the purposes of media, social, and aesthetic appearance at the cost of content. Thus, the narrator succeeds the "leading artist" of the daily *Dream Mirror*, Castringius, soon after his arrival only to realize that what matters about the production of art for the media in the Dream Realm is *not* to deliver meaning, pose questions or challenge authorities. What determines its value is its power to "*make a show*": "And that's what counted in the Dream Realm, *to make a show of being something*, anything" (70, emphases in original). And as "position overrules painting," he receives the same amount of money, "whatever I delivered, a lot of pictures or nothing at all" (69). Similarly, in the society of the Dream Realm a work of art does not serve to encourage contemplation, change perspectives, and initiate changes but is mainly appreciated for maintaining social structures as a status symbol: in the higher circles "[a]rt objects are valued above all for their practical use," translating to their eligibility to show off someone's social rank: "Our Croesus, Alfred Blumenstich, the director of the Dreamland Bank, has a gallery of valuable paintings, including a Rembrandt and a genuine Grünewald, the existence of which no one in your world even suspects. It's called 'The Seven Sins Eating the Lamb of God'" (89)—an ironic remark both on the society's superficiality and the narrator's inability to recognize it as such. Closing the circle, the narrator's comments on and eclectic enumerations of Castringius' works critiques the painter's view on art as being profoundly determined by an aesthetic discourse whose golden rule states "Art is a safety valve!"

> Before I arrived Castringius had his simplest period. Three or four lines and the picture was finished. He called it "Greatness." The most important works had titles such as *The Head, He, She, Us, It*! They placed no limits on the imagination. For example, a head in a flower vase—it could mean anything. However, when the public began to take notice of me, Castringius was forced to produce something more substantial. "Plumb the depths of the subject matter, that's the answer!" was his obstinate maxim. Now came works such as *Mad Pope Innocence Dancing the Cardinals' Quadrille*.
>
> Kubin [1909] 1990: 107f., emphases in the original

While before the narrator always maintained the role of a distant albeit uncritical observer, it is after viewing these paintings, ironically, that he fully merges with the mindset of "the other side" (and it is only shortly after this that he meets and *sees* Patera for the first and only time). By metonymic extension his pseudo-formalist remarks read as a caricature of an aesthetic "Dream Manifesto" where artistic value is calculated by number of lines and title words: fewer lines and more words equaling higher value. They disclose a longing for an(y) aesthetic system and a refusal to engage with its aesthetic consequences that result in a ridiculous aesthetics without program which glorifies form for form's sake, leads to a complete loss of reference, and results in profound arbitrariness: these pieces of art truly and sadly "could mean anything."

The story's third part finally shows the destructive power released by such decontextualized meaning and artifacts. For, increasingly, a life of its own awakens in the Dream Realm's escapist parallel world: people's outer appearances metamorphose such as the narrator's charwoman who changes from a young lady to "a bustling old woman with a wrinkled face" (101) overnight; communication goes awry with uninvited people such as craftsmen or musicians repeatedly and randomly showing up at unexpected places; and a general decline prevails, art being no exception: "Precious *objets d'art* succumbed to an irresistible *inner* decay without any reason being apparent" (227, emphases in original), which soon manifests in inexorable outer decay: "The precious objects had clearly lost the will to live. The valuable vases and china were covered in a delicate network of tiny cracks; magnificent paintings developed black spots which spread over the whole picture; engravings became porous and disintegrated" (238). This decay, however, is not "a sickness of inanimate matter" as the narrator diagnoses, but an expression of the Dream Realm's general disposition:

a pervasive "*inner* decay" materializing the "promised land's" blind spot: the priority of form over content. Initiating the Dream Realm's ultimate apocalypse, this "Confusion of the Dream" (179) thus draws a line from the history's decontextualization for the sake of the Dreamer's dream—art as convention—back to the story's recontextualization for the sake of the reader's reality.

Art as communication

In his philosophical story, "Voyage to Faremido" (1916) about the first fictional robot society and culture, Hungarian writer Frigyes Karinthy shifts the perspective on the relation between the alien other and alien art to the present and the problem of communication. Being one of two sequels to Jonathan Swift's *Gulliver's Travels* (1726) and telling about the adventures of "Gulliver's fifth journey" the narrative designates dialogue as its main aesthetic subject and principle already on a paratextual level.[19] Throughout the story, other intertextual references include various Enlightenment utopian-dystopian narratives ranging from Voltaire (*Micromégas*, 1752) to Jean Paul (*Der Maschinemann/Machine Man*, 1789), as well as contemporaries such as H. G. Wells' scientific romances and Samuel Butler (*Erewhon*, 1872).

The story links this abundant "tissue of quotations" (Barthes 1977: 146) on the level of (literary) language composition to the issue of composition as language: it follows Gulliver in a hydroplane to the land of Faremido after his ship has been under attack from the Germans at the height of the First World War. The foreign land's name derives from the language of its inhabitants, the Solasis: huge robots who converse in music. The idea of exploring the alien other by means of musical language derives from another source, probably—next to Swift—the most important one. Already in the 1620s, Francis Godwin had written his famous *The Man in the Moone* (1638). The story's framework sounds familiar: Spaniard Domingo Gonsales escapes the British fleet in an air carriage pulled by large birds that bring him to the moon—a paradisiacal place populated by the Lunars who blend "pastoral and utopian stereotypes" in order to evoke "an attitude typical of early modern travel writers: it accommodates the unknown to a conventional perspective" (Capoferro 2010: 154). This certainly also accounts for the Lunar language: while it "consisteth not so much of words and letters, as of tunes and uncouth sounds" (Godwin 2009: 108), it allocates each tone on the musical scale to a corresponding letter in the Latin alphabet, thus more resembling a "cipher" than a language (Knowlson 1968: 360). The Solasi's language in Karinthy's story inverses this perspective: similar to François Sudre's constructed language Solresol,[20] it derives from the originally medieval system of solmization in which each note corresponds to a particular syllable—the well-known do (ut), re, mi, fa, sol, la, si, do—and thus pushes the concept of fictional musical language a step further.[21]

The link between musical composition and communication is not new to science fiction writing of the time either, as Samuel Butler's singing statues in his seminal novel *Erewhon* (1872) show. A hybrid "Stonehenge of rude and barbaric figures" (Butler 1985: 66), they guard and mark the entrance to the alien world of Erewhon: "The inhuman beings [...] had made their heads into a sort of organ-pipe, so that their mouths should catch the wind and sound with its blowing" (67). Their music resembles Handel's compositions for the harpsichord, as the narrator realizes upon his return to England (68). At the time of the meeting between the narrator and the statues, however, the communication with the alien other by means of alien art fails and the narrator flees the sphinxlike statues: "I rushed away from them into the mist [...] I heard their ghostly chanting, and felt as though one of them would rush after me and grip me in his hand and throttle me" (67f.). Yet, the singing statues prepare the ground for the literary dialogue between artificial life and the arts at the time and sketch a rough picture of the musical machines in Karinthy's story. For Gulliver's first encounter with the Solasi's singing at the aerial border to Faremido has quite a different effect:

> Now I realized why I felt such deep happiness: For an hour already a chord chimed around me, so soft and bright, that I believed to be bathing and swimming in this tone such as in cool liquid. I listened attentively and discovered that four simple notes were being repeated. The enchanting charm of the chord was created by the colour and softness of these notes rather than by their sequence. [...] f, d, e, c—or, according to the solfa notation: Fa-re-mi-do. At this moment we touched down.
>
> Karinthy 1916: 7

Gulliver listens silently to the Solasi and their unusual singsong, and is unable to say anything. Both initial encounters with the alien other by means of alien art thus differ diametrically: while Butler's narrator encounters the singing statues as "fiends" (1985: 67) with an anxiety that shapes their (failing) interaction, and by extension that between arts and technology, Karinthy's Gulliver meets the "beautiful" musical machines as friends and with an attitude of Swiftian curiosity, thus paving the way for the story's further discussion of the relation between the arts and technology.

Following this pivotal scene, the story focuses on the narrator's integration in the Solasi robot society and his adaptation to their language. A typical technique both in the Swiftian and utopian/dystopian tradition, this process of assimilation allows the narrative to address a number of aesthetic challenges regarding the relation between human and machine and between machine and art and to contextualize them in the modern present. One of the story's most interesting effects in this regard is how it turns the problem of communication with the alien other by means of alien art from a systematic into an evolutionary challenge and thus extends the concept of evolution: to language and the arts— intertextual and inter-art relations *avant la lettre*.

A short look at Gulliver's stay in Faremido captures the setting of this development. Upon his arrival, Gulliver encounters the Solasi Sido, which lays the ground for a "case study" of the alien other, as happened before from Lilliput to Brobdingnag (see Swift 1994: 12ff. and 97ff.). As he does not speak the language yet, this first encounter follows a rather "monological" procedure, which, however, inspires a range of important reactions: Gulliver experiences the emotive function of language,[22] begins to challenge the essential difference between man and machine and, more generally, man's creations, and links his thoughts to a mimetic concept of language, art and literary form, placing them in the context of the media revolution at the turn of the century. His critical (and retarding) reflections lead him to acknowledge the Solasi singsong as a genuine language that he wants to adopt, and the Solasi as a more advanced society within which he seeks a place. Against this backdrop, Gulliver's first truly dialogical interaction with a group of Solasi takes up and advances the previous considerations: he explores language as a code, that is, its meta-linguistic function, and extends his genealogical approach to the relation between the human and his creations to an evolutionary concept of language and the arts. This prepares Gulliver's ultimate encounter and friendship with Midore, the chief Solasi. Their comparison of the role of language and the arts in Faremido and on Earth raises Gulliver's earlier reflections to a new level. In their discussion they address language's poetic function in a way that suggests to transfer the notion of evolutionary encounters to inter-art relationships and not least the reader's encounter with the story—who, after all, is the one unraveling the Barthian "tissue of quotations" thus recomposing the story. It is only then that events come to a full circle for Gulliver. He learns that it was ultimately he who has served as a "case study" for the Solasi from the beginning. They found him an interesting example for an intelligent "disease," which they classified as Remisolami-Sidore, who, unlike other human beings, is capable of learning their language. Linking science fiction narrative techniques to contemporary discourses, predominantly Darwin's theory of evolution, this reversal of perspective thus challenges allegedly established binaries (of foreign/self, man/machine, art/non-art, author/reader, etc.) and invites the reader to redefine the alien other and alien art.

The story's three encounters—with Sido, the Solasi society, and Midore— illuminate this development and "literarization" of intertextuality and inter-art relations. Reversing the narrative procedure in Kubin's novel, the story begins by examining the role of art at the turn of the century, particularly within the context of the media revolution. Gulliver's first encounter with Sido serves as a background for these reflections. Sido is the first Solasi Gulliver meets in Faremido. While he still ponders "who might be the man" (Karinthy 1965: 10) that controls the machine, the robot begins voicing a similar singsong to that which welcomed Gulliver:

> This time it was [...] a different, deep, rhythm, with a rising final inflection which I cannot, unfortunately, express in the chromatic scale—but roughly in the following sequence: g, a, a, g-sharp, g, g-sharp. I heard this phrase several times, while the eyes stared at me. The sounds stirred me strangely—as if I were addressed in a foreign language that does not know any text.
>
> Karinthy 1965: 10

While Gulliver listens to the voice within the framework of familiar grammatical structures ("a rising final inflection"), he, at the same time, reaches the limits of any sign system he is familiar with; the singsong remains untranslatable. It is the resulting ambiguity that opens the realm to the emotive qualities beyond when the music "stirred him strangely." He then draws on what has already been a popular remedy for Wells' time-traveling narrator: the imitation of the unfamiliar sound (Wells 2002: 26). Gulliver repeats the sequence a few times, which Sido ultimately answers with a sequence of three different notes. The game starts afresh and continues with a chain of other sequences until Sido leaves abruptly. Despite its dialogical procedure, the conversation is still based on a monological structure: Gulliver's utterances are a repetition of but not engagement with Sido's singsong. In his following reflections, Gulliver critically links this experience to man's relation to his creations and to a mimetic concept of art: an approach that measures art's value by its capacity to express "forms of life, forms and colours, history and feelings to such perfection" (Karinthy 1965: 14) that they surpass real life. As a consequence, he claims that, "[m]ankind reached a point where the painting of a nude fetched ten times as much as the woman who served as the painter's model." Both Gulliver's "monological" encounter with Sido and an artist's mimetic encounter with his subject ultimately lack social and artistic engagement.

The story contextualizes this discussion within changes medial at the turn of the century, particularly the invention of film: Gulliver's comparison of living actors on a theater stage and their flickering images on a movie screen reads as a literary anticipation of Walter Benjamin's thoughts in *The Work of Art in the Age of Mechanical Reproduction* (1936). It already implies the imperative of an aesthetic (re)definition of moving pictures, which the narrative takes up in some ideas for "cinematic narration"—for instance when Gulliver approaches and gets an aerial overview of Faremido, as if in an extreme long shot, while he and the Solasi examine each other in fragmented detail, as if in an extreme close-up.

Gulliver's following encounter is with a group of Solasi and culminates in "a regular concert [...] the machines made music" (Karinthy 1965: 15). For the narrative, this encounter is also the point at which to introduce a poetological perspective that links the problem of dialogue to the reader function, expands the concept of evolution to art, and addresses the transition from the spoken to the written word. When meeting this group of Solasi, Gulliver for the first time realizes that "in this country they speak with music" and begins to interact with the alien creatures. While he uses sign language and gestures to refer to various things in the surrounding area, they offer him the corresponding "translations," which he, in turn, learns by heart: they introduce themselves as "so, la, si," their land as "fa, re, mi, do," and their palace as "mi, fa, re." As this inner-fictional dialogue proves successful, the story adds a new dimension with Gulliver directly addressing and inviting his reader to "sing" the original words "as this is the only way they make sense" (16). In what follows, this link between the narrative's (implied) multi-code level of composition and the reader function allows the story to expand the concept of evolution to language while it, at the same time, implicitly (and—in its Swiftian style—overtly) extends it to literature. Gulliver's reflections on the relation between the Solasi and human beings and the different role of music in both societies introduce this thought. He not only accepts the alien creatures as a physically and cognitively superior species, but he also appreciates their emotional and communicative advancement: "As for the force of their emotions and passions, it is characteristic that they use [...] the means which *we* employ only for the expression of our most complex and heightened feelings—the medium of music" (1965: 19, emphasis in the original). Broadening the idea of a linguistic evolution to an artistic one, this comparison finally allows the story to condense its different threads of thought at the entrance of the Solasi factory where Gulliver reads some "golden signs or letters": intertwining the Solasi's (re-)production to the written (re-)production of the sung sign introduces and illuminates the idea of autopoiesis of both, the alien creature and alien art.

Against this backdrop, Gulliver finally—after months of assimilation and language acquisition—meets Midore, the chief Solasi, with whom he explores and reflects on both the origin and categorization of self and alien other as well as language and alien art. Covering a broad range of theories on human existence Gulliver draws the line from philosophy to biology to mathematics, while, at the same time, Midore questions their shared distinction between soul and reason—thus challenging one of the fundamental binaries of the Western world. At the heart of their discussion lies Gulliver's account of his acquisition of the Solasi language in comparison to man's languages and another binary, the distinction between concrete and abstract sign systems:

> [W]e never dreamt of the possibility of expressing concrete thoughts by musical sounds. [...] I explained that we expressed our feelings through it [...]. This amazed him [Midore] because for the *solasis* these were synonymous. He could not understand how we failed to notice that emotion expressed thought, that in turn created the emotion—and *vice versa*. I told him that we sometimes combined these two, expressing our thoughts through emotions, and I spoke of songs which were the framework for this process, the spoken word being combined with a musical accompaniment or set to a melody.
>
> Karinthy 1965: 27, emphases in the original

Like the musical language of the Solasi, Karinthy's story thus encourages its reader to explore literary language and its potential to reveal the immediate and concrete—from a philosophical point of view, unlike Kubin and contemporaries who engaged with concrete poetry such as Apollinaire.

This final holistic approach concurs with Karinthy's more general definition of literature as a universal language, which he illustrated in one of his letters to H. G. Wells in 1925:

Literature is certainly more than art and represents man as a whole with skin and hair, with soul and reason, with eyes and ears and so on—quite in contrast to an *actual* artist who only ever represents one sense: the painter the eye, the musician the ear, the sculptor the sense of touch, the poet the soul, the philosopher reason.

Karinthy 1989: 67, my translation, emphasis in the original

Such a holistic concept of literature, however, also implies a holistic, cross-medial mode of reading, which *The Voyage to Faremido* encourages its recipients to adopt: it invites the reader to engage with the text, to enter a dialogue with literature as if with another person.

Art as cognition

Russian author Evgenij Zamyatin extends the science fictional redefinition of the role of art. While Kubin problematizes the conventionalization of art and Karinthy rehabilitates art's communicative potential, Zamyatin's *We* (1921), an early model for Orwell's *Nineteen Eighty-Four* (1949), shifts the perspective in a twofold way: the novel redefines art, particularly music, as a mode of cognition with a reversed narrative view. Rather than focusing on a narrator's entry to an alien world it tells the story of a narrator's alienation and escape from a familiar world—an escape from a totalitarian system that is initiated and mediated by aesthetic experiences. Within this context, both the fictional concept of the alien other and alien art are redefined as a hybrid figure from within: the alien is not what lies beyond a boundary of a political or artistic (or any other) system but is an inherent part of it.

In the future totalitarian "One State," a true panoptic[23] and Taylorist[24] society, creativity is considered a disease prevalent until the modern era when humanity suffered from that "ancient sickness of dreaming" (Zamyatin 2007: 67), which allowed him only to create pieces of art through "'inspiration,' a strange form of epilepsy" (17). The novel, the journal of D-503, tells the story of such a "disease": the narrator is one of the chief engineers responsible for the *Integral*, a spaceship that will allow the state's "Benefactor" to extend his absolute power to outer space. A faithful servant to the system, D-503 plans on recording his work in his journal. When he meets I-330 and listens to her playing the synesthetic music of modern composer Alexander Scriabin, however, he is "incurabl[y]" (79) "infected"—a condition that worsens with his regular visits to the Ancient House: a museal and liminal place at the One State's boundary, the Green Wall. Paralleling the Integral's further progress and his very own creative development, that is his "decline," D-503's story explores a process of increasing alienation, stages varying liminal experiences and increasingly intertwines scientific and poetic narration, contrasting the language of an experimental setup with synesthetic writing, ellipses, and metaphorical speech. The story reaches its climax when he ultimately enters a secret passage and crosses to "the other side" (to revert to and reread Kubin's title) beyond the Green Wall where he meets the MEPHI, a parallel society that plans on overthrowing the One State. The novel's end, however, remains open: while the MEPHI initiate an uprising, all One State citizens, including the narrator, are subjected to the "Great Operation" (202) in an attempt to reinstate order and cure the "sickness (a soul)" (203).[25] In contrast to the previous stories, this narrative links science fiction writing and D-503's alienation and social exclusion (due to his "incurable" sickness) in order to assume a "perspective of second order" from within (employing places of transition such as doors, thresholds, passageways)—a twist that is mirrored by Zamyatin's literary position and the novel's complicated publication history that began at the newly instated Soviet censorship bureau.[26]

Ancient art and (hi-)story are literally marginalized and displaced in the One State: the Ancient House is the only place that assembles art from the past from Homer to Pushkin. It is also, revealingly, a (secret) transitional space where behind a mirror[27] D-503 finds the entrance to a secret passageway that literally undermines this hermetically closed system's boundary and leads to the other side beyond the Green Wall. Tellingly, it is this place of ancient culture and art that links the technocratic world inside to the natural world outside.

Beyond the Ancient House, the One State is, at first glance, presented as a truly technocratic construction where art, if at all, exists as a mechanically reproducible derivate of technology. It builds, however, upon an elaborate aesthetic system that affects all areas of life from architecture via entertainment to intimacy: the One State's transparent glass façades, the musicometer's "mathematical composition[s]" (17) and the "pink ticket" system for sexual intercourse read like a constructivist caricature that engages with contemporary aesthetic concepts and their social and cultural consequences. In fact, drawing the line back to Kubin, *We* is another example for a mode of science fiction writing that critically links "aesthetics and bureaucracy":

Both are human productions after all, and the engineer Zamyatin is a true constructivist whose World State is decidedly a work of art of the epoch of Malevich and El Lissitsky [...] *We*'s revolutionaries are iconoclasts rather than freedom fighters, and the sexual repression of the state is closer to Loos' condemnation of ornament and Le Corbusier's hygienic spaces than to Puritan settlements or Roman Catholic monasteries.

Jameson 2005: 202

Zamyatin's novel hence does what all utopian/dystopian and science fictional novels do: it engages with the present rather than with the future (or past) and, more specifically, contextualizes contemporary aesthetics and re-reads them as linked to their role and function for the development of the story.

It is the music of Alexander Scriabin (1872–1915) that holds a particular place in this development: his colorful music[28] triggers a moment of initiation and point of no return for the narrator when, one day, he attends a public talk on the comparison between old and new music. Before introducing the newly invented musicometer, a mechanical musical instrument, the "phonolector" presents I-330 playing Scriabin's music at the old grand piano—which brings D-503 into a state of ecstasy:

She sat and played. It was wild, convulsive, colourful—like everything back then: lacking even a shadow of rational mechanics. And, of course, all those around me were right: they were all laughing. Except a few including me – but why wasn't I? Yes, epilepsy is a psychic sickness—a pain ... a slow, sweet pain—a sting—and you wish it would go deeper, hurt more. Then, slowly—sunshine emerges. Not our kind of sunshine, the pale-bluish-crystalline kind, which disperses evenly through our glass bricks—no: it was a wild, rushing, burning sun, expelling itself, shedding itself in little tufts.

The person sitting next to me glanced to the left—at me—and giggled. For some reason, I distinctly recall seeing on his lips: a microscopic spit bubble jump out and burst. This bubble brought me to my senses. I was myself again.

Zamyatin 2007: 18

This musically induced loss of control is marked by a reference to epilepsy, the "psychic sickness," which initiates the process of alienation and exclusion that is to follow throughout the narrator's steps of developing a soul. Additionally, a change in the narrator's writing links his own musically liminal experience to a poetically liminal experience for the reader: his language changes from a very linear, scientific writing (stressed by the inclusion of some mathematical equations to the journal) to a stream of consciousness narration that employs a number of poetic devices from ellipses to metaphor. It is particularly the image of the yellow sun (the note *d* as opposed to the bluish *e* in Scriabin's chromatic scale), that will recur throughout the narrator's various stages of inner change and lead him on to leave his Platonic cave: shining through the fabric of I-330's yellow dress, the golden smile of a Buddha in the Ancient House, the bricks of a yellow wall behind the mirror. This moment of musical reception thus establishes a dual mode of musical narration, oscillating between mathematical rhetorics and colorful images, that intensifies and characterizes all future encounters with alien art in D-503's process of alienation.

What follows are various visits to the Ancient House with I-330 that increasingly expand the narrator's musical and poetic liminal experience from the arts to all areas of his life: from everyday life to (breaking) the law. It is here that he "rehearses" his ultimate, actual transition to "the other side"—not least reflected in the place's frequent connotation as a theater stage. It metonymically condenses the human condition and imagination, personified in the figure of I-330 in whose eyes, "two terrifyingly dark windows," D-503 reads "a very unknown, strange life" (Zamyatin 2007: 26). Likewise, the Ancient House is a place whose opacity and polyvalence contrast with the One State's aesthetics of transparency and "clarity": behind a "creaky, opaque door" (24) the narrator enters "chaos" and "disorderly space[s]" that assemble countless artifacts from the past. Amongst them "stood that strange, 'grand' musical instrument, amid the wild, disorganised, crazy multicolour of tones and shapes—like that ancient music" (25). The musical liminal experience thus expands into a more profound cultural liminal experience, characterized by a cultural "language" and an interplay of objects, signs, and meanings that the narrator has difficulties to decode. The same accounts for D-503's interaction with I-330, for whom the Ancient House turns into a stage to perform a role that is not part of the One State's protocol: she dresses in "a short, old-fashioned, bright-yellow dress, a black hat, black stockings" (27), a costume to seduce the narrator—an emotional liminal experience which he is soon prepared to encounter:

> The heavy, creaking, opaque door closed and just then, with great pain, my heart opened wide and then wider still: all the way open. Her lips: mine. I drank and drank, then broke away and silently looked into the eyes thrown upon to me . . . and again . . .
>
> The semi-darkness of the room, the blue, the saffron-yellow, the dark-green Morocco leather, the golden smile of the Buddha, the twinkle of the mirror.

And my old dream is so understandable now: everything is impregnated with golden pink sap, and it was about to overflow its edges, about to gush—

Ripened. And, inevitably, like the iron and the magnet with sweet obedience to their precise, immutable laws, I poured myself into her. There was no pink ticket, there were no calculations, there was no One State, there was no me. There were only gentle, sharp, clenched teeth and there were golden eyes thrown wide open to me—and through them I slowly went inside, deeper and deeper still. And silence— except in the corner, thousands of miles away, where drops were dripping into the sink. I was the universe, and eras and epochs passed as drop followed drop . . .

                                                                Zamyatin 2007: 65f.

This pivotal scene brings D-503's alienation process to a close: in having prohibited intercourse he transgresses not only his own emotional but also the state's juridical boundaries. At the same time, his alienation induces yet another poetic liberation by encouraging him to explore and experiment with hitherto unfamiliar narrative techniques. Colorful enumerations build chains of meaning (unlike in Kubin's novel) that link distant places: from the Ancient House's semi-darkness to Orient and Occident back to the mirror's heterotopia and beyond. Lyrical images intertwine present, past, and future, condensing "eras and epochs" in one drop of water. Unexpected juxtapositions link different realms of meaning creating new metaphors and modes of synesthetic writing ("audible scent," 118).

These multifaceted liminal experiences promote such profound inner changes that a doctor at the "Bureau of Medicine" ultimately tells the narrator: "you've developed a soul" (79). It is only then that he is prepared for the transition to the other side. In his wish to leave his Platonic cave, he explores the yellow-brick passageway beyond the mirror but is only successful in going beyond the heavy door at its other end, when he ultimately joins forces with I-330. This ultimate, very physical liminal experience refers back to his very first, aesthetic liminal experience when listening to Scriabin's music:

An intolerably colourful uproar, a whistle, daylight [. . .] Then I opened my eyes wide and I was face-to-face, in actuality, with the very thing, which no living person today had seen until now—other than through the cloudy glass of the Wall, which weakened, obscured, and reduced it by a thousand times.

The sun . . . it wasn't our sun, evenly distributed along the mirrored surfaces of the streets: it was live splinters and incessantly jumping dots, blinding your eyes and spinning your head. And the trees were like candles jutting right up into the sky; like Spiders on gnarled paws squatting on the earth; like mute, green fountains.

                                                                Zamyatin 2007: 135f.

This is where the story and its narrator's alleged (creative) "disease" reach their climax. The sudden immediacy of impressions ("as if a bomb had exploded in my head") shifts the narrator's boundaries of sensual perception and poetic expression, condensed in the numerous ellipses, insertions, and parentheses of the whole journal entry of that day. The liberation from rigid discursive, historic, and poetic structures, however, does not last and the novel's end is left open: after being subjected to the "Great Operation" it is only the narrator's writing that is left and prevents his story from decline: "The handwriting is mine. And this now is the exact same handwriting, but, happily, it is only the handwriting that is similar. None of the ravings, none of the ridiculous metaphors, none of the feelings: only the facts" (202). Yet, it is that very handwriting, in its materiality as a journal, that traces the narrator's alienation process, reflects, in every sentence, the dialogue between artistic and technological language and suggests to redefine art as a means of cognition.

Postmodern prospects

Following the three stories *The Other Side* (1909), "Voyage to Faremido" (1916), and *We* (1921), the discussion traced a development of the alien other and literature's perspective on alien art(s) that shed light on significant shifts in the modern era and signified meaningful changes beyond. While both Kubin's novel and Karinthy's story focus on their protagonists' and narrators' processes of entering new worlds, one in diagnosing how artistic strategies turned conventional and the other in rehabilitating art's communicative potential, they lay the ground for a more fundamental transition in Zamyatin's novel: the alienation of a protagonist and narrator from a familiar world and his ultimate transition into a new world linked to a redefinition of art as a means of cognition. Drawing on these reflections upon the aesthetic and "historical present," the three stories also explore the more general relation between literary writing and other artistic modes such as painting and music. They stage an interplay and perform a dialogue between the immediacy of painting and music and the mediacy of the written wor(l)d which creates alternate modes of literary expression. Within this context, both the fictional concept of the alien other and alien art are redefined as a hybrid figure from within: the alien is not what lies beyond a boundary of a political or artistic system but is an inherent part of it.

Notes

1   See Arjun Appadurai's famous definition of "*the imagination as a social practice*":
    "The imagination is now central to all forms of agency, is itself a social fact, and is
    the key component of the new global order" (2003: 31, emphasis in the original).

2   This includes language as a primary structure, and stretches to works of fiction as
    a secondary structure (literature, film, music, etc.).

3   Roland Barthes defines the present as the true subject of utopian writing:
    "the mark of utopia is the everyday; or even: everything everyday is utopian"
    (1989: 17). Fredric Jameson extends this definition to science fiction in general:
    "Science Fiction is generally understood as the attempt to imagine unimaginable
    futures. But its deepest subject may in fact be our own historical present"
    (2005: 345).

4   Despite its long tradition, the attempt at distinguishing science fiction and
    utopian/dystopian writing still raises more questions than it solves and is, to say
    the least, problematic. For the purpose of this essay, however, Fredric Jameson's
    rough distinction shall suffice. Following Darko Suvin he argues "[u]topia to be a
    socio-economic sub-genre of that broader literary form" (Jameson 2005: xiv), that
    is science fiction. Against this background, I would also argue that John
    Huntington's definition of utopia/dystopia, which he presented in his seminal
    analysis of H. G. Wells' works: the "two-world structure" as a "juxtaposition of two
    incongruous worlds" (Huntington 1981: 240), works as a general characteristic of
    both *science fiction* and *tales of transnationalism*.

5   The creatures speak "a strange and very sweet and liquid tongue" but "made no
    effort to communicate with me" (Wells 2002: 22f.).

6   Depending on its complexity these dialogical constellations multiply the more
    the story's structure resembles a Chinese box or employs the matryoshka
    principle. In Wells' story the dialogue between the recipient's present world and the
    story is reflected within the story in a dialogue between the Time Traveller's
    narrative and his listeners' present world. The dialectic structure is mirrored in the
    contrast between the Time Traveller's turn-of-the-century British home and the
    world in the year 802.701. In that very future the tension and dialogue between
    different worlds continues in the conflict between the upper earth realm of the
    Eloi and the underground realm of the Morlocks. On an aesthetic level this
    dialectic structure is mirrored and multiplied, for example by numerous
    intertextual references.

7   Irina Rajewsky distinguishes three subcategories of intermediality. 1. medial
    transposition: "a production-oriented, 'genetic' conception of intermediality," e.g.
    film adaptations; 2. media combination: "a communicative-semiotic concept,

based on the combination of at least two medial forms of articulation," e.g. comics;
3. intermedial references: "a communicative-semiotic concept, but here it is *by definition* just *one* medium—the referencing medium (as opposed to the medium referred to)—that is materially present," e.g. the musicalization of literature (Rajewsky 2005: 51ff., emphases in the original).

8 Darko Suvin famously defined science fiction "as the *literature of cognitive estrangement*" (1972: 372, emphasis in the original). However, in science fiction "the attitude of estrangement—used by Brecht in a different way, within a still predominantly 'realistic' context—has grown into the *formal framework* of the genre" (375, emphasis in the original).

9 All page numbers refer to the German original (Kubin 1990), all translations are taken from the digital pre-edition of a new English translation that will be published in summer 2014: *The Other Side*, M. Mitchell (trans.), London/ Sawtry: Dedalus.

10 For a more detailed discussion of his work in general and art quotes in Kubin's work in particular, see Rauchenbacher (2011).

11 In this regard, the story may be read as an answer to H. G. Wells' *The Time Machine* (1895) and reverses one of Wells' main themes: historical amnesia.

12 There is only one painting portraying a painter as viewed from the front. It is part of the paratext and strongly resembles a photograph of Kubin of 1904 (see alfred-kubin.blogspot.de, accessed 31 March 2014), particularly with regard to posture and light incidence (the face, as if in reference to the novel's title, half in shadow). On the other hand, however, it introduces the story world even before the fly-title, both as regards its style and position, and thus challenges the boundary between the non-fictional and fictional realm: it is painted in a similar fashion as the other pictures in the novel and it frames the narrative together with a map of the Dream Realm on the very last page. Within the story most illustrations take a personal perspective with many of them unfolding inner pictures, thus crossing the boundary between the narrator's outer and inner perspective (Kubin 1990: 115, 181, 259, 276, 317). There is only one picture showing the narrator himself—from behind: revealingly at a moment where he speaks of his very last day at home before his journey to the utopian Dream Realm.

13 These are two functions of book illustration that in some way or other shape the discussion of book art: "Illustration *reacts*, is chronologically subordinate to the text, *interprets* what is preexisting and predetermined" (Neugebauer 1996: 8, my translation, emphases in the original); and: "Two functions are to be distinguished: book illustration as decoration and embellishment of a belletristic or religious work or with a documentary function for the illustration of a scientific text" (Walther 1988: 81f., my translation).

14 In his Inaugural Lecture on "The Order Of Discourse" at the Collège de France in
   1970, Foucault distinguishes three modes of discourse regulation: exterior
   "procedures of exclusion" (1981: 52), internal "principles of classification, of
   ordering, of distribution" (56), and structural strategies "determining the condition
   of [both] their application," thus resulting in "a rarefaction [. . .] of the speaking
   subjects" (61). While the Dream Realm develops all three of them to perfection, its
   further development shows the destructive consequences of a discursive order for
   its own sake.

15 The German original speaks pointedly of "*Komödienobrichkeit*" (Kubin 1990: 77).

16 One of the illustrations accompanying and commenting upon the Dream Realm's
   demise draws a terrifying picture of the ubiquitous death that the state's ultimate
   apocalypse brought about (Kubin 1990: 305): a heap of corpses in a gateway
   invoking pictures of the First and Second World War and particularly of the
   liberation of the concentration camps in 1945; for instance as shown in Alain
   Resnais' 1955 documentation *Nuit et brouillard* (*Night and Fog*, cf. picture 2 at
   www.welt.de/kultur/history/article12333057, accessed 31 March 2014).

17 The narrator's particular, old-fashioned, illustrations are the questionable ticket to
   the utopian world of the past: "*You* [. . .] were selected because certain of your
   drawings made an impression on the Master" (Kubin 1990: 18).

18 The role of irony is particularly interesting in relation to the narrative perspective
   in the novel: being a first-person narrative, various ironic "meta commentaries"
   introduce a "second," authorial perspective that shines through the narrator's voice
   every now and then and is, most importantly, present in the caricature of the
   story's characters.

19 Ulrich Broich defines a narrow concept of intertextuality (as opposed to Julia
   Kristeva's very broad notion) as a process of communication that is only successful
   under certain conditions: "Intertextuality in this narrow sense presupposes the
   success of a specific communication process, in the course of which not only
   author and reader are aware of a text's intertextuality, but where, additionally, each
   of both communication partners takes the respective other's awareness of that
   very intertextuality into account" (1985: 31).

20 François Sudre introduced his concept of *Solresol* in his *Langue musicale
   universelle* (1827, published posthumously in 1866). At the turn of the century the
   language gained increasing popularity with Bolesla Gajewski's *Grammaire du
   Solresol* (1902). What is particularly interesting about *Solresol* is that its complexity
   derives from the interplay between different sign systems (letters, tones, colors,
   and gestures) rather than the number of signs (which is limited to seven, as in the
   solfa notation)—something that Karinthy's story alludes to, for instance when
   describing the "color and softness" (Karinthy 1965: 7) of the music.

21 Already in the beginning of the twentieth century, Karinthy's contemporary and famous composer and pedagogue Zoltán Kodály introduced the solmization method to Hungarian musical pedagogy.

22 See Roman Jakobson's distinction of the six functions of language (2007).

23 In *Discipline and Punish* Foucault discusses Jeremy Bentham's concept of the Panopticon, the ideal prison and "laboratory of power" (1995: 204), as a social structure: "The Panopticon [...] must be understood as a generalizable model of functioning; a way of defining power relations in terms of the everyday life of men. [...] Utopias, perfectly closed in upon themselves, are common enough. [...] But the Panopticon must not be understood as a dream building: it is the diagram of a mechanism of power reduced to its ideal form; [...] it is in fact a figure of political technology that may and must be detached from any specific use" (205).

24 In *The Principles of Scientific Management* (1911) Frederick Winslow Taylor suggests various strategies to link industrial production and scientific study in order to improve production efficiency—a model that the novel's One State reflects in its system of "tickets" that determine and terminate all private and public—social, sexual, educational, industrial, etc.—activities.

25 For a discussion of mental sickness as a mechanism of exclusion from a discourse, see Foucault (1981: 52ff. and 1995).

26 Initially, the novel was planned to be published in 1921. Censorship, however, prevented the publication and, as a consequence, the novel was first released in English language in 1924. It was only in 1952 that a first edition of the book was available in Russian.

27 Foucault discusses the mirror as a "heterotopia," a transitional space that intertwines incompatible places (2005: 44ff.).

28 Russian composer and musician Alexander Scriabin was himself synesthetic and invented a color organ, the *clavier à lumières*, for his piece "Prométhée. Le Poème du feu" "Prometheus: Poem on Fire" (1910).

References

Appadurai, A. (2003), *Modernity at Large*, Minneapolis, MN: University of Minnesota Press.

Assmann, P. (1999), " 'Daß sich unter ihren Augen das Moderne in ein Chaos verwandelt, ist ein Genuß.' Kubin diesseits und jenseits der Anderen Seite," in J. L. W. Freund and C. Ruthner (eds), *Der Demiurg ist ein Zwitter*, Münich: Fink.

Barthes, R. (1977), "The Death of the Author," in S. Heath (ed.), *Roland Barthes. Image Music Text*, London: Fontana Press.

Barthes, R. (1989), *Sade, Fourier, Loyola*, R. Miller (trans.), Berkeley, CA and Los Angeles: University of California Press.

Benjamin, W. (1968), *The Work of Art in the Age of Mechanical Reproduction*, H. Arendt (ed.), London: Fontana.

Broich, U. (1985), "Formen der Markierung von Intertextualität," in U. Broich and M. Pfister (eds), *Intertextualität. Formen, Funktionen, anglistische Fallstudien*, Tübingen: Niemeyer.

Butler, S. (1985), *Erewhon*, London: Penguin.

Capoferro, R. (2010), *Empirical Wonder: Historicizing the Fantastic, 1660–1760*, Bern: Peter Lang.

Delany, S. R. (1980), "Generic Protocols: Science Fiction and Mundane," in A. H. T. De Lauretis and K. M. Woodward (eds), *The Technological Imagination: Theories and Fictions*, Madison, WI: Coda Press.

Foucault, M. (1981), "The Order of Discourse," in R. Young (ed.), *Untying The Text: A Post-Structuralist Reader*, Boston, MA and London: Routledge & Kegan Paul.

Foucault, M. (1995), *Discipline and Punish. The Birth of the Prison*, New York: Random House.

Foucault, M. (2005), *Die Heterotopien/Les hétérotopies. Der utopische Körper /Le corps utopique. Zwei Radiovorträge*, M. Bischoff (trans.), Frankfurt am Main: Suhrkamp.

Godwin, F. ([1638] 2009), *The Man in the Moone*, W. Poole (ed.), Plymouth and Peterborough: Broadview Press.

Huntington, J. (1981), "Thinking by Opposition: The 'Two-World' Structure in H.G. Wells's Short Fiction," *Science Fiction Studies*, 8.3: 240–54.

Jakobson, R. (2007), "Linguistik und Poetik," in S. H. D. Birus (ed.) *Poesie der Grammatik und Grammatik der Poesie*, Berlin and New York: De Gruyter.

Jameson, F. (2005), *Archaeologies of the Future. The Desire Called Utopia and Other Science Fictions*, London and New York: Verso.

Karinthy, F. ([1916] 1965), "Voyage to Faremido," *Capillária*, Budapest: Corvina Press.

Karinthy, F. ([1916] 1989), *Die neuen Reisen des Lemuel Gulliver*, Berlin: Verlag Neues Berlin.

Knowlson, J. R. (1968), "A Note on Bishop Godwin's 'Man in the Moone': The East Indies Trade Route and a 'Language' of Musical Notes," *Modern Philologies*, 65.4: 357–61.

Kubin, A. ([1909] 1990), *Die andere Seite. Ein phantastischer Roman*, München: Edition Spangenberg.

Lippuner, H. (1977), *Alfred Kubins Roman "Die andere Seite"*, Bern and München: A. Francke.

Neugebauer, R. (1996), "Aspekte literarischer Buchillustration im 20. Jahrhundert," in R. Neugebauer (ed.), *Aspekte der literarischen Buchillustration im 20. Jahrhundert*, Wiesbaden: Harrassowitz Verlag.

Rajewsky, I. O. (2005), "Intermediality, Intertextuality and Remediation: A Literary Perspective on Intermediality," *Intermédialités*, 6: 43–64.

Rauchenbacher, M. (2011), "Alfred Kubin," in M. R. K. Fliedl and J. Wolf (eds), *Handbuch der Kunstzitate*, Berlin and Boston, MA: De Gruyter.

Schwanberg, J. (1999), "In zwei Welten: das literarische und zeichnerische Werk Alfred Kubins," in J. L. W. Freund and C. Ruthner (eds), *Der Demiurg ist ein Zwitter*, München: Fink.

Suvin, D. (1972), "On the Poetics of the Science Fiction Genre", *College English*, 34.3: 372–82.

Swift, J. (1994), *Gulliver's Travels*, London: Penguin.

Taylor, F. W. (1911), *The Principles of Scientific Management*, New York and London: Harper & Brothers.

Van Zon, G. ([1726] 1991), *Word and Picture. A Study of the Double Talent in Alfred Kubin and Fritz von Herzmanovsky-Orlando*, New York: Peter Lang.

Walther, K. K. (1988), *Lexikon der Buchkunst und Bibliophilie*, München: Saur.

Wells, H. G. ([1895] 2002), *The Time Machine*, New York: Modern Library.

Zamyatin, Y. ([1921] 2007), *We*, London: Vintage.

3

Assimilating Aliens: Imagining National Identity in Oskar Panizza's *Operated Jew* and Salomo Friedlaender's *Operated Goy*

Joela Jacobs

University of Chicago, USA

In the 1871 constitution of the German Empire, the Jewish population of Germany was granted equal citizenship rights.[1] This process shifted the so-called Jewish Question[2] about the position of Jews in Germany from the struggle for legal equality towards a discourse about the nature of assimilation, which was intensified by increasing Jewish immigration from Eastern Europe around 1900. The debate about what constituted German culture and identity focused on the relationship not only between German Christians and Jews, but also between the assimilated German Jewry and newly arriving orthodox, Yiddish-speaking Jews from Eastern Europe. These changes complicated already complex notions of cultural assimilation, appropriation, and belonging. Answers to the Jewish Question took shapes as different as the Zionist dream of a Jewish state or conversion to Christianity. Yet many approaches shared a focus on the foreign or alien nature of Jewish culture within Germany, which consequently would either have to be radically integrated or expelled, despite examples of successful coexistence that allowed for the acceptance of cultural difference. The image of the "Jewish alien" as a figure of otherness persistently occurred in aesthetic and literary representations, which often satirically commented on the political and cultural facets of the Jewish Question. Those exaggerated caricatures of stereotypes show particularly well the ways in which not only Jewish, but also German identity was imagined and constructed at the time.

In the following pages, I will examine such a pair of satirical and even gruesome texts, published almost thirty years apart, yet in conversation with each other, which engage with the question of Jewish assimilation by exploring the alien characteristics with which the figure of the Jew was imbued. The first text is *Der Operierte Jud* (*The Operated Jew*), written by the non-Jewish Oskar Panizza[3] in 1893, and the second is *Der Operierte Goy* (*The Operated Goy*), which was conceived as a response to Panizza's text by the Jewish author Salomo Friedlaender[4] in 1922. Both texts belong to the micro-genre of the literary Grotesque[5] and they present a figure's assimilation process through satirically exaggerated means. The authors' dissimilar backgrounds with respect to the Jewish Question and the texts' different political settings within the Wilhelmine Empire and the Weimar Republic, respectively, make them a fascinating case study of the role of literature in the shifting discourse about Jewish assimilation in Germany around 1900. Reading the texts together shows a variety of attitudes toward Jewish assimilation throughout this tumultuous time, and it provides two distinct perspectives on the imagination of the Jew as alien that are nonetheless negotiated through similar literary strategies.

In Panizza's *The Operated Jew*, a Jewish figure undergoes extreme physical operations, behavioral training, and speech therapy in order to "become a Goy." His transformation, while initially successful, falls apart in a gruesome manner on his wedding day, and at first glance, this story by a non-Jewish author seems to suggest that any attempt at assimilation is doomed from the beginning because it is a mere act of mimicry. However, by examining the notions of the pure and the hybrid in the text, I will demonstrate that the text problematizes the concept of national identity as such and satirizes the paranoid imagination of German society. In Friedlaender's *The Operated Goy*, an über-Aryan figure falls in love with a Jewish woman and converts to Judaism with body, mind, and soul in steps similar to Panizza's protagonist. While the direction of the change in the text is the opposite, both its transformative and narrative strategies are deliberately the same. I will show that this similarity expands the satirical target of the text from German society to the Jewish community, thus complicating its reading as a strictly oppositional counter-narrative to Panizza's text. Addressing both inner-Jewish conflicts between Western and Eastern European Jewry and the Zionist project, Friedlaender's text poses the provocative thesis that German and the Jewish nationalism employ similar principles of exclusion based on the notion of an essential quality of identity whose purity has to be retained. As a set, the two texts allow me to illustrate the complex problems that arose amidst attempts to define both German and Jewish identity within and against one another in the early twentieth century.

The Operated Jew

The protagonist of Panizza's *Operated Jew* is in every way an amalgamation of exaggerated stereotypes, and as such, he appears like an imagined collage of anti-Semitic insults. His name, Itzig Faitel Stern, is that of a Jewish stock figure,[6] and his appearance, from the shape of his nose to his dark, curly hair, follows anti-Semitic physiognomic typecasting. Against the foil of the white, male German Christian, the narrative constructs the image of a Jewish figure whose "antelope's eye with a subdued, cherry-like glow swam in wide apertures of the smooth velvet, lightly yellow skin of his temple and cheeks" (Zipes 1991: 48). By likening Faitel's appearance and behavior to that of animals, the text calls into question whether its alien protagonist is fully human, and the use of colors is designed to suggest racial difference. Not only are Faitel's species and race described as foreign, but he is also depicted as overly sexual and effeminate, particularly after he receives blood donations from several young Catholic women.[7] In addition, remnants of his religious and cultural practices continue to resurface as misplaced elements, for instance in his constant back-and-forth movement that is reminiscent of Jewish prayer. The construction of Faitel's alienness thus rests on central categories such as species and race, gender and sexuality, as well as religion and culture, which serve both to define normative national identity and to establish Faitel as foreign through his not-belonging to the right categories, or his violation of these categories' supposed clear-cut nature. Faitel's assimilative endeavor cannot succeed because the normative exclusivity of nineteenth-century German national identity does not allow for any inclusion of otherness. The satirically exaggerated stereotypes of the text therefore serve not primarily to target Jews as foreign—though they certainly give a gruesome picture of the range of anti-Semitic insults[8]—but rather to showcase the impossible demands of assimilation by means of hyperbole and the use of similar stereotypes about Germans. The text ultimately destabilizes the notion of an inherent purity or mythical essence of national identity, and therefore challenges seemingly clear-cut normative categories such as race or gender that are used to reinforce belonging and exclusion.

Faitel's story is told by a narrator who is transfixed by the latter's foreignness throughout the story: "It would take a linguist, a choreographer, an aesthete, anatomist, a tailor, and a psychiatrist all in one to grasp and fully explain Faitel's entire appearance, what he said, how he walked, and what he did"

(Zipes 1991: 47). Faitel appears to be so fundamentally different that a slew of experts is required in order to define, categorize, and make him comprehensible in familiar categories. In line with racial pseudo-science and the colonial endeavors of the time, Faitel is to be mapped and charted like a foreign territory. The normative parameters of comparison in this process are equally stereotypical ideas of German national identity that "*imagine* [. . .] the Teutonic genre like some young stalwart, blond and naïve, who walked about smiling with great ignorance" (57, emphasis mine). Yet while meticulously logging every aspect of Faitel's appearance and behavior over the course of many pages, the narrator repeatedly emphasizes his own difficulty in describing Faitel, which seems to indicate that Faitel is too alien to be imagined at all. The text paints a gruesomely exaggerated image that is based on the greatest degree of difference from the German template as possible—dark skin and eyes, a crooked posture, speech that hybridizes several languages and dialects, including animalistic sounds and foreign movements—so that Faitel is introduced to the reader's imagination as the most alien and foreign figure conceivable. In consequence, he is reduced to an object of curiosity and study, rather than a subject in his own right, and not only the operations performed on Faitel's body in the text, but also the narrative dissection of his every move strip him of his humanity:

> There was certainly a great deal of what I [the narrator] would call medical or rather anthropological curiosity in this case. I was attracted to him in the same way I might be to a Negro [. . .]. Perhaps there was also some pity here, but not much. I observed with astonishment how this monster took terrible pains to adapt to our circumstances, our way of walking, thinking, our gesticulations, the expressions of our intellectual tradition, our manner of speech.
>
> Zipes 1991: 52

In his alien manner of speech, the goal of Faitel's attempts at adaptation is "to become such a fine gentilman just like a goymenera and to geeve up all fizonomie of Jewishness" (55). To transform his physiognomy into that of a goy and gentile man, Faitel visits the very specialists invoked earlier. These doctors and scientists reinforce the narrator's descriptions of Faitel's alienness by asking "whether it was certain that Itzig's parentage was human" (1991: 54), and they devise a plan to change Faitel's body, gestures, language, and overall behavior through a series of surgical operations and a regime of intensive retraining in exchange for copious amounts of money. Just as difficult as it was for the narrator to describe the alien Faitel, it is now impossible "to give the reader an account of all the garnishings, changes, injections and quackeries to which Itzig Faitel Stern submitted himself [...] so he could become the equivalent of an Occidental human being" (Zipes 1991: 57). Faitel's "becoming human" consists of making himself appear different, or rather, familiar to others. His bones are broken, his hair straightened and bleached along with his skin, and his movements are restricted by a spiked belt "as they do with dogs" (1991: 56). Actors, gymnasts, and language teachers are hired to re-animate this German cyborg in the "right" ways. His transformation ultimately allows him to be no longer perceived as alien, but as a "dumb, awkward German lad [...]. He called himself Siegfried Freudenstern [...]. Faitel was now an entirely new human being" (58). Unrecognizable to his old acquaintances, the blond, tall, and upright Siegfried Freudenstern is now able to live a different life filled with the prospects of someone who matches the normative description of a German man and a human being. Fitting in allows him to disappear into bourgeois boredom, but it also requires him to leave behind every trace of his former self. Yet the narrator undermines this restrictive definition of assimilation even further by deeming it merely an act of imagination, or of seeing what one wants to see, for "[o]f course, the formation of the teeth, the padded lips, the nasal pitch in Faitel's face had to remain absolutely fixed to prevent a monster from becoming visible. And whoever had an eye for such things could recognize the sensual, fleshy, and jutting Sphinx-like face in Freudenstern's profile" (68). The narrative suggests that assimilation, which is, on the surface of the text, defined as a transformation process that results in becoming someone else, is in fact perceived as a continuous act of imitation that requires one to go to extreme lengths in order to adhere to a norm that is bound to produce doppelgängers. It is therefore conceived of as an act of deception that can only result in living a lie.

The problematic notion of disguising one's true self in order to fit in is based on the idea of an essence that determines one's identity. The text locates this essence in the soul, and it shows through in a person's shibboleth, i.e. the elements of speech that give away one's social or regional origin: "Faitel had heard about the chaste, undefined Germanic soul, which shrouded the possessor like an aroma. This soul was the source of the possessor's rich treasures and formed the shibboleth of the Germanic nations, a soul which was immediately recognized by all who possessed one" (48). As a word with Hebrew roots, the phrase "the shibboleth of the Germanic nations" showcases the hybrid nature of language itself, since German cannot do without foreign words to communicate specific expressions. It is therefore an ironic commentary on the bourgeois German fears of Jewish assimilation, and the term "shibboleth" is also the narrative in a nutshell: it either reveals someone as an authentic member of a community or it exposes him as a fraud.

In the text, the image of the blond German archetype and his particular shibboleth is destabilized by the diversity of the German population itself, and the treatment of language most poignantly negotiates the notions of purity and hybridity. Faitel is tasked to learn standard German, or *Hochdeutsch*, because his hybrid language combines German dialect, French influence, and a range of sounds that are identified as animalistic. His language is considered as alien as his body, taking the anti-Semitic caricature of the *mauschelnde Jude*[9] (mumbling Jew) to the extreme. Yet contrary to the narrator's statements, Faitel is actually not the example of compromised or aberrant language that he is made out to be. He barely speaks in the text, but instead, a vast number of languages and dialects are spoken by others and extensive phonetic spelling goes along with this.[10] Throughout the narrative it thus becomes clear that a German language standard does not exist in practice, but is rather defined by degree of difference from Faitel's manner of speech:

> Since it was hopeless to raise the level of his Palatinate-Yiddish to that of the related pure high German, an attempt was made to bring his former sing-song on the right track through its direct opposite. A private tutor was engaged, and Itzig was to repeat his clear nasal-sounding manner of speech like a schoolboy, sentence by sentence, so that he learned high German like a totally new, foreign language. [...] And now he was examined to determine which German dialect contained the least tonal affinity with Faitel's Palatinate-Yiddish. At first, the specialists considered Pomeranian. But this was too harsh[11] for Faitel. Finally, they agreed upon the Hannoverian dialect.
>
> Zipes 1991: 56f.

Even though the region around Hannover is often considered the "cradle of *Hochdeutsch*", the text makes clear that the selection criterion is rather which German dialect is most different from Faitel's, and can, yet, be imitated by him with the greatest success. This circumstance is ironized when Faitel privately imitates the Germans around him who are supposedly *Hochdeutsch* speakers. The phrases he successfully copies are heavily inflected with the local dialect, which notably differs both from *Hochdeutsch* and from Faitel's usual Yiddish phrasing and word order in the surrounding lines.[12] This makes clear that *Hochdeutsch* is hardly the condition for belonging to German society that it is made out to be; rather, the true shibboleth is the "right" regional dialect.

Despite Faitel's mastery of the "right" language, he is nonetheless exposed as an imitation in the very moment that should establish his transformative success: "Only one thing was still missing, for it was also important to reproduce this human race [...]. A blonde Germanic lass had to help preserve the results that had been garnered through fabulous efforts" (Zipes 1991: 64). But when his wedding day arrives, Faitel drinks too much, and subsequently his old behavior, manner of speech, and ultimately also his physical features return in front of the horrified guests. Described in even more gruesome terms than before, Faitel appears at once like an animal, with a different skin color and religion, sexually deviant and losing the meticulously learned language and gestures. He violates the same categories of belonging as before and exposes the paranoid fear that is caused by this transgression when he says:

> "I vant you shood know dat I'm a human bing jost as good for sumtink as any ov you!" [...A] bloodthirsty, swelling, crimson visage spewed saliva from flabby drooping lips, and gushing eyes glared at them. [...] Faitel jumped from his chair, clicking his tongue, gurgling, and tottering back and forth while making disgusting, lascivious and bestial canine movements with his rear end. "[...] Waiterá, vere iss mine copulated Chreesten bride? [...]" His arms and legs, which had been stretched and bent in numerous operations, could no longer perform the recently learned movements, nor the old ones. [...] Everyone looked with dread at [...] the Jew.
>
> Zipes 1991: 72f.

Whereas Faitel attests to his humanity using his old language, the description reinforces his dehumanized status. It seems that Faitel has been rendered truly alien by the operations society required of him, as he is now painfully stuck in the hybrid space between his old and new existence. Everyone flees in terror at the sight of this unraveling "de-assimilation," and the story ends with the image of a "counterfeit of human flesh, Itzig Faitel Stern" (74). Both Faitel's assimilated life and his marriage fall apart before they have fully begun, and Panizza's story therefore ends not only with the failure of assimilation, but also that of reproduction, which was supposed "to help preserve the results that had been garnered through fabulous efforts."

The Operated Goy

Friedlaender's story from 1922, *The Operated Goy: A Counter-Narrative to Panizza's Operated Jew*, is written in direct response to Panizza's text and turns its premise upside down. The story undoes the gruesome ending and instead presents German-Jewish intermarriage as the path to a society that no longer knows the category of race. In Friedlaender's narrative, an Aryan nobleman converts to Judaism and lives out his life in Jerusalem with his Jewish bride and many children. Just like Faitel, he undergoes complicated operations to match a stereotypical physical image, and his transformation into a Jew is only complete and acceptable after he has learned Hebrew *and* Yiddish, and once "[h]e talked with arms, legs, and tongue, a man after Jehovah's own heart" (Zipes 1991: 84). The goal of his conversion is to attain his bride's hand in marriage with her parents' approval, so this case of successful linguistic reproduction ultimately also equals sexual reproduction and preserves assimilation for future generations.

Friedlaender's narrative reverses the outcomes of Panizza's text in order to hold a mirror up to German society and criticize its increasingly one-sided and paranoid view of assimilation more explicitly. Written by a Jewish author one year before the failed *Hitlerputsch*, the text anticipates the worsening anti-Semitism and militarism of German society, but it also speaks to the contemporary Zionist project and comments on the relationship between assimilated Western and orthodox Eastern European Jewry. To that end, Friedlaender's narrative introduces a semblance of Shakespeare's "two households, both alike in dignity," which are set up as polar opposites through their respective German and Jewish identity, but are shown to have maintained the same values of purity of identity for centuries: (cf. the Montagues and Capulets). As far as purity of race was concerned, the house of Gold-Isaac[13] was the Jewish counterpart to the family of Count Rehsok: "ditto, ever since the destruction of Jerusalem, and ever since the dispersion of the Jewish people in many different countries, the family had never become contaminated by alien blood" (Zipes 1991: 79). Just as Friedlaender's story is identified as a counter-narrative (*Gegenstück*) to Panizza's text in its subtitle, these two houses are called counterparts (*Gegenstücke*); yet their differences in heritage underscore the similarities in the manner they construct and preserve the purity of this heritage, or bloodline. Both texts criticize this particular conception of pure identity by demonstrating through satirically exaggerated means how destructive it can be. Even though Panizza's narrative depicts the failure of changing one's identity and Friedlaender's story presents a successful transformation, both texts show that the categories of the German and the Jew are socially constructed, based on racial pseudo-science, and meant to reinforce the self by excluding the other. Thirty years after Panizza's narrative, Friedlaender's text emphasizes that the situation has far from improved and organized anti-Semitism is on the rise. But his story also extends the critique of exclusionary German national identity to Jewish identity and the contemporary Zionist debates.

The two houses in Friedlaender's narrative are the noble German line of the von Reschok's with their successful son Kreuzwendedich and the Jewish dynasty Gold-Isak with their beautiful daughter Rebecka. From their names to their physical features, both of the main figures reinforce a slew of stereotypes about the kind of identity their families represent. Kreuzwendedich's name (literally: cross-turn-around) signifies his impending act of conversion, or turning around, and the cross (*Kreuz*) alludes both to his Christian identity and to the *Hakenkreuz* (swastika) he wears as an early Nazi supporter. His demeanor is military, his cultural references boast of Nordic mythology, and his appearance is identified as perfectly Aryan. The text contrasts Kreuzwendedich's tall, blond, and blue-eyed appearance with many of Faitel's pre-transformation characteristics and re-inscribes them into Rebecka's Eastern European, Yiddish-speaking father. Rebecka and her Western, assimilated mother, on the other hand, are shown to disrupt stereotypical gender roles with their strong-willed behavior, but this feeds a multiplicity of other typecasts, such as that of the Jewish matriarch and the dangerously seductive beautiful Jewess. Accordingly, Rebecka Gold-Isak is made out to be an exotic, dark-haired beauty, whose name is associated with her prestigious Jewish lineage and indicates the stereotypical wealth of her family.

Count Kreuzwendedich is known for his pronounced anti-Semitism and seeks to distance himself from any contact with Jews and Jewish culture through a warning system that betrays his pure paranoia: "As soon as anything Hebrew showed itself, [his servant made] a shrill sound with a silver whistle. Of course, it would be superfluous to remark that the Count's Great Dane was carefully trained to bite any Jew who came too close. In addition, the raven Hugin could correctly chirp the well-known Borkum anti-Semitic hymn" (Zipes 1991: 77).[14] This multi-species vanguard relies not only on visual cues, but also the supposedly unfailing "*foetor judaicus*" (78), an anti-Semitic concept that dates back to the Middle Ages, according to which Jews have a distinctly different body odor.[15]

The idea that someone's identity would be so clear-cut and obvious that one could smell it reinforces the idea of a Jewish and a German essence that both texts locate in one's blood or soul. In fact, Panizza's story also contains a scented shibboleth, if you will, when it speaks of "the chaste, undefined Germanic soul, which shrouded the possessor like an aroma." The mention of *foetor judaicus* turns this aroma into a foul smell that underpins both texts' criticism of national identity based on a mythical, pure essence.

Rebecka is infuriated by Kreuzwendedich's anti-Semitic behavior and decides to confront him. In order to fool his warning system, she disguises herself as a Germanic Venus figure and thus undergoes the first transformation of the text. But her successful intervention has an unexpected side-effect: Kreuzwendedich falls in love with her, and Rebecka realizes that her retribution would be most effective "if I [...] marry him out of revenge" (Zipes 1991: 78). She begins a campaign to transform Kreuzwendedich into the Jewish groom her parents demand. "Fascinated by his inimical strangeness, she felt hate, vanity, and fury mixed with love. She yearned ardently to overcome everything, that is, she yearned for complete assimilation and incorporation of the enemy" (79). This uncanny image of consumption combines cannibalism and intercourse in a threatening melee.[16] Through the melding of oppositions such as love and hate, death and life, devouring and giving birth, the notions of assimilation and anni-hilation become synonymous. While Faitel belonged neither here, nor there after his failed assimilative endeavor, Kreuzwendedich will be fully absorbed by the Jewish community at the end of the story, so that cultural assimilation ultimately comes to mean cultural annihilation.

None other than Sigmund Freud himself is hired by Rebecka to make Kreuzwendedich aware that he is in love with a Jewish woman, and once he has overcome his shock, he tackles the project of conversion without hesitation. Kreuzwendedich studies Hebrew, learns about Jewish laws, traditions, and prayers, and submits to his circumcision. He takes on the new name Moses, or Moische, Mogandovidwendedich (*Mogandovid*, i.e. the Star of David, replaces the cross in his name), and reverses his last name from Reschok into Koscher. Yet this transformation into an assimilated Jew proves to be not quite enough; rather, Rebecka demands a (re)turn to "more authentic" Eastern European Jewish roots that suggests an uneasy hybrid status for assimilated Western Jewry. Whereas Faitel's hair was turned blond and straight, and his nose, legs, and back straightened, Kreuzwendedich's tall Aryan body is now darkened, curled, hooked and twisted with medical help to resemble "a true Jew." Moreover, he learns Yiddish "as well as all the gestures that go along with it" (Zipes 1991: 83f.), which serve to authenticate his intellectual, spiritual, and physical conversion into what is imagined to be "the most Jewish." He is now accepted by her family and can finally marry Rebecka, which will lead to the ultimate fulfillment of his assimilatory success through reproduction. And indeed, Moische and Rebecka Koscher live out their lives "as enraged[17] Zionists [...] near Jerusalem" (85) with their five sons.

Friedlaender's story ends by assessing the long-term effects of Kreuzwendedich's case on humankind:

> Since then, anti-Semitism has noticeably slackened. Certain orthopedists are feared and resisted by people who are still proud of the purity of their race. [...] One no longer bases everything on racial differences. Racial blood has stopped being considered a special kind of vital juice. Meanwhile, Professor Friedlaender gathers it in bottles and continues to transfer it undauntedly from one vessel into another.
>
> Zipes 1991: 85f.

In a world in which one's skin color can be changed like one's hair color, categories such as race lose their power. Kreuzwendedich's total transformation results in a radical change of the way humankind conceives of identity: it is no longer understood as an unchangeable result of one's blood or physical properties, rather, it becomes mutable and mobile. At the forefront of this development is Professor Friedlaender, who is Kreuzwendedich's orthopedic surgeon, but also the author's namesake. He was tasked with the "perverse task, in a certain way to do the reverse, that is, to act as a caco-orthopedist" (83).[18] This applies not only to the operations conducted on Kreuzwendedich, but also to the author Friedlaender, whose awareness of anti-Semitic stereotypes in addition to his familiarity with Jewish culture leave him in the perverse situation that he can create the "best" anti-Semitic image. He feels tasked to do so, around the one-year anniversary of Panizza's death, in order to call attention to the increasing anti-Semitism of the unstable Weimar Republic, but also to point out that inner-Jewish conflicts as well as Zionism and other national projects are in danger of relying on similar notions of authenticity, purity, and exclusion. Rather than focusing on the supposed difference between nations, Friedlaender says, "I shall defend the sublime, beautiful, good, pious, intelligent *human being* that is just as much in the German as it is in the Negro and the Jew" (letter to Fritz Lemke, 29 February 1936, translated excerpt in Zipes 1991: 124f., emphasis in the original).

Even though Friedlaender's and Panizza's stories end on vastly different notes, they nonetheless caricature the same paranoid fear of assimilation and expose the supposed pure essence of both German and Jewish identity as an imaginary construct. The genre of the literary Grotesque allows the imagination to run particularly wild, in a way that is now confined to a distinct historical moment. In 1975, Gershom Scholem calls Friedlaender's Grotesques "a literary form that became impossible after Hitler and is virtually inaccessible today [...]; this genre [...] almost knocked me off my chair with laughter at the time" (2003: 58). Today, the comedy of these Grotesques belongs to a bygone era that has been overshadowed by the Holocaust and its devastating deployment of the very racial stereotypes that these works so irreverently challenge.

Notes

1 This nonetheless still excluded access to certain professions and certainly did not preclude anti-Semitism.

2 The expression has encompassed questions about the civil, legal, and national status of Jews within Western European societies since the mid-eighteenth century and later also included the question of a Jewish state. In the mid-nineteenth century, the term was increasingly negatively appropriated by anti-Semites and ultimately the Nazis, who proposed their horrific "Final Solution" to the Jewish Question in 1941.

3 The trained physician and multi-faceted Munich author Oskar Panizza (1853–1921) faced persecution and censorship throughout his life both for his provocative writing about sexuality and disease, as well as his criticism of the Wilhelmine Empire and the Catholic Church. He wrote in all major genres and was part of the "Munich Moderns" until he was forced into exile in Paris. He infamously served the longest prison sentence for a work of art under Kaiser Wilhelm's rule, and spent the last years of his life in voluntary confinement in an asylum. His grotesque and neo-romantic short prose is an assemblage of fantastic figures, such as a Sudanese dancer who changes the color of his skin by way of mind-control and an Indian chief who is pondering the mass suicide of his people out of spite for his colonizers.

4 The German–Jewish philosopher Salomo Friedlaender (1871–1946) wrote grotesque and satirical prose, so-called *Grotesken* (Grotesques), under the pseudonym Mynona (anonymous in German spelled backwards), which he also

performed on popular reading tours. Friedlaender was actively involved in both the literary and philosophical debates of his time and called himself "a synthesis of Immanuel Kant and Charlie Chaplin" (cf. Kuxdorf 1990: 3). His philosophical texts, which negotiate Kantian ideas in the school of Ernst Marcus, were widely received and spurred debates within his illustrious circle of friends, which included Martin Buber, Alfred Kubin, Gustav Landauer, and Else Lasker-Schüler. Persecuted by the Nazis, Friedlaender died in exile in Paris.

5 A literary Grotesque is a short prose piece that upsets bourgeois sensibilities, or in Friedlaender's own words, that "angers and shocks the almost unexterminable philistine in us—who, out of forgetfulness, naively feels good in the middle of a caricature of genuine life—by exaggerating the caricature to the point of being Grotesque, until it succeeds in driving him [the philistine] out of the merely imagined paradise of his customs" (Friedlaender, "Grotesk" (1921), reprinted in Kuxdorf 1990: 62f., my translation). For more details on the history of the grotesque and its elements, cf. Fuß (2001).

6 The name was first used as an anti-Semitic pseudonym in the eighteenth century and was given to literary figures like Veitel Itzig in Gustav Freytag's 1855 novel *Debit and Credit* (cf. Althaus 2002: 145). Itzig is the Hebrew name Israel transformed into colloquial or dialectal German. Israel was a metonym for a Jewish person and associated stereotypical characteristics (257f.). The name Faitel evokes a variety of typically Eastern European and Yiddish names, whereas Stern alludes to the Star of David and was a popular choice among Ashkenazi Jews who adopted German names in the course of Emancipation.

7 Cf. contemporary anti-Semitic depictions of Jewish men as effeminate in Gilman (1993b) and the blood-related stereotype of male menstruation in Gilman (1998).

8 Decades later, the text has hardly been considered in its own right or in the context of Panizza's oeuvre, but mainly served as an example for the gruesome anti-Semitic stereotyping of Jewish bodies (cf. Geller 2011 and Gilman 1993a, 1993b). Eric Santner recognizes though that "[w]hat is at stake here, then, is not simply Panizza's ridicule of German vulgarity and stupidity, which is no doubt also present in the text, but rather his suggestion that, in a sense, 'the German' does not exist" (1996: 127).

9 Originally, "speaking like Moses" meant "speaking Yiddish," but also "to cheat," "to make secret agreements" (cf. Althaus 2002).

10 Panizza himself adopted a unique phonetic spelling for all of his writing in the very year *The Operated Jew* was written and increasingly so until the end of his life. His spelling resonates with his Lower-Franconian dialect, and after giving up his German citzenship, Panizza invoked his Huguenot family heritage by speaking

only French towards the end of his life in an act of defiance against Kaiser Wilhelm. These two linguistic influences precisely mirror Faitel's language make-up. For a more detailed exploration of the use of language in the text, see Jacobs (2012).

11 Zipes mistranslates Faitel's reaction to Pomeranian: he considers it too harsh (*hart*), not too hard/difficult (*schwer*).

12 Cf. for instance Panizza (1981: 275).

13 Zipes anglicizes the family names. Gold-Isak becomes Gold-Isaac and Reschok is turned into Rehsok to underscore that it reads kosher backwards.

14 At the end of the nineteenth century, many health resorts, and particularly the island Borkum, advertised that they did not host Jews. The Borkum song, which was played daily by the health resort band and sung by the guests, says in its third stanza: "On this green Island reigns a truly German spirit. Therefore everyone who is blood-related to us flocks to you joyously. [. . .] We keep Germania's noble crest pure forever! But who approaches you on flat feet, with crooked noses and curly hair shall not enjoy your beach; out with him, out with him!" (Bajohr 2003: 171, my translation). The animal names and species evoke Nordic mythology, such as Odin's raven Hugin.

15 Cf. Geller (2011: 273).

16 The castration anxiety alluded to by this combination foreshadows the topic of Kreuzwendedich's circumcision and evokes the *vagina dentata* myth.

17 Zipes' translation says "committed," but the original reads "*enragierte*" (enraged/raging), not "*engagierte*" (engaged/active), which suggests that he includes Zionism in his satirical critique (cf. Friedlaender 2008: 606).

18 κακός = ugly, bad, evil.

References

Althaus, H. P. (2002), *Mauscheln: Ein Wort als Waffe*, Berlin: De Gruyter.

Bajohr, F. (2003), "*Unser Hotel ist judenfrei*": *Bäder-Antisemitismus im 19. und 20. Jahrhundert*, Frankfurt am Main: Fischer.

Friedlaender, S./Mynona (2008), *Gesammelte Schriften, Band 7: Grotesken, Teil I*, H. Geerken and D. Thiel (eds), Herrsching: Whaitawhile.

Fuß, P. (2001), *Das Groteske: Ein Medium des kulturellen Wandels*, Köln: Böhlau.

Geller, J. (2011), *The Other Jewish Question: Identifying the Jew and Making Sense of Modernity*, New York: Fordham University Press.

Gilman, S. (1993a), *The Case of Sigmund Freud: Medicine and Identity at the Fin de Siècle*, Baltimore, MD: Johns Hopkins University Press.

Gilman, S. (1993b), *Freud, Race, and Gender*, Princeton, NJ: Princeton University Press.

Gilman, S. (1998), *Creating Beauty to Cure the Soul: Race and Psychology in the Shaping of Aesthetic Surgery*, Durham, NC: Duke University Press.

Jacobs, J. (2012), " '. . . und die ganze pfälzisch-jüdische Sündfluth kam dann heraus': Monstrosity and Multilingualism in Oskar Panizza's *Der operirte Jud*," in *Zeitschrift für interkulturelle Germanistik*, 3.2: 61–74.

Kuxdorf, M. (1990), *Der Schriftsteller Salomo Friedlaender/Mynona: Kommentator einer Epoche*, Frankfurt am Main: Peter Lang.

Panizza, O. (1981), *Der Korsettenfritz: Geschichten*, München: Matthes & Seitz.

Santner, E. (1996), *My Own Private Germany: Daniel Paul Schreber's Secret History of Modernity*, Princeton, NJ: Princeton University Press.

Scholem, G. (2003), *Walter Benjamin: The Story of a Friendship*, New York: The New York Review of Books.

Zipes, J. (1991), *The Operated Jew: Two Tales of Anti-Semitism*, New York: Routledge.

4

Canned Foreign: Transnational Estrangement in Yoko Tawada

Silja Maehl

Brown University, USA

In "Canned Foreign," one of the better-known texts by Japanese-German writer Yoko Tawada, the narrator purchases a can in a German store depicting a Japanese woman. Upon opening it she discovers that the can contains tuna, and due to her inability to read the German label, the correlation between can and content comes as a surprise. "The woman seemed to have changed into a piece of fish during her long voyage (89)." Her wonder lays bare the bizarre orientalism of "the West" and its absurd stereotypes of "the East" (turning her into the Japanese woman in the can) and her naïveté seemingly complies with this orientalism. At the same time, she undermines the demand to master cultural codes and read "properly": instead of extracting the "correct" meaning, she imagines and confers new meaning on what she sees.

"Canned Foreign" follows the theme of most of Tawada's early story-essays written in German and published in *Talisman* (1996), namely the alienating encounter of a female Japanese narrator with the German culture and language.[1] Tawada is an exophonic writer, which means that she also writes in an adopted language. Very few readers and critics can read the author's entire bilingual work in the original—Tawada lives in Germany while publishing simultaneously in Japanese and German—which represents and depicts cultural otherness in a uniquely challenging way. Scholarship on Tawada continuously calls attention to the large variety of cultural and linguistic themes in her work, which has been discussed, for example, in terms of gender, surrealism, postcolonialism, translation, and media studies.[2]

I suggest that Tawada's writing also shares certain themes and strategies commonly associated with science fiction, all of which have always been central to her work: alienation and the encounter with the foreign, poetic estrangement (which I will discuss vis-à-vis Bertolt Brecht's and Darko Suvin's concepts of estrangement), the commingling of material and virtual spaces as well as the central role of travel and concomitant forms of mobility.³ Bringing her into dialogue with science fiction, on the one hand, further emphasizes the particular openness and transgressive potential of her work—be it between national languages or genres—and, on the other hand, draws attention to the intersections between certain transnational tales and science fiction, a genre that is itself notoriously difficult to define.⁴

Science fiction imagines the crossing of frontiers in time and space, between different species and worlds, to which Tawada adds language as a new and foreign world to be discovered; her latest collection of poems is tellingly entitled *Abenteuer der deutschen Grammatik* (2010, *Adventures of German Grammar*). Writing in two languages simultaneously evokes an alienated relationship with both languages and semiotic processes in general and fuels the author's persistent move beyond binaries (foreign versus familiar, surface versus depth, sign versus meaning, material versus virtual, etc.). By means of metalinguistic reflections and defamiliarizing techniques, such as paying attention to the materiality instead of the meaning of words, she employs estrangement, which is also central to science fiction, albeit not limited to it, as an aesthetic strategy. Knowledge, perception, and language become detached from fixed cultural contexts and can thus enter into new relations, which for Tawada are transcultural.

The story-essays in *Talisman*—the ones I will be discussing are translated and included in *Where Europe Begins* (2002)—blur the boundaries between short story, essay, autobiography, and, at times, travelogue.⁵ More often than not, the first-person narrators are anonymous aliens in a foreign country, culture, and language. They dissolve all grounds for identification by not presenting themselves as complex psychological characters, but functioning as placeholders for experiences of alienation; in this manner they are similar to those of modernist writers such as Franz Kafka or Samuel Beckett.⁶ Tawada's focus lies not so much on the foreigner as a specific person coping with these experiences and having to assimilate to the foreign country and culture, but rather on general experiences of foreignness.

One of the literary techniques in Tawada's German texts is an inversion of the Western anthropological and ethnological tradition. While the ethnologist becomes part of a foreign community in order to report back home, the gaze of her narrators is directed towards European customs and everyday culture (*Alltagskultur*).⁷ The author toys with the German audience's expectation of reading a (semi)autobiographical account of migrant writing. In the following pages I will relate her strategy to that of the early European travel narrative—a genre that science fiction draws upon. While these Enlightenment stories also portray fictional foreigners encountering Western society, Tawada's twentieth-century texts are written in a foreign language for a foreign audience.

Outsiders inside

"Sometimes women's hair styles gradually go up and up, until a revolution suddenly brings them down again. There was a time when because of their enormous height a woman's face was in the middle of her body. At another time her feet occupied the same position; her heels were pedestals supporting them in mid-air" (184). Taken from Montesquieu's *Lettres persanes* (*Persian Letters*, ([1721] 1993), this is not a description of the denizens of some remote planet, continent or island, but the account of two Persian noblemen, instructing themselves in European manners and culture, who are amazed by the capricious fashion of Paris and all things French. Three centuries later, the foreigner in Tawada's story "The Talisman" paints a similarly strange picture, this time of a city that turns out to be Hamburg: "In this city there are a great many women who wear bits of metal on their ears. They have put holes in their earlobes especially for this purpose [...]. At first glance, the city doesn't strike me as particularly dangerous. Why, then, do so many women wear talismans on the street?" (91). Puzzled about their meaning, the narrator misinterprets earrings as protective charms.

This perspective "through strangers' eyes"—to use the title of Sylvie Romanowski's book on Old Regime France (2005)—has its tradition in Enlightenment narratives of naïve outsiders: in a reverse move to the spread of European imperialism and colonialism, numerous fictional foreigners came from Peru, America, or Persia to France, observing this new and alien world. Montesquieu's epistolary novel served as inspiration for Francoise de Graffigny's *Lettres d'une Péruvienne* (*Letters from a Peruvian Woman*, 1747) and Voltaire's *L'Ingénu* (1767) among others. By means of contrast with other worlds, these non-European outsiders (who are, due to their extended stay, also insiders) reflect on and thus determine the identity of French culture while at the same time highlighting the problems plaguing it.[8] In eighteenth-century literature, the foreigner becomes a vehicle of cultural critique: like the trope of the "noble savage," other worlds provide a fictive exotic standpoint for criticism.[9] To be sure, the cultural outsiders in the *Persian Letters* are far from being alien others but instead represent the act of Europeans looking at themselves; as Romanowksi aptly puts it, the outsider topos "constitutes a compromise between the absolutely other (and hence incomprehensible) and the completely similar (and therefore unable to critique society)" (2005: 37).

Edward Said has famously argued that the difficulty for the traveler is that he or she never really leaves home however long the journey: "There is a rather complex dialectic of reinforcement by which the experiences of readers in reality are determined by what they have read, and this in turn influences writers to take up subjects defined in advance by readers' experiences" (1994: 94). He concludes that travel or guidebooks, as texts that direct and govern what should be seen, "can *create* not only knowledge but also the very reality they appear to describe" (94, emphasis in the original). Tawada's representation and simultaneous deconstruction of "East" and "West" are influenced by the distinction discussed by Said in *Orientalism* between "Orient" and "Occident" and their complex relations of power and hegemony.[10] "The Talisman" is indeed reminiscent of Said's account: "My guidebook, for instance, says that in Europe you should never ask people you don't yet know very well anything related to their bodies or religion" (Tawada 2002: 91). The text demonstrates how travel is biased and predetermined. By the same token, reading (and, of course, writing) never takes place from a clean slate but is influenced by the society and the discourse from which it emerges as well as other readings. The comical misinterpretation in "The Talisman" arises from the conclusions the narrator draws from the information provided by her travel guide: "Gilda replied indifferently that the earring was simply a piece of jewelry and had no meaning at all. As I had supposed, Gilda was reluctant to discuss the earring's significance" (93). The narrator applies the advice not to ask questions relating to body or religion and assumes that the earring is indeed a religious object. Under the gaze of the foreigner, many more quotidian objects and habits of Western life turn into superstitious relicts and unconsciously magical rituals. The foreigner disturbs the social order by rendering customary cultural knowledge absurd.

Wonder and estrangement

"Everything interests me, everything surprises me: I am like a child, whose organs are still delicate, so that even the most trivial things make an impression on them" (Montesquieu [1721] 1993: 104). The sense of wonder that Montesquieu's Persians experience in Paris is paralleled in Tawada's narrators who observe their surroundings with child-like wonder, seeing the fantastic and extraordinary in the everyday. Yet, the naïveté of her narrators is called into question, and ultimately subverted, by her texts' frequent overt and covert challenges to the very notion of identity.[11] Instead of being a personal characteristic, naïveté thus serves as a mechanism of estrangement. By the same token, reading and decoding are interrupted: signs are no longer transparent, enabling one to read and understand their meaning, but opaque; the materiality of the letters prevent their functioning as script. While it is hardly disputable that language creates and guides knowledge, language itself as the very medium that is supposed to mediate becomes the centre of attention in Tawada's texts.

"Canned Foreign"—originally published together with "The Talisman" in *Das Fremde aus der Dose* (1992)—begins as follows:

> In any city one finds a *surprisingly* large number of people who cannot read. Some of them are still too young, others simply refuse to learn the letters of the alphabet. There are also a good many tourists and workers from other countries who live with a different set of characters altogether. In their eyes, the image of the city seems *enigmatic*, veiled.
>
> Tawada 2002a: 85, emphasis mine

Right away, Tawada's narrator experiences moments of wonder: a "surprisingly" large number of people who cannot read and through whose eyes the image of the city seems "enigmatic." By the end of the story it will become clear that the city's enigma is not a riddle that waits to be solved or some hidden meaning that needs to be unveiled. The enigmatic character of the city is not portrayed negatively but instead points to a complexity of seeing and reading that is all too often overlooked and forgotten when meaning becomes cliché-ridden—in short, canned. In order to highlight the human tendency towards stereotypes, the text refers to "the image of the city," to its construction as a site for "tourists and workers from other countries," who each arrive in it with general stereotypes and personal expectations in mind. The experiences of foreignness as well as the alienation and prejudice described in "Canned Foreign" are common to all major cities across the world—and they are intensified for those who cannot read: children, illiterates, and others who "simply refuse to learn the letters of the alphabet."

The narrator, who proves to be Japanese, is detached enough from German to see the actual letters instead of entering into the automated process of signification. In fact, it remains unclear whether she knows how to read German at all: "I already knew the alphabet when I arrived in Hamburg, but I could gaze at the individual letters for a long time without recognizing the meaning of the words" (Tawada 2002a: 85). Under her gaze, the letters are surface appearances similar to the images and pictures on billboards. In her imagination, they become animated:

> For example, every day I looked at the same posters beside the bus stop but never read the names of the products. I know only that on one of the most beautiful of these posters the letter S appeared seven times. I don't think this letter reminded me of the shape of a snake. Not only the S, but all the other letters as well differed from live snakes in that they lacked both moisture and flesh. I repeated the S sounds in my mouth and noticed that my tongue suddenly tasted odd. I hadn't known a tongue, too, could taste of something.
>
> Tawada 2002a: 86

The letter "S" appears seven times—a magical number not only in Tawada. As in "The Talisman," the taken-for-granted is rendered strange, in this case the letter "S," which the narrator perceives sensually instead of cognitively. Like most of Tawada's protagonists, she encounters the foreign script with her senses. Despite her claim that "S" does not remind her of a snake—after all the letters of the alphabet are not read pictographically like ideograms—she conjures it nevertheless.[12] The pronunciation of "S" sounds like the sizzling of a snake (in the English "snake" as well as the German *Schlange*), which emphasizes the acoustic function of the alphabet in contrast to the ideograms' embeddedness in the visual. By being reduced to fragments, the words in which the letter "S" occurs are stripped of their communicative function. Instead, "S" is incorporated into the body ("I repeated the S sounds in my mouth and noticed that my tongue suddenly tasted odd"). Although the letter lacks "both moisture and flesh," the "S" sounds affect the feeling in the narrator's tongue, which takes on an alien snake-like life of its own: the snake is now part of the snake charmer, so to speak, and it thus remains open whether, in this scenario, language is in control of the speaker or vice versa.

A similar process of animation takes place in "From Mother Tongue to Linguistic Mother," another text originally published in *Talisman*. The longer the narrator stares at the foreign words, the more alien they become—for instance the German personal pronoun *es* ("it"):

Besides, I didn't believe that the word "it" had no meaning. The very moment you say "it's raining," an "it" is established that pours water out of the sky. If you ask how "it" is going, you imply that there is an "it" that can influence people's well-being. And yet nobody paid *it* much attention. It didn't even have a proper name. But it kept working away busily and effectively in all sorts of areas, living modestly in a grammatical gap.

Tawada 2006: 142

First, "it" indeed lives in a curious grammatical gap: in the sentence "it didn't even have a proper name," it can be read as a pronoun (it) *as well as* a proper name (It). Second, *es* and the letter "S" share the same pronunciation. Finally, *es* is also the term for the Freudian unconscious *Es* (in English "it" stands in more skewed relation to "id"). Tawada's German wordplay with "S" and *es* opens up a horizontal web of acoustic resemblances and associations that add to and counteract customary meanings. As Gizem Arslan aptly describes, in this disintegrating feature of Tawada's style, the sensory capacities of text "resist participation in unified semantic systems" (2012: 227).

The narrator eventually meets Sasha, an illiterate German woman (with a gender-neutral name), who is special in the sense that she is not only unable to read but also unable or unwilling to read something *into* the narrator's Japanese physiognomy. The narrator frequently experiences other people's unease with the incapability to decipher her foreign face like a text: "It's curious the way the expression of a foreigner's face is often compared to a mask. Does this comparison conceal a wish to discover a familiar face behind the strange one?" (86). In contrast, Sasha's interested and intently observing gaze does not evaluate her surroundings. Like the otherness of all others in Tawada, disability is not seen as impairment but rather as an original intensification of perception. In the absence of a naturalized environment that provides stable references, Tawada's illiterates—the narrator, Sasha, and her handicapped friend Sonia—experience an openness towards that which is new and strange. These outsiders are aware of the illusion of mastery that comes with speaking a language fluently, which the narrator describes as follows:

Most of the words that came out of my mouth had nothing to do with how I felt. But at the same time I realized that my native tongue didn't have words for how I felt either. It's just that this never occurred to me until I'd begun to live in a foreign language. Often it sickened me to hear people speak their native tongues fluently. It was as if they were unable to think and feel anything but what their language so readily served up to them.

Tawada 2002a: 87–8

Their otherness prevents Sasha and Sonia from resorting to stereotypical questions such as "Is it true what I read that the Japanese . . ." or "In Japan do people also . . ." (87).

All three story-essays discussed thus far, "Canned Foreign," "The Talisman," and "From Mother Tongue to Linguistic Mother," are literary manifestos against habitual and conventional bonds. In the latter text, the motif of the snake returns in the shape of an office utensil that embodies detachment from such bonds:

> One of the writing utensils I liked best was the staple remover, or *Heftklammerentferner*. Its wonderful name was the incarnation of my longing for a foreign language. This little object, which reminded me of a snake's head with four fangs, was illiterate, though it belonged to the writing utensils. In contrast to the ball point or the typewriter, it could not write a single letter. All it could do was remove staples. But I was especially fond of it because it seemed magical when it unfastened all the sheets of paper stapled together.

Tawada 2006: 143, emphasis in the original

The staple remover, which is personified as being illiterate, "reminds" the narrator of a snake. The German verbs *sich erinnern* (to remember) and *an etwas erinnern* (to remind somebody of something) mean two very different things: whereas the first is reflexive and refers to a single person's memories, the latter is transitive and can set in motion a plurality of (horizontally oriented) comparisons. Being reminded of something by something else is a characteristic sensation of Tawada's narrators, whose primary function is to pursue idiosyncratic avenues of association beyond well-trodden semantic paths. As a new and unusual metaphor for a foreign language, the staple remover ("its wonderful name") loosens the relation between sign and meaning, container and content, and releases the magical potential of language out of its "can."

Like the wonder expressed by Tawada's narrators, the reader's estrangement is achieved through a certain relation and balance between what is familiar and what is foreign: while complete familiarity forestalls our curiosity, not being able to know or understand overwhelms us. It is this dynamic that brings the author's work close to science fiction, which is not merely about a futuristic setting, a voyage into space, or an alien invasion. Darko Suvin famously defines it as a mode or mechanism as well as a literary form when he argues for it as a "genre whose necessary and sufficient conditions are the presence and interaction of estrangement and cognition, and whose main formal device is an imaginative framework alternative to the author's empirical environment" (1979: 7–8). Carl Freedman insists that "the category of science fiction, like any other generic category, is best used to analyze tendencies within a literary work rather than to classify entire works in one or another pigeonhole" (2000: xvi). Like Suvin, he emphasizes that "the estrangement of science fiction need not be limited to the technological estrangements popularly associated with the genre."

Estrangement was first developed into a literary theory in 1917 by the Russian formalist Viktor Shklovsky as *ostraneniye*, a variety of stylistic techniques intended to counter habitualization and increase awareness of the process of sense-making. After a visit to Moscow, these ideas among others led Bertolt Brecht to develop the action- and praxis-oriented theory of "epic theater," in which the audience of the "scientific age" would not empathize and identify with the characters, as in Aristotelian poetics, but would be educated instead to look with a high level of awareness, thus critically reflecting upon what they observe. In his "Short Organum for the Theatre" (1948), he writes: "A representation that alienates is one which allows us to recognize its subject, but at the same time makes it seem unfamiliar" (1992b: 192). Tawada's prose (as well as her plays) demonstrates such an alienation described by Brecht, who in turn was famously influenced by Chinese and Japanese theater. In "Alienation Effects in Chinese Acting Theatre" (1936) he uses and describes the term for the first time, explaining how this theater stands in contrast to the European stage's characteristic illusions: "The artist's object is to appear strange and even surprising to the audience. He achieves this by looking strangely at himself and his work. As a result everything put forward by him has a touch of the amazing. Everyday things are thereby raised above the level of the obvious and automatic" (1992a: 92). As in Brecht, the sensation and effect of wonder are central to Tawada's "cognitive estrangement," to use Suvin's language.[13] In Tawada, wonder often occurs when quotidian objects and habits are observed closely (too closely) through the distorting mirror of another culture and a second language.

The strange journey of reading

In a preface to *Where Europe Begins* (originally published as a preface to *Talisman*), Wim Wenders calls Tawada's work "a voyage of discovery and adventure" explaining how "[t]he book is a travelogue. It relates the experience of a traveler, and as the reader you experience all sorts of things yourself and you travel far and wide while reading it, Where do these travels take you?" (Wenders 2002: x). Wenders' question is hardly rhetorical as Tawada's German readers have difficulties recognizing their homeland; in fact, it is not only Germany but the binary opposition between "native" and "foreign" that is rendered unrecognizable, leading Wenders to draw an interesting comparison with early science fiction: "Like in a novel by Jules Verne, fantastic new spaces keep opening up before your inner eye, and with conflicting emotions and mixed feelings I rediscovered in its pages my fatherland and mother tongue" (xii). Referring to *Talisman* as "a model of utopian storytelling," he continues as follows: "[It] is not set in Rothenburg-on-the-Tauber, not in Hamburg or Tokyo. It is not a book about 'Europe' versus 'Asia' or the other way around. Rather, it is a book that comes to us from a no-man's land where words, names, signs have no meaning any more, a place where everything is put into question" (xiii). Tawada's Germany is a "no-man's land" first, because the characteristics and quotidian details are not necessarily German but generally Western, and second, because the "West" is both an actual and an imagined place. Wender's argument is that what we imagine shapes the actuality of what we see and vice versa. *Tokyo-Ga* (1985)—a film diary of Wenders' journey to Tokyo, a city he came to know through the films of Yasujiro Ozu—is precisely about the impossibility of distinctly separating the "native" from the "foreign," the "virtual" from the "real."[14] I understand Tawada's "no-man's land" as the space of a potent estrangement, in which the author makes her German readers see what is strange in the familiar and at the same time evokes a process of transnational imagining.

Both travel and reading are experiences and sensations of encounter: "All narratives take the reader or listener on a journey, and many of them tell the story of a journey too" (Beer 1996: 55). They are connected, on the one hand, by a desire to experience and indulge in the unknown and, on the other hand, by the need to know, to understand and to interpret, which usually entails a need to possess and to master. Like travel, reading (as mobility without moving) informs what can be seen, and preconditions what is valued (cf. Beer 1996: 37). According to Wenders, Tawada's "no-man's land" points to a utopia, in which spoken and written language become obsolete because, as Wenders says, "the only actions that count are perceiving, taking in, feeling and relating the experience of it all" (2002: xiii). Without clearly recognizable signs and codes, perception can misguide, yet it is precisely this misguidance that brings relief from experience that is canned.

The material and the virtual

Transnational movement is also always a physical encounter with, and a taking-in of, foreign languages. Like "Canned Foreign," the literary essay "Erzähler ohne Seelen" ("Storytellers Without Souls)," also published in the German collection *Talisman*, performs estrangement through observations on language. The text is a reflection on travel and storytelling and a reference to Walter Benjamin's "The Storyteller." It is inspired by a number of associations and contemplations on the German word for cell, *Zelle* ("This word lets me imagine a large number of tiny spaces alive within my body," Tawada: 2002c: 101). What is only implied here is that *Zelle* resonates in the pronunciation of the German *Erzähler* ("storyteller") and enables a word play by means of which *Erzähl-Zellen* ("storytelling cells," 2002c: 103) sounds like *erzählen*. (In a curious way, the English translation allows for a similar relation between cell and storytelling as "cell" rhymes with "tell".) The narrator, once again an anonymous foreigner, compares different sorts of cells, from spaces inhabited by prisoners and monks—which is the oldest meaning of "cell"—to telephone booths:

> It's beautiful when a phone booth is lit up at night on a dark street. In the section of Tokyo where I grew up, there was a park full of ginkgo trees. In one corner of the park stood a phone booth that was very popular with young girls. From dusk to midnight it was continuously occupied. Probably the girls could develop their talent for telling stories better in this cell than at home with their parents.
>
> Tawada 2002c: 101–2

This scene reminds the narrator of a Japanese folktale, in which an old man finds a girl from the moon inside the trunk of a bamboo tree.[15] Moving from the image of the tree to a futuristic vision she continues: "The nocturnal phone booth might also have been a spaceship that has just landed in the park. The moon men have sent a moon girl to Earth to inform them about our life. The girl is just making her first report. What would she say about the park? Would she have much to report so soon after her arrival?" (102). Another example of story-telling is a confessional of a Catholic church: "But unlike a modern phone booth, the confessional was made of wood and stood there like a tree whose roots have grown deep into the earth. It couldn't fly away like a spaceship. So there are story-telling cells that stay in one place, and others that appear to be mobile" (103). What lies at the center of these passages is the embeddedness of the virtual in the material and vice versa, as well as the seamless transition from the organic to the technological. What applies to "Storytellers Without Souls" can be said about the author's work in general: the virtual does not function merely as a synonym for the digital, nor can it be clearly separated from the real, but is presented as an extension of the mental, the imagination, and thus as a defining feature of the human.

Considering the estranging ways in which Tawada often describes physical travel by train or plane makes a spaceship almost appear as merely one more mode of transportation. Christina Kraenzle traces the theme of virtual mobility, "from plane travel to the flow of information along telecommunications highways" (2007: 92), in *Überseezungen* (2002). This virtual mobility is already at work in the earlier text "The Talisman":

> Once [Gilda] knocked on my door in the middle of the night and said there was something wrong with her computer. I was really quite surprised she'd woken me up for this, since she knew I didn't know the first thing about computers. But soon I understood what the matter was: Gilda claimed that there was an alien being living inside her computer and producing sentences. She kept discovering sentences in her essays that she definitely hadn't written herself.
>
> Tawada 2002b: 94

Here, common experiences with computers—for instance, spell-checking systems that take on a life of their own—are narrated like a nocturnal ghost story. The narrator, ostensibly inexperienced in matters of information technology, suggests a talisman as remedy. When Gilda happens to paste some stickers on her computer, the narrator assumes that these are supposed to ward off the evil force. The meaning she attributes to Gilda's action is, once again, a "misunderstanding" of cultural codes.[16]

Tawada was to address the topic of electronic ghosts—and thus the question of how reading and writing change with the use of electronic media—in later texts such as "Der Apfel und die Nase" ("The Apple and the Nose") in *Überseezungen* and "E-mail für Japanische Gespenster" ("Email for Japanese Ghosts"): "The letters on my screen seem to me more ghostly than brushstrokes on paper, because they are at once there and not there. They are only shadows on the surface of electronic water" (Tawada 1999: 221, my translation). In this text she imagines falling into "the turquoise ocean of the computer screen" (220). Water is a central trope and organizing principle in Tawada's work: fluid and mutable qualities do not exclusively belong to this natural element but extend to the porous borders between the sensuous and the cognitive, the corporeal and the virtual. Whereas pencil and typewriter (which figure interestingly in Tawada's text "From Mother Tongue to Linguistic Mother") keep us from forgetting the materiality of these processes, the computer with its seamless writing and editing functions is a medium that can indeed be considered fluid.

"Canned Foreign" unsettles the belief in complete legibility and unconditional decoding; yet what alternative kind of reading does Tawada suggest? What can the future of reading look like beyond the practice of decipherment? In the chapter "Ways of Reading" in *Does Writing have a Future?* Vilém Flusser explains how "[u]ntil now, *to read* was understood to be the unraveling of a mystery [. . .] But it is also possible to translate *to read* as 'to guess'" (2011: 84). Flusser describes this other way of reading as "dealing with a reversal of the vectors of meaning: no longer does the reader draw a meaning from what is read; rather he is the one who confers meaning on what is read" (85). The link to Flusser proves interesting as his critique of alphabetic writing draws attention away from the sense-making role of letters to that which writing, as Flusser criticizes, intends to supersede: ideographic writing and magical-mythical thought. Tawada explicitly draws on him when foregrounding the body of letters (*Schriftkörper*) as well as the non-European history of the Latin alphabet: "The alphabet always reminded me of the Near East. Vilém Flusser wrote: 'A still shows the two horns of the Semitic steer, B the two domes of the Semitic house, C the humps of the Semitic camel in the Near Eastern desert.' One writes the alphabet in order to evoke the desert in language" (2007: 12, my translation). When Tawada intends to evoke the desert in the Latin alphabet, she foregrounds its material history within processes of abstraction.

It is not only the Latin alphabet that remains entangled with and anchored in the material world, but the human body also consists of information that can be read—as the dreaded physiognomic reading of the foreign narrator's face in "Canned Foreign" demonstrates. How Tawada conceives bodies, languages and media, and the material and the virtual as inextricably intertwined can be seen when the narrator in "Canned Foreign" is unable to—or refuses to—cognitively grasp the differences between the Japanese and German cultures and instead experiences them sensually:

> Every attempt I made to describe the difference between two cultures failed: this difference was painted on my skin like a foreign script, which I could feel but not read. Every foreign sound, every foreign glance, every foreign taste struck my

body as disagreeable until my body changed. The Ö sounds, for example, stabbed too deeply into my ears and the R sounds scratched my throat.

Tawada 2002a: 87

The body's inscription with signs, be it letters or racial markers such as skin and hair color, has its counterpart in language's materiality. Reading the sign for a Chinese restaurant called "The Green Dragon," the protagonist Sasha compares the traditional Chinese ideogram for dragon, 龍, to the actual animal: "And in fact it *is* possible to see the image of a dragon in this character: the little box in the upper right-hand corner might be a dragon's head, and the lines on the right side remind me of a dragon's back" (2002a: 88, emphasis in the original). She conjures a dragon in a way similar to the narrator's animation of "S." Sasha knows, of course, that the sign is not a "picture" of a dragon: "she asked me whether I, too, could *write* it." However, just because the sign is script does not make it less alive as the text suggests; or, in the words of the narrator in "Storytellers Without Souls": "Even my writing lives" (Tawada 2002c: 103).[17]

Working against the idea of "cultural content" (Tawada 2002a: 90), the author creates a translingual network between the alphabet and ideograms by comparing letters and signs to animals, more precisely to animals with scales: the snake, the dragon, and the fish. While each of these animals can be associated with specific cultural meanings—the snake as a Western biblical symbol, the dragon as a symbol of China's imperial power, the tuna fish as a symbol of Japan as a major fish-consuming and -trading nation—they can also enter into very different relations, for example, with one another. Dragons are often depicted as snakes with legs or wings, a relatedness that is supported by the fact that dragon, *lóng* (龍), can also mean serpent. Just as in "E-mail für Japanische Gespenster," in which the dual-language keyboard unexpectedly transforms alphabetical letters into ideograms, virtuality in "Canned Foreign" is also a transcultural experience: while media technologies offer a key to understanding the interaction between humans and machines and the process of globalization, they are also central to understanding Tawada's writings, in which she underlines the fact that the alphabet is transnational *avant la lettre*. She calls attention to the intermediality of language, introducing a new perspective onto the Latin alphabet and its material and virtual qualities. In ways similar to science fiction, words are estranged from their communicative function and instead serve as inspirations for the creation and discovery of new "language worlds"[18]—as in the case of *Zelle* in "Storytellers Without Souls."

Conclusion

Unlike Montesquieu's wondering wanderers and the travel narratives of the Enlightenment, Tawada's narrators in "Canned Foreign" and "Talisman" do not compare the new foreign world with their own. Whereas the *Persian Letters*, a political and religious satire and critique, puts its French readers imaginatively into the place of foreigners, maintaining a clear separation between "native" and "foreign," European and non-European, Tawada's "first contact" narratives are written from an exophonic perspective: she writes in her adopted language of German for a German audience. Tawada combines an outsider's perspective on the West with twentieth-century poetic estrangement mechanisms. In addition to the estrangement familiar from Russian formalism or Brecht's epic theater, she employs a reversal of perspective that is common to science fiction. Through science fiction we are exposed to fictional societies whose norms are the diametric opposite of our own; estrangement is produced by means of the disparity between the reader's empirical reality and the world of the science fictional text.[19] Tawada introduces her German readers (and, by extension, her Western audience through translation) to an entirely unfamiliar perspective by drawing attention to surface phenomena within a society that is accustomed to the value of depth—whether in a person or a text. Her perspective on the alphabet can be described as "the flattening of all metaphor" (Kim 2010: 346) and a foregrounding of the optic and the acoustic. Moreover, Tawada reminds us that language is not only a tool to describe the world, but is also the creator of what it describes: animating language (in the sense that the letter "S" is reminiscent of a snake) is then a reversal of the fact that language animates our world.

As Gillian Beer writes in her foreword to this collection: "In science fiction we learn to look at the world as a different place." At the same time, science fiction can do more than momentarily dazzle us with an entirely unfamiliar world. It presents us with "a world whose difference is concretized within a cognitive continuum with the actual" and thus distinguishable from the "irrationalist estrangements of fantasy or Gothic literature" (Freedman 2000: xvi). Just as Tawada's narrators are situated at once outside and inside the foreign language and culture, so their naïveté and wonder are strategies that allow for foreignness to remain in between that which is known and that which remains unknown. Accepting the possibility of not knowing is especially crucial in a society whose (Enlightenment) values are grounded on rationality and knowledge as power. In a manner similar to actual travel, reading Tawada can take a Western audience to a place that resembles home but is, in Wim Wenders' words, a "no-man's land." Her distanced observers counteract normative paradigms of knowledge and understanding through which the foreign is all too often "canned" instead of experienced with an open mind.

Notes

1 Her more recent work, namely *Das nackte Auge* (2004) (*The Naked Eye*) and *Schwager in Bordeaux* (2008) (*Good Brother in Bordeaux*), relocates these experiences from Germany to France. *Überseezungen* (2002) (Overseatongues) combines the hitherto dominant East-West axis with a North-South axis, for example in a story-essay on Afrikaans.

2 Chantal Wright, for instance, points out how Tawada's strategy of sometimes juxtaposing Japanese and German in her German texts is reminiscent of postcolonial writing (2013: 13).

3 It is beyond the scope of this article to link Tawada's German works to contemporary writers of (postcolonial) science fiction—such as Larissa Lai's *Salt Fish Girl*—which I believe would be a promising project. For the connection between postcolonialism and science fiction, on which such a project can be grounded, see Jessica Langer's *Postcolonialism and Science Fiction* (Palgrave Macmillan, 2011). Relating Tawada's work to the supernatural as well as the uncanny, the fantastic and the marvelous (as Tzvetan Todorov discusses them in *The Fantastic*) would also be worth a thorough investigation.

4 In 2012, Yoko Tawada published a dystopian science fiction text about the 2011 nuclear disaster in Fukushima, entitled "Fushi no shima" and translated as "The Island of Eternal Life" in the collection *March was Made of Yarn*, in which a Japan set in the future is catapulted back into an isolation reminiscent of the Edo period. To my knowledge, Leslie Adelson (2011) is the only critic who discusses aspects of science fiction in Tawada, more specifically time travel, parallel worlds, and futurity. Her focus lies on Tawada's German essays "Zukunft ohne Herkunft" and "Eine Heidin in einem Heidenkloster."

5 The other two German collections of short fiction are *Überseezungen* (2002) (*Overseatongues*) and *Sprachpolizei und Spielpolyglotte* (2007) (*Speech Police and Polyglot Play*).

6 Tawada has written on Kafka in her dissertation entitled *Spielzeug und Sprachmagie in der europäischen Literatur* (2000) (*Toys and Language Magic in European Literature*); Beckett in turn is one of her predecessors in bilingual writing.

Canned Foreign

89

7 Tawada scholars have pointed this out repeatedly, grounding their discussion on an often-quoted passage in "Storytellers Without Souls," reflecting the possibility of a "fictive ethnology," in which "not the described but the describer is imaginary" (2002: 110).

8 In her foreword to this volume, Gillian Beer highlights how travel literature and science fiction lie close together. There is also a conceptual link between science fiction and early thought-experiments about other worlds (e.g. Cyrano de Bergerac's *L'Autre Monde ou les États et Empires de la Lune* (The Other World: Comical History of the States and Empires of the Moon, 1657). Compare, for instance, Roger Luckhurst who traces science fiction back to exotic travel narratives, which "had always bordered on fantasmatic invention along the pathways of global trade routes, as in the fabulated China described in the works of Marco Polo" (2005: 15).

9 Cf. Romanowski (2005: 35).

10 Next to *Orientalism*, Roland Barthes' *Empire of Signs* and Julia Kristeva's *Chinese Women* are also influential works for Tawada. The dialogue with Barthes has been well documented by critics such as Andrea Krauß ("Talisman. Tawadische Sprachtheorie," in Aglaia Blioumi (ed.), *Migration und Interkulturalität in neueren literarischen Texten*. München: Iudicium, 2002: 55–77).

11 Compare, for instance, John Kim's insightful article on personal pronouns in Tawada's "Eine leere Flasche" ("A Vacuous Flask"), published in *Überseezungen*.

12 I also read this sentence as an evocation of the Freudian concept of negation, which suggests that certain unconscious ideas are permitted to the conscious only in the inverted form of denial.

13 Compare Maria S. Grewe's dissertation (2009), in which she discusses Brecht's estrangement effect vis-à-vis Tawada's poetic construction of the foreign.

14 *Tokyo-Ga* translates to "Tokyo Images." In his film, Wenders comments on Ozu's work as follows: "As thoroughly Japanese as they are, these films are, at the same time, universal. In them, I've been able to recognize all families, in all the countries of the world, as well as my parents, my brother and myself. For me, never before and never again since has the cinema been so close to its essence and its purpose: to present an image of man in our century, a usable, true and valid image, in which he not only recognized himself but from which, above all, he may learn about himself."

15 This tale is in fact a version of the tenth-century proto-science fiction story "Taketori Monogatari," translated into English as "The Tale of the Bamboo Cutter."

16 The stickers themselves illustrate the arbitrary relation between the image (a car, a nuclear power plant, a gun) and the words written above ("no thanks"), or rather between signified and signifier.

17 To my knowledge, Tawada's work has not yet been discussed in connection with animal studies, which would be a fruitful project, especially if it includes her Japanese work (this extends to the motif of disgust, a liminal concept and in many ways a reminder of our "animal history").

18 Science fiction (along with fantasy and other related genres) has produced an abundance of fictional idioms and languages, two famous examples being the totalitarian "Newspeak" in George Orwell's *Nineteen Eighty-Four* and *Star Trek's* Klingon language.

19 In this collection, Matthew Goodwin, for instance, shows how in "Sugar on the Lips" by José Luis Alverdi it is not the US government that restricts movement of Mexican migrants, but the government of Mexico. Emilie McCabe demonstrates how using a homonormative society like the *hwarhath* in Eleanor Arnason's novel *Ring of Swords* estranges us readers from our understanding of human sexuality and the norm of heterosexuality. That the aesthetic device of inversion or reversal is, of course, not exclusive to science fiction is demonstrated by Joela Jacobs in her analysis of the literary grotesque in Oskar Panizza and Salomo Friedlaender.

References

Adelson, L. (2011), "The Future of Futurity: Alexander Kluge and Yoko Tawada," *The Germanic Review,* 86: 153–84.

Arslan, G. (2012), "Orientation, Encounter, and Synaesthesia in Paul Celan & Yoko Tawada," in O. Amihay and L. Walsh (eds), *The Future of Text and Image: Collected Essays on Literary and Visual Conjunctures,* Newcastle upon Tyne: Cambridge Scholars Publishing.

Beer, G. (1996), *Open Fields. Science in Cultural Encounter,* Oxford: Clarendon Press.

Brecht, B. ([1936] 1992a), "The Alienation Effect in Chinese Theatre," in J. Willett (ed.), *Brecht on Theatre. The Development of an Aesthetic,* New York: Hill & Wang.

Brecht, B. (1992b), "A Short Organum for the Theatre," in J. Willett (ed.), *Brecht on Theatre. The Development of an Aesthetic,* New York: Hill & Wang.

Flusser, V. (2011), *Does Writing have a Future?*, Minneapolis, MN: University of Minnesota Press.

Freedman, C. (2000), *Critical Theory and Science Fiction,* Hanover and London: Wesleyan University Press.

Grewe, M. S. (2009), *Estranging Poetic: On the Poetic of the Foreign in Select Works by Herta Müller and Yoko Tawada,* dissertation at Columbia University.

Kim, J. N. (2010), "Ethnic Irony: The Poetic Parabasis of the Promiscuous Personal Pronoun in Yoko Tawada's 'Eine leere Flasche' (Vacous Flask)," *The German Quarterly,* 83.3: 333–52.

Kraenzle, C. (2007), "Traveling Without Moving: Physical and Linguistic Mobility in Yoko Tawada's *Überseezungen*," in D. Slaymaker (ed.), *Yoko Tawada: Voices from Everywhere*, Lanham, MD: Lexington Books.

Luckhurst, R. (2005), *Science Fiction*, Malden, MA: Polity.

Montesquieu ([1721] 1993), *Persian Letters*, London: Penguin Books.

Romanowski, S. (2005), *Through Strangers' Eyes. Fictional Foreigners in Old Regime France*, West Lafayette, IN: Purdue University Press.

Said, E. (1994), *Orientalism*, New York: Vintage Books.

Suvin, D. (1979), *Metamorphosis of Science Fiction: On the Poetics and History of a Literary Genre*, New Haven, CT: Yale University.

Tawada, Y. (1992), *Das Fremde aus der Dose,* Graz and Wien: Verlag Droschl.

Tawada, Y. (1996), *Talisman*, Tübingen: Konkursbuch Verlag Claudia Gehrke.

Tawada, Y. (1999), "E-mail für Japanische Gespenster," in *Rituale heute: Theorien – Kontroversen – Entwürfe,* Berlin: Reimer.

Tawada, Y. (2002a), "Canned Foreign," in *Where Europe Begins*, S. Bernofsky and Y. Selden (trans), New York: New Directions.

Tawada, Y. (2002b), "The Talisman," in *Where Europe Begins*, S. Bernofsky and Y. Selden (trans), New York: New Directions.

Tawada, Y. (2002c), "Storytellers Without Souls," in *Where Europe Begins,* S. Bernofsky and Y. Selden (trans), New York: New Directions.

Tawada, Y. (2006), "From Mother Tongue to Linguistic Mother," *Manoa*, 18.1: 139–43.

Tawada, Y. (2007), "An der Spree," in *Sprachpolizei und Spielpolyglotte,* Tübingen: Konkursbuch Verlag Claudia Gehrke.

Wenders, W. (2002), Preface to *Where Europe Begins*, S. Bernofsky and Y. Selden (trans), New York: New Directions.

Wright, C. (2013), *Portrait of a Tongue. An Experimental Translation*, Ottawa: University of Ottawa Press.

Filmography

Tokyo-Ga (1985), directed by Wim Wenders, Leipzig, Germany: Arthaus, 2006, DVD.

Part Two

Alien Anxieties

5

Human Subjects—Alien Objects?
Abjection and the Constructions of Race
and Racism in *District 9*

Andrew M. Butler

Canterbury Christ Church University, UK

There is a moment in a review of *District 9* (Neill Blomkamp, 2009) when Joshua Clover anticipates that the film will be "a neat allegory of apartheid, with the marooned race of repulsive and sad-sack aliens standing for the dispossessed" (2009: 8). Similarly, Eric D. Smith suggests that the film "at first seem[s] an allegory for the suspension of constitutional law during the officially declared South African State of Emergency in the latter days of apartheid policy (1985–1990)" (2012: 149). In this essay I want to map *District 9*'s representation of inter-species hybrids within the complex situation of apartheid-era South African interracial relations and discuss some of the issues surrounding science fiction as allegory. I will consider 'race' as being an ideological category and, following Julia Kristeva's notion of the abject, a psychological construction that nevertheless has a material existence. I will be posing the question of to what extent *District 9* is itself racist.

District 9 begins in the style of a documentary: an alien spaceship appeared above Johannesburg in 1982. The million or so aliens found on board were ferried down to District 9, below the ship, and left to scavenge in what becomes a shantytown. The aliens were nicknamed "prawns" by humans and, because of crime and violence, kept separate from the rest of the city. Twenty-eight years later, the aliens are to be forcibly moved to a new area, District 10, an operation outsourced by the South African government to a multinational corporation, MNU. Their executive, Piet Smit (Louis Minaar), puts his barely competent son-in-law Wikus van de Merwe (Sharlto Copley) in charge. During the failed eviction of extraterrestrial Christopher Johnson (Jason Cope), van de Merwe is contaminated by a fluid and begins to metamorphose into a human-alien hybrid.

MNU now view him as an exploitable asset and begin to experiment on him. He escapes back to District 9, in the hope that Johnson can save his humanity.

It might be suggested that the film has two protagonists rather than one. The film's mock-documentary sections present the hapless van de Merwe, assembled from myriad interviews, news reports, security footage, and other footage. He is identified but not identifiable with. The aliens meanwhile cannot speak for themselves and are only represented from the outside, as the alien other. We may, of course, choose to reject this documentary discourse as the diegesis is intercut with the style of continuity editing that can allow audience identification, first with Johnson and then with van de Merwe as he crosses the species divide. In the non-documentary sections, the editing humanizes van de Merwe more than it does Johnson. We identify, if we can, with a member of an alien species or a fool.

District 9 is not the first science fiction film to displace racial difference onto distinct species. Darko Suvin's definition of science fiction as the "*literature of cognitive estrangement*" (1979: 4, emphasis in the original) allows for an interaction between the world as we know it and as it can be imagined. As an allegory, a real-world scenario can be shifted in time and/or space to allow a form of commentary upon it. As Eric Greene suggests: "Addressing a problem through allegory may potentially allow the audiences to focus on the story without paying attention to the underlying conflicts and themes" (1996: 151). With real people being removed from the situation, it might be that a calmer reaction may result. For example, the Planet of the Apes mythos—the original five films, a television series, an animated series, novelizations, comic books, and a rebooted film series—was initially created during the Vietnam War, the rise of the counterculture, and an ongoing struggle for Black Civil Rights. The original scriptwriter Rod Serling was initially attracted to the class stratification of the apes in Pierre Boulle's 1963 novel. Through the project's development the theme shifted to an examination of race relations. Greene's reading of the film suggests that it portrays "white gentiles as orangutans, white Jews as chimpanzees, and African Americans as gorillas" (55). The hierarchy within the community of apes may be thought to reflect real-world values. The orangutans are consistently represented as in control, law-givers, and perhaps are the most privileged grouping. Greene identifies the chimpanzees with Jews, a group that was in an ambiguous position in 1960s America: they are "pacifists, intellectuals, scientists, and political radicals, [who] still face discrimination in their quests for better positions and are denied true authority" (31). They have some benefits, but are not fully part of the central power structure. In contrast, the gorillas, "inherently stupid, physically powerful, and belligerent" (150), come to represent white stereotypes of African Americans.

In *Planet of the Apes* (Franklin J. Schaffner, 1968), four human astronauts crash on what they take to be an alien planet, one of them dying on impact, another being killed when they are captured by gorillas. The two survivors find a society of silent human slaves ruled by apes; in the American context whites were slave owners and so, if the audience identifies with George Taylor (Charlton Heston), they may begin to understand better the status of the subjugated. As the sequence progresses, so the real-world contexts and analogues change—notable events in Civil Rights history included the assassination of Martin Luther King, the conviction for voluntary manslaughter of the leader of the Black Panther Party Huey Newton, the release of the first blaxploitation films, and Shirley Chisholm becoming the first African American woman to run for a Democratic presidential nomination. The emphasis of the series shifts to anxieties about race. In Adilifu Nash's words, *Conquest of the Planet of the Apes* (J. Lee Thompson, 1972) and *Battle for the Planet of the Apes* (J. Lee Thompson, 1973) "pandered to white political paranoia and possibly black political fantasy" (2008: 131). In *Conquest*, African American MacDonald (Hari Rhodes) helps talking chimpanzee Caesar (Roddy McDowell) to escape from the experiments of scientists and the white characters observe that of course MacDonald would have sympathy for an ape. As Greene notes: "within the first few moments of his appearance, the film establishes and comments upon the expectation that because he is a black man, MacDonald will be compassionate towards the apes" (2006: 102). Compassion is a positive value, but the film offers—not necessarily uncritically—the assertion that he is a traitor to the human species. It also taps into old racist hierarchy, such as Carolus Linnaeus' division into *Homo Europaeus, Asiaticus, Americanus*, and *Africanus*, thus situating African Americans closer to animals than Westerners. We have a slippage between race and species.

The construction of race

'Race' is a much-contested concept that may be an ideological construction. Science fiction writer Samuel R. Delany points to the novelist and social commentator James Baldwin's observation that, it suddenly struck him that there *were* no white people—that is to say, "whiteness," as it indicated a race was purely an anxiety fantasy to which certain people had been trained immediately to leap (and, Baldwin realized, felt wholly inadequate to make that leap) whenever they encountered certain other people whom they coded as black or nonwhite.

Interviewed in Dery 1994: 190, emphasis in the original

The processes of oppression and othering work both ways. Someone from one culture meets someone who seems different from them, and in the articulation of that difference sameness is also articulated. Baldwin insists that "white people are not white: part of the price of the ticket is to delude themselves into believing that they are" (1985a: xiv). He adds: The price the white American paid for his ticket was to become white—and, in the main, nothing more than that, or, as he was to insist, nothing less" (xx). The ticket is the entry to the promised land, in particular to America as quasi-utopia and one of the prices seems to be to leave the homeland behind. In an account of a visit to a small Swiss village, Baldwin notes the European reactions to him and his skin color and adds: "one's imagination of other people is dictated, of course, by the laws of one's own personality and it is one of the ironies of black-white relations that, by means of what the white man imagines the black man to be, the black man is enabled to know who the white man is" (1985b: 84). The establishment of race as an apparently identifiable human characteristic has a material and political purpose.

The concept of race emerged in its modern form in the era of the Western encounter with the East, Africa, and, especially, the Americas. Scientists sought the causes of physical differences between people on different continents, and in the eighteenth century Georges-Louis Leclerc, Comte de Buffon, suggested that "quasi-permanent change from an original stock could take place as a result of climate, geography and especially food" (quoted in Bernasconi 2001: 16). The problem for scientists of the eighteenth and nineteenth centuries was how to account for the perceived racial differences within the span of history allowed for by a reading of the Bible. As Robert Bernasconi observes: "One solution was that some of these people were simply not human" (2001: 18). The scientific division of human beings into races offers a value judgment and a hierarchy, as well as continuing the pre-scientific, Platonic sense of the Great Chain of Being from God down via angels, humans, animals and plants, to rocks into the Linnaean classification of living things into phyla, kingdoms, orders, families, genera, and species. Race was a potential subdivision of species.

Buffon argued that if two animals could reproduce and create fertile offspring, then they were of the same species; this would begin to articulate all kinds of anxieties about interracial reproduction. With a certain amount of understatement, Paul Gilroy notes: "Science, the master cipher of a future with boundless promise, has not always been an ally of the political movements involved in disaggregating modern race-thinking" (2000: 339). There is no doubt that the ideology of race facilitated the horrors of the slave trade, although Bernasconi argues that "[t]he fact that the scientific concept of race was developed initially in Germany rather than in Britain or America suggests that it was not specifically the interests of the slave owner that led to its introduction" (2001: 21).

Bernasconi locates the beginning of the scientific notion of race in the writings of the Enlightenment philosopher Immanuel Kant, who repeatedly assumes that there are four races—Whites, Negroes, the Hunnish, and the Hindu—"which persistently preserve themselves in all transplantings (transpositions to other regions) over prolonged generations among themselves and which also always beget half-breed young with other variations" (2007a: 85). These categories do not map onto our contemporary notion of ethnicities, Whites including Moors, Arabs, the Turkish-Tataric, the Persian "as well as all other peoples from Asia who are not specifically excluded from it by the remaining divisions" (2007b: 87). Kant ascribes the skin and behavioral differences to a predisposition to an original climate, especially air and sun, with the sense that there are four different "germs" within individuals that develop the characteristics of the given race. In defining the human, Kant regrets that there are no aliens to compare them against: "The highest species concept may be that of a *terrestrial* rational being, however we will not be able to name its character because we have no knowledge of *non-terrestrial* rational beings" (2007b: 416, emphases in the original). David Clark (2001) notes how Kant laments the non-existence of such aliens. Rationality and varying degrees of rationality—presumably most developed in the White race—are central to defining the human and the possibilities of human progress.

Kant's contribution to the wider sense of progress toward utopia during the Enlightenment period is critiqued by Jean-François Lyotard's version of postmodernity (1984). Scientific thought and method—rationality—ends up justifying the slaughter or enslavement of a huge number of people across lines of class, race, sexuality, gender, and so forth. One of the most visible examples of the consequences of racial distinctions is the South African political system of apartheid, which is allegorized in *District 9*.

Apartheid, South Africa, and *District 9*

Nash argues: At its best, SF cinema is an allegorical site that invites the audience to safely examine and reflect on long-standing social issues in an unfamiliar setting, providing the possibility of viewing them in a new light. At its worst, the process of allegorical displacement invites audiences to affirm racist ideas, confirm racial fears, and reinforce dubious generalizations about race [...] without employing overt racial language or explicit imagery.

Nash 2008: 146

In fact, the situation is more complicated than Nash describes it: texts are poly-valent and may be both reflective and offensive at the same time. A film, in particular a Hollywood film, is not a single-authored work. The scriptwriter's or scriptwriters' intent may be modified by the director, producers, actors, camera operators, designers, editors, and so on. Further, as a multimillion-dollar enter-prise that might be viewed by many different audiences, there might be an attempt to appeal to a broad range of markets from across the ideological spec-trum. Popular films may attempt to have multiple meanings to appeal to several audiences of differing political persuasions; it might be that in my reading of an unstable text I am myself being racist.

I am also uneasy at considering science fiction as allegorical in its aesthetic. The genre works by implication and encourages extrapolation. The audience's inferences may be too literal to sustain allegory. Allegory requires that we recog-nize that fictional X is standing in for real-world Y, but in reading science fiction we focus on X and are distanced from Y. Writing of the cognate genre, fantasy, Rosemary Jackson argues "one object does not *stand for* another, but literally slides into it, metamorphosing from one shape to another" (1981: 42, emphasis in the original). The distance between symbol and reality may not be maintained; in science fiction a symbol becomes 'reality.' It also needs to be noted that science fiction pays attention to the causes, effects, and interrelation of events: this is part of its cognitive processes. A narrative set on a desert planet, which is *really* an allegory for Morocco, has at best lazily "filed the serial numbers off" and at worst has failed sufficiently to think through the combination of historical and geographical events that have led to such a society. Allegory can make poor science fiction. Nevertheless, as audiences we cannot help but notice parallels. In his analysis of *District 9*, Ben Walters argues that "[i]nitially the 'prawns' seem a fairly obvious analogue for black South Africans, especially under apartheid:

they are barred from participation in large parts of society and live in townships subjected to violent raids by the authorities. The clicks of their language even suggest Xhosa" (2009: 57). The "prawns" may be an allegorical denotation of a race, but the denotation risks being racist.

Apartheid was intended to prop up white minority rule in a former British and Dutch colony. Prior to 1923, the African population had been largely rural, but the growth of industry and a need for domestic servants required workforces conveniently be situated in townships; these

> were to be sited as far as possible from white residential areas, but reasonably close to industrial areas. Spatial separation was to be reinforced by buffer zones and by natural or other barriers. And townships were to be designed and sited in such a way that they could be cordoned off in the event of riot or rebellion, and the resistance suppressed in open streets.
>
> Maylam 1990: 69–70

The Group Areas Act of 1950 classified four racial groups—White, Black, Coloured, and Indian—although in practice the last two groups seemed to be connected, the Coloured communities could be subdivided into an Indian group, a Chinese group, the other Asiatic group, the Cape Coloured, the Cape Malay, the Griqua, and other Coloured people (Western 1981: 77). The disparate range of nationalities and ethnic identities constituting a single 'race' indicates the ideological processes at work and the staying power of the Linnaean taxonomy. The White settlers included immigrants of British, Dutch, French, and German heritages. In a series of ideological acts with material consequences, people were labeled White, Coloured, or Black, determining their place of residence and work, social network and freedom of travel.

Segregating townships displaced people. The temporary accommodation that Blacks and Coloureds were moved to in the 1950s and 1960s all too often became permanent. Bill Freund notes "the new sites are almost invariably poorly provided with the most basic amenities—clinics and access to doctors, schools, electricity, good water supply, etc." (1984: 57). Forced removals destroyed businesses and led to the breakdown of existing social structures—often deliberately so. Freund writes that "the resettled appear traumatised, unable to reorganise community life or to create effective structures of resistance" (60). Apartheid policies were an attempt to maintain the social structure, but they also produced the anger and dissatisfaction that fueled the African National Congress's continued resistance.

The film's diegesis diverges from the extra-diegetic world in 1982. Whilst the 1980s saw the creation of a Tricameral Parliament with three elected chambers, White, Coloured, and Indian, it was dominated by the White representatives and the Black majority population remained disenfranchized in designated quasi-independent homelands. Bombing campaigns attacked both the White and non-White populations. Cultural, sporting, and economic boycotts put the system under more strain—South Africa's industry was increasingly confined to its domestic market. Twenty-eight years later, roughly 2010, would be the post-apartheid South Africa, indeed the post-Nelson Mandela era. Clover objects: "Though there are elements of apartheid's history mixed throughout the movie—as with the forced relocation of the aliens from Johannesburg to distant town-ships—that history doesn't provide a consistent or coherent structure" (2009: 8). Armand White asserts its story "makes trash of [...] Apartheid history by constructing a ludicrous allegory for segregation that involves human beings (South Africa's white government, scientific and media authorities plus still-disadvantaged blacks) openly ostracizing extraterrestrials in shanty-town encampments that resemble South Africa's bantustans" (8). The word "apartheid" is not used in the film—we can only assume that if such a system occurred, it has been dismantled as there are enough Blacks and other non-Whites (albeit not in positions of power) to suggest that an equivalent shift has happened.

The name of *District 9* echoes the real-world District Six, "one of Cape Town's oldest suburbs. A racially mixed, working-class neighborhood, it was known for its community atmosphere and harmony" (Rudakoff 2004: 138). Situated on the port side of Cape Town, the area was home to various workers, immigrants, freed slaves, and merchants. Conditions in Cape Town were harsh, with high "incidence of infant mortality, illegitimate births, and tuberculosis mortality" (Scott 1955: 154). Disease was perceived to spread from non-Europeans to Europeans, both where they lived together and where non-Europeans were in domestic service to Europeans. John Western notes that there was an "automatically assumed connection between visible physical dilapidation and supposed social dysfunction" (1981: 144). Disease is given a moral value that in turn has political implications. Authorities would label the razing of non-White and mixed-race areas as slum clearance, although the replacement accommodations were hardly any better.

The District Six removals were carried out by the Department of Community Development (Beyers 2008: 360). Scott C. Johnson (2009) records: "Nearly 70,000 people were summarily evicted from the only homes they had ever known. Some

1,800 houses were torn apart. The complete razing of the community took 15 years, a process its engineers drew out at length to further fragment already destabilized areas." Whilst the long drawn-out evictions aimed both to create a Whites-only area and "to excise the fact of heterogeneity and hybridity of which District Six was emblematic" (Beyers 2008: 360), only the latter was successful. Beyers argues: "Today a large portion of District Six remains undeveloped, lying empty as what is often referred to as a scar in the centre of the city [...] due to concerted opposition first from the popular sectors [...] but also from developers and corporations— who did not want the mark of District Six on their name" (360). It remains as evidence of government-led racism, and as inspiration for novels, poetry (Kruger 2001), photography, a museum (Beyer 2008), and of course *District 9*. Smith notes:

> Despite the fact that first contact with aliens occurs in 1982, squarely in the midst of the National Party's reign [...] neither the party nor the state plays a significant role in the film, the eponymous slum of which is not cleared until *28 years later*, more than 15 years after the election of the African National Congress and the official end of the apartheid order; in fact, the absent South African state is significant only in the conspicuous ceding of the authority to MNU, and no representative of state power (neither human nor architectural nor symbolic) appears in the film.
>
> Smith 2012: 149, emphasis mine

This outsourcing of authority to a multinational corporation is typical of the postmodern world and the erasure of the nation-state as described by Lyotard (1984). The (largely) white filmmakers—some South African, some New Zealander—are themselves part of a multinational corporation.

The (largely) white producers of science fiction repeatedly create narratives in which an identificatory but naïve white protagonist realizes the dystopian nature of their society. Ashley Dawson notes that *District 9*—along with *Avatar* (James Cameron, 2009)—uses such narrative to confront apartheid. A social realistic version typically begins with the disappearance of a domestic servant:

> [T]he protagonist [...] becomes involved, believing that justice will quickly be done and things set aright. Of course, his efforts not only fail to produce justice, but in addition show him the venality of the apartheid system's treatment of nonwhites. In the course of his odyssey, the protagonist is increasingly alienated from the complacent white people with whom he has heretofore lived; these people in turn ostracize him, closing ranks against a perceived race traitor.
>
> Dawson 2012: 149

John Rieder compares *District 9* to both *Avatar* and *Inglourious Basterds* (Quentin Tarantino, 2009), suggesting that the two science fiction films represent "the white male protagonist's achievement of sympathetic identification with the racial other" (2011: 47). Both stage the revenge of the non-White/alien other against the White/human population. Whereas the narrative of *Avatar* seems to be one of appropriation—Jake Sully (Sam Worthington) is able to achieve in a brief period what the Na'avi have struggled to do in a year—Rieder sees van de Merwe's transformation as more positive although "slow and torturous" (49).[1] Van de Merwe's disenfranchisement from home, family, job, and human abilities is a repetition of the thousands of disenfranchisements of District Six. Mocke Jansen van Veuren suggests *District 9* "sketches a wish-fulfilment that leads to an imagined redemption through becoming the other" (2012: 58). The transition remains unresolved by the end of the film—readable in terms of the shift from apartheid South Africa to the rainbow coalition to the post-Mandela era, in which the country has been absorbed into a neoliberal, globalized system of capital dominated by American corporations (Smith 2012: 150–2). We have a last glimpse of van de Merwe or, rather, an alien who we take to be him, holding a tin flower. This might be a symbol of hope, but the ending is open. Where does the White working class stand in contemporary South Africa? Where does the Black?

To read the aliens as allegorical representations of Black or Coloured South Africans is as problematic as the equivalent reading of the Planet of the Apes mythos. Whilst the intent might be to explore and critique interracial relations—perhaps due to growing levels of White anxiety—the connotations risk being racist. We can slip from the thought that "these gorillas are like African Americans" to "African Americans are like gorillas." To argue that the aliens are like the non-White South Africans (some of whom are subtitled despite speaking in English in the documentary sections) is to invoke the impression of the non-Whites as alien—indistinguishable, subtitled, somewhere between prawns and insect drones, violent, dirty, vomiting, and, in Roger Ebert's view "loathsome and disgusting" (2009). Whilst the trajectory of the plot allows sympathy with Christopher Johnson, it is hard to transcend the visceral gut reaction. Aside from Johnson, none of the aliens have names; his son is the only other identifiable identity. To parrot the old racist accusation: "They all look the same."

A third grouping in the film are the Nigerians, characterized as "voodoo/mercenary/cannibal" (van Veuren 2012: 573), and forming what Smith calls "a cartoonishly sinister stereotype" (2012: 154). Accusations of cannibalism have long been a means of connoting barbarism. The film's Nigerians are associated with guns and violence, and their leader, Obesandjo (Eugene Khumbanyiwa), wants to eat van de Merwe's arm. White notes he "sits in a wheelchair, big, black and scary. By this point *District 9* stops making sense and becomes careless agitation using social fears and filmmaking tropes" (2009). A further potential racist representation is the decision of the filmmakers to subtitle the Nigerians, despite much of their dialogue being comprehensible. Many of the White characters have strong Afrikaans accents, including van de Merwe, but the assumption is that they will be understood. The Nigerians, like the aliens (who are also subtitled), are situated as other. Van Veuren suggests that "[t]he film is unable to deal within its own vocabulary with the black body" (2012: 573). Black characters are either "over the top" stereotypes, sources of fear, or sidelined figures such as Fundiswa Mhlanga (Mandla Gaduka), a novice MNU agent forced to give up his armored jacket to his white superior. "Nigerian" itself is a complex identity: the former British colony of Nigeria consists of a number of ethnic groupings, the most numerous being Yoruba, Hausa, Igbo, and Fulani. Adéle Nel notes that the Nigerians, "like the aliens, [. . .] find themselves strangers in South Africa" (554).

The White community is also descended from a range of immigrants from a range of European nationals, predominantly of Britain and the Netherlands. Van de Merwe begins as a hapless, inefficient, and racist petty bureaucrat within the MNU structure, hardly a character designed to elicit audience sympathy at the beginning of the film. "Van de Merwe" is a Dutch name ("from the Merwede," a river in the Netherlands) that is also used in South Africa. It has connotations of being a fool, the name having been used in jokes in much the same way as other forms of humor. Piet Smit lies to Sandra van de Merwe (Marian Hooman) and is quick to libel van de Merwe with allegations of alien sex. MNU's supreme military commander Koobus Venter (David James) is typical of the thoughtless, sadistic, violent army stereotype and an analogue to *Avatar*'s Colonel Quaritch (Stephen Lang).

Van Veuren suggests that "the overall effect is that of a kind of puppet theatre of stereotypes" (2012: 571). The White, Nigerian, and alien communities all collapse into homogeneous identities, each of which is negative. Clover argues that the film "seems to dislike pretty much every human, and human position, it can conjure up; if the aliens represent some fraction of humanity, well, it doesn't like them much either. It's driven [. . .] by a profound and remorseless contempt for present humanity" (2009: 8). If the White, Nigerian, and alien communities are respectively conflated into three homogeneous groups, is the film's equal opportunity xenophobia racist? In a similar way, the treatment of various nation-alities in *The Mummy* (Stephen Sommers, 1999) might excuse its utilization of civilization/savagery, damsels in distress, and white man's burden maneuvers. The use of irony and satire makes the attribution of motives difficult. Van Veuren argues that the racism of *District 9*'s characters—whether White or Nigerian—is displaced onto the aliens as a focus for disgust over food consumption, bodily fluids, and ugly appearance, suggesting that they become versions of both the apartheid era shack dweller and post-apartheid era black working class (2012: 573–4).

Abjection

Van de Merwe is disgusted both by the invasion of his body by alien fluids and bodily parts and by the ejection of these: "he had started to haemorrhage black blood from his nose, lost fingernails, defecated in his pants at a surprise party and vomited black liquid over the cake, sprouted an alien claw from his left arm" (van Veuren 2012: 570–1). The British structural anthropologist Mary Douglas argues that we "desire to keep the body (physical and social) intact" (1970: 166). An uneasy margin lies between the body and the not-body and a range of phenomena trouble the precise edges of that self: "[s]pittle, blood, milk, urine, faeces or tears [...] bodily parings, skin, nail, hair clippings and sweat" (145). Societies develop rituals as "an attempt to create and maintain a particular culture [...]. Any culture is a series of related structures which comprise social forms, values, cosmology, the whole of knowledge and through which all experi-ence is mediated" (153). Specific cultures divide aspects of their society by space or time into distinct zones with policed boundaries. Abominations, hybrid cases that straddle boundaries, are rejected and expelled, whether from the individual body or the body of society. In the diegesis of *District 9*, van de Merwe is ejected from human society; in the extradiegetic world non-Whites were ejected from being complete citizens in South Africa.

Apartheid can be seen as a political manifestation of what psychoanalytic critic Julia Kristeva calls abjection. As van Veuren puts it: "a theoretical exposition of the psychological origins and mechanisms of loathing and disgust" (2012: 549). Kristeva draws upon the Freudian psychosexual development of the child, starting with the oral phase in which the child–mother dyad seems to be all there is to the world. The child eventually emerges as a subject, distinguished from the object world. Between the subject and object worlds is an uneasy, ill-defined boundary, associated with the abject. This boundary may be further damaged when the subject is met with some kind of uncanny or threatening experience, which returns them to the oral phase, to the point before the separation from the maternal. Linking back to the experience of breast feeding, Kristeva describes the disgust felt (by some) when observing the thin skin that has developed on the surface of cooling milk, and the loss of control of the body—perspiring, stomach-churning, even vomiting—that ensues. She argues that "[f]ood loathing is perhaps the most elementary and most archaic form of abjection" (Kristeva 1982: 2). Humans find the consumption of cat food by aliens disgusting and van de Merwe experiences this disgust when he has to eat it: "Wikus is simultaneously attracted and repulsed by the cat food he hungrily devours but then, nauseated, spits out" (van Veuren 2012: 579). Buffon suggested that ingesting certain foods led to a "quasi-permanent change from an original stock" (quoted in Bernasconi 2001: 16); a change of diet is thought to lead to a change of species. Van de Merwe's crossing of the human/alien and the human/animal boundary destabilizes the figure of the alien: gone is the simple relationship of the alien as the animal, the non-White, the non-human.

I have already mentioned Obesandjo's wish to consume van de Merwe's arm. Nel notes, "it is clear that cannibalism can be viewed as an abject act par excellence" (2012: 555). The oral phase of Freudian psychosexual development is associated with cannibalism—there is almost a desire to eat the mother. Nel describes the practice of *muthi* or *muti*, "African holistic healthcare where, among others, human body parts and vital organs are used to make medicine" (555). To Western eyes this is barbaric and savage, distinct from the occidental metanarrative of medicine. But Obesandjo would not be a cannibal: van de Merwe's arm is precisely non-human. It is an assertion of the (Nigerian) self over the outside world and an incorporation of an alien other into the self.

Abject racism underlies the political ideology of apartheid. Derek Hook suggests that at the heart of racism is "a rudimentary attempt to affect a kind of ego-coherence, with the set of base responsive emotions connected to such an attempt, indeed, with the exaggerated affect that comes with the desperate urgency of the wish to divide self from other" (2004: 685–6). The intention of apartheid is to keep the clean and proper boundaries of Whiteness, by defining Blacks and Coloureds as other, policing the social, economic, and political distinctions. This extends to the designation of space—whilst Johannesburg is a city sprawl, the townships are defined (by the authorities) as slums. The 'civiliza-tion' of the White spaces is distinguished from the 'wasteland' of the townships. Jacques Derrida breaks down the word 'apartheid,' analyzing its operation of separation and distinction:

> The word concentrates separation, raises it to another power and sets separation itself *apart*: "apartitionality," something like that. By isolating being apart in some sort of essence or hypostasis, the word corrupts it into a quasi-ontological segregation. At every point, like all racisms, it tends to pass segregation off as natural—and as the very law of the origin.
>
> 1985: 292, emphasis in the original

There is useful, civilized, and clean space separated by apartheid from wasted, savage, and dirty space, as the detritus of White society is expelled—*District 9* was filmed in heavily polluted Chiawelo, an area of Soweto. The waste spaces are inevitably associated with feces, urine, and corpses. District 9 had been desig-nated by law as the holding space for aliens. Van de Merwe, as the empowered representative of MNU government, has the right to expel the aliens to a substi-tute space, District 10, the next in the series. The ritual is committed with a signature—an alien hand print—that is clearly as much theater as authentica-tion. But once he crosses the human/alien boundary, van de Merwe no longer has authority. He is expelled from family, society, and species.

Conclusion

Science fiction has a long history of using allegorical techniques. The American frontier, the Second World War, the Cold War, the Korean War, the Vietnam War, feminism, Civil Rights, and apartheid have all offered cognition points to be estranged. The various others of science fiction—aliens, androids, clones, cyborgs, or robots—become metaphorical stand-ins for non-White ethnicities, women, homosexuals, the working class, or other non-privileged groups. The self to that alien other all too often defaults to a single category of White, male, heterosexual, and middle class. Fictional representations of encounters between humans and such others may offer a nuanced commentary upon the known real world from an estranging distance or may replicate racism, sexism, homophobia, or classism.

'Race' is an ideological construction, largely a product of the demands of capi-talism. Whilst the concept of race predates the slave trade, it facilitated the treatment of humans first as others and then as property, "the slave was actually manufactured to fulfill a function: as a servomechanism, as a transport system, as furniture, as *3/5* of the human, as a fractional subject" (Eshun 1998: 113, emphasis in the original). Kodwo Eshun argues that slaves are aliens. However, the aliens in *District 9* are not even slaves: aside from their exploitation by the Nigerians, they are outside the economic system, a surplus underclass that 'needs' to be expelled, maintaining the clean and proper nature of the ruling group. Hook argues that "if we view racism as subject to the dynamics of abjection we are able to appreciate how racism may come to be fixed as a kind of bodily logic which would hence assume a naturalising bent in the process" (2004: 693). Racism imagines an unclean, impure body that then is taken as evidence to justify racism. The slippage between different meanings of race—from part of a species to an entire species, from the human race to the master race—is part of the work of abjection.

The metamorphosing van de Merwe, straddling the human-alien boundary, has had his blood polluted (the traditional model of racial transmission) or his DNA mutated (the contemporary, more 'scientific' discourse) by an extra-terrestrial fluid, another abject liquid. Van de Merwe is transformed from a family joke to an isolated (almost) hero. Compare this to the typical anti-apartheid film, where "[t]he protagonist's abjection is redeemed, however, by his newfound status as hero of the antiapartheid movement" (Dawson 2011: 337). Is van de Merwe redeemed? At best he may have atoned for his actions. It is Christopher Johnson who may redeem his people and it is surely no accident that his name both contains the name "Christ" and that his initials are those of Jesus Christ.

District 9 offers the viewer a means of thinking through the construction of race through a text that invites an allegorical reading of apartheid South Africa. The film's failure to differentiate the aliens beyond the characters of Johnson and his son—to be cissexist, where are the female aliens?—its depiction of Nigerians and its incorporation of the (potential) redemption of a white character risks falling into racist discourse. White argues that "District 9 confirms that few media makers know how to perceive history, race and class relations" (2009). On the other hand, the filmmakers might just be making a film about humans and aliens, with no allegory intended. To dismiss the filmmakers as racist risks being an act of political correctness, declaring them unclean. It is another act of abjection, of drawing boundaries.

An allegorical reading is only one of the reading strategies that a viewer may deploy. Any lack of nuance on the specific issues of South African history might say more about the consumers than the producers. The viewer may work to isolate the similarities and differences between the researchable extra-diegetic and inferred diegetic histories, policing the fidelity of the translation from reality to narrative. Better than an allegorical reading would be a looser sense of estrangement. Even better may be if this reflection on the political operations of abjection and power structures within the extra-diegetic world may help to change them.

Note

1 Cf. Bianca Westermann's essay in this volume.

References

Baldwin, J. (1985a), "The Price of the Ticket," in *The Price of the Ticket: Collection Nonfiction, 1948–1985*, New York: St Martin's Press.

Baldwin, J. (1985b), "The Stranger in the Village," in *The Price of the Ticket: Collection Nonfiction, 1948–1985*, New York: St Martin's Press.

Bernasconi, R. (2001), "Who Invented the Concept of Race?: Kant's Role in the Enlightenment Construction of Race," in R. Bernasconi (ed.), *Race*, Oxford: Blackwell.

Beyers, C. (2008), "The Cultural Politics of 'Community' and Citizenship in the District Six Museum, Cape Town," *Anthropologica*, 50: 359–73.

Clark, D. L. (2001), "Kant's Aliens: The Anthropology and Its Others," *CR: The New Centennial Review*, 1: 201–89.

Clover, J. (2009), "Allegory Bomb," *Film Quarterly*, 63: 8–9.

Cook, G. P. (1991), "Cape Town," in A. Lemon (ed.), *Homes Apart: South Africa's Segregated Cities*, Bloomington and Indianapolis, IN: Indiana University Press.

Dawson, A. (2011), "Extract from a Report on the Origins of the Present Crisis," *Women's Studies Quarterly*, 39: 332–8.

Derrida, J. (1985), "Racism's Last Word," *Critical Inquiry*, 12: 290–9.

Dery, M. (1994), "Black to the Future: Interviews with Samuel R. Delany, Greg Tate, and Tricia Rose," in M. Dery (ed.), *Flame Wars: The Discourse of Cyberculture*, Durham, NC and London: Duke University Press.

Douglas, M. (1970), *Purity and Danger: An Analysis of Concepts of Pollution and Taboo*, London: Penguin.

Ebert, R. (2009), "Review of *District 9*," RogerEbert.com, 12 August 2009, http://rogerebert.com/reviews/district-9-2009, accessed 1 February 2014.

Eshun, K. (1998), *More Brilliant than the Sun: Adventures in Sonic Fiction*, London: Quartet.

Freund, B. (1984), *The Making of Contemporary Africa: the Development of African Society Since 1800*, Bloomington, IN: Indiana University Press.

Gilroy, P. (2000), *Between Camps: Race, Identity and Nationalism at the End of the Colour Line*, London: Allen Lane.

Greene, E. (1996), *Planet of the Apes as American Myth: Race and Politics in the Films and Television Series*, Jefferson NC: McFarland.

Hook, D. (2004), "Racism as Abjection: A Psychoanalytic Conceptualisation for a Post-apartheid South Africa," *South African Journal of Psychology*, 34: 672–703.

Jackson, R. (1981), *Fantasy: The Literature of Subversion*, London and New York: Routledge.

Johnson, S. C. (2009), "The Real District 9: Cape Town's District Six," Newsweek www.newsweek.com/real-district–9-cape-towns-district-six–78939, accessed 1 February 2014.

Kant, I. (2007a), "Anthropology from a Pragmatic Point of View," in G. Zöller and R. B. Louden (eds), *Anthropology, History, and Education*, Cambridge: Cambridge University Press.

Kant, I. (2007b), "Of the Different Races of Human Beings," in G. Zöller and R. B. Louden (eds), *Anthropology, History, and Education*, Cambridge: Cambridge University Press.

Kristeva, J. (1982), *Powers of Horror: An Essay on Abjection*, New York: Columbia University Press.

Kruger, L. (2001), "Black Atlantics, White Indians, and Jews: Locations, Locutions, and Syncretic Identities in the Fiction of Achmat Dangor and Others," *The South Atlantic Quarterly*, 100: 111–43.

Lyotard, J.-F. (1984), *The Postmodern Condition: A Report on Knowledge*, Manchester: Manchester University Press.

Maylam, P. (1990), "The Rise and Decline of Urban Apartheid in South Africa," *African Affairs*, 89: 57–84.

Nash, A. (2008), *Black Space: Imagining Race in Science Fiction Film*, Austin, TX: University of Texas Press.

Nel, A. (2012), "The Repugnant Appeal of the Abject: Cityscape and Cinematic Corporality in *District 9*," *Critical Arts*, 26: 547–69.

Rieder, J. (2011), "Race and Revenge Fantasies in *Avatar*, *District 9* and *Inglourious Basterds*," *Science Fiction Film and Television Studies*, 4: 41–56.

Rudakoff, J. D. (2004), "Somewhere, Over the Rainbow: White-Female-Canadian-Dramaturge in Cape Town," *TDR: The Drama Review*, 48: 126–63.

Scott, P. (1955) "Capetown a Multi-Racial City," *Geographical Journal*, 121: 149–57.

Smith, E. D. (2012), *Globalization, Utopia, and Postcolonial Science Fiction: New Maps of Hope*, Basingstoke: Palgrave Macmillan.

Suvin, D. (1979), *Metamorphoses of Science Fiction: On the Poetics and History of a Literary Genre*, New Haven, CT: Yale University Press.

van Veuren, M. J. (2012), "Tooth and Nail: Anxious Bodies in Neill Blomkamp's *District 9*," *Critical Arts*, 26: 570–86.

Walters, B. (2009), "Review of *District 9*," *Sight + Sound*, 19: 57.

Western, J. (1981), *Outcast Cape Town*, London: George Allen & Unwin.

White, A. (2009), "From Mothership to Bullship," *NY Press*, 13 August, http://nypress.com/from-mothership-to-bullship, accessed 1 February 2014.

Filmography

Avatar (2009), directed by James Cameron, Los Angeles, CA: 20th Century Fox, 2010, DVD.

District 9 (2009), directed by Neill Blomkamp, Culver City, CA: Sony Pictures Home Entertainment, 2010, DVD.

Inglourious Basterds (2009), directed by Quentin Tarantino, Universal City, CA: Universal Pictures, 2009, DVD.

Planet of the Apes (1968), directed by Franklin J. Schaffner, Los Angeles, CA: 20th Century Fox, 2006, DVD.

6

The Interplanetary Logic of Late Capitalism: Global Warming, Forced Migration, and Cyborg Futures in Philip K. Dick's *The Three Stigmata of Palmer Eldritch*

Andrew Opitz
Hawaii Pacific University, USA

Imagine a dystopian future in which climate change has reshaped the surface of the planet, radically disrupted the global economy, and forced the migration of millions of people who must now find shelter and employment in lands far from home. The wealthy predictably use their resources to protect and isolate themselves in sheltered enclaves, while the poor have no choice but to relocate to refugee camps and work colonies where they are subjected to constant surveillance, and from which there is little hope of escape. This vision now seems less like science fiction and more like a plausible projection of what the twenty-first century has in store for much of the world's population. Some would say that the process of migration, dispossession, and segregation is already well underway as vulnerable populations near sea level and in drought-prone regions leave home out of necessity while wealthier countries seek to block the flow of immigrants. Long before global warming became a topic of public debate, however, the bleak conditions just described served as the backdrop for Philip K. Dick's 1965 novel *The Three Stigmata of Palmer Eldritch*—a remarkably prescient text that, while not as well known as some of the author's more Hollywood-friendly work, reads as a powerful critique of our dystopian present.[1] This essay will examine Dick's novel, its historical context, its vision of the future, and its relevance to our current global situation—a world in which capital crosses borders freely while most of the Earth's population remains trapped on islands of poverty as ice caps melt and sea levels rise.

My goal is not to promote *The Three Stigmata of Palmer Eldritch* as a prophetic text that anticipates our world from fifty years in the past, but rather to read it as an imaginative work of cultural criticism that accurately identifies destructive forces active when the novel was written and, if anything, amplified in our world today. "Science fiction is generally understood as the attempt to imagine unimaginable futures," Fredric Jameson notes, "but its deepest subject may in fact be our own historical present" (2007: 345). Dick's novel of ecological disaster, forced migration, rapacious corporations, consumerism, genetic manipulation, social atomization, and drug-induced solipsism is rooted in the cultural landscape of the late twentieth-century California in which it was written, but its points of overlap with our world give the text a contemporary resonance. There are also places where, understandably, given the half century since publication, the story feels quite dated, focused on technologies and cultural priorities that seem out of step with the present. These too are worthy of closer attention, for they tell us something important about what we have gained and lost in the years since the 1960s.

First published in 1965, *The Three Stigmata of Palmer Eldritch* tells the story of a rapidly warming Earth on which the wealthy live in shielded estates and exclusive condos, while ordinary workers are either exterminated by the harsh climate or forced to relocate to colonies on other moons and planets in the solar system. Oppressed by endless work on wasted worlds far from home, the colonists turn to hallucinogenic drugs as a form of escape. Much of Earth's economy comes to depend on selling drugs and drug paraphernalia to the desperate colonists. Without both their labor and their appetite for escapist fantasies, the whole system would fail. Into this interplanetary dystopia steps a cyborg industrialist, Palmer Eldritch, who claims to have discovered a superior self-help drug that will enable people to remake reality to suit their personal ambitions and desires. This powerful new hallucinogen initially seems to offer unlimited freedom to its users, but they soon find themselves trapped in a never-ending bad trip where they cannot tell what is real and repeatedly see disturbing visions of Eldritch's physical features—a robotic hand, artificial eyes, and steel teeth. These cyborg enhancements are the "stigmata" of the title, and indicate to the users that their minds have been invaded by Eldritch. They lose track of reality, and even their most private thoughts are polluted by the presence of the dealer who sold them the product that cost them both their privacy and their dreams.

Readers are first introduced to the world of the novel through the eyes of Barney Mayerson, a "precog" consultant employed by P.P. Layouts, Inc., a company that manufactures a popular doll named "Perky Pat Christensen" and the miniaturized accessories and home furnishings that fill her world. Like all "precognatives," Barney is able to see glimpses of the future. His employer uses this miraculous future sight to anticipate consumer trends and plan product development and marketing strategies. He is the primary character in the novel, and like many of Dick's protagonists he is decidedly average in terms of his career—a worker drone rather than a captain of industry or a down-and-out vagrant. As Jameson observes, Dick's heroes tend to be "Capraesque [...] small employees such as record salesmen, self-employed mechanics and petty bureaucrats [...] caught in the convulsive struggles of monopoly corporations and now galactic and intergalactic multinationals, rather than in the *Star Wars* feudal or imperial battles" (2007: 347, emphasis in the original).[2] Barney falls comfortably into the "petty bureaucrat" category.

Barney's boss is a difficult man named Leo Bulero, the fabulously rich CEO of P.P. Layouts who owns a vacation home in Earth orbit (where he keeps his mistress) and who has undergone e-therapy (evolutionary enhancement) to expand his intelligence and develop a thick brown coconut-like skin to shield his body from the intense heat and solar radiation now plaguing Earth. On the surface, P.P. Layouts is a doll company devoted to the "Perky Pat" and her handsome boyfriend "Walt Essex." It soon becomes clear, however, that the company's true wealth depends on an illegal drug trade involving a hallucinogenic lichen processed into a product called Can-D, which allows its users to temporarily translate themselves into the glamorous lives of Walt and Perky Pat, massproduced fantasy characters that combine Barbie and Ken with the carefree beach party lifestyle of Frankie Avalon and Annette Funicello. Without Can-D, Pat and Walt are just dolls with miniature houses and cars. With the drug, they open up an alternative world of conspicuous consumption that users can inhabit. Colonists on outer moons and planets are especially drawn to Can-D and the layouts because the drug allows them to briefly revisit an Earth/California environment that they will never see again and, indeed, due to the ravages of global warming, no longer even exists in reality.

P.P. Layouts is basically in the business of selling nostalgic fantasies to desperate refugees. Nostalgia is not the only thing on offer, however. Unlike Mattel's Barbie and Ken, Pat and Walt are anatomically correct vessels that can become home to the consciousness and libidos of several Can-D users at the same time. In addition to fantasies of homecoming, Perky Pat opens up the possibility of group sex through vivid hallucinations in which multiple people occupy the lover dolls simultaneously. In one particularly striking scene, Mars colonist Sam Regan tries to use the Perky Pat layout to have an affair with fellow refugee Fran Schein. Before they can consummate the relationship, however, other drug users, including their real-world spouses, enter the Walt consciousness and ruin the mood. Then, the spell of the drug begins to fade:

> Already Sam Regan could feel the power of the drug wearing off; he felt weak and afraid and bitterly sickened at the realization. So goddam soon, he said to himself. All over; back to the hovel, to the pit in which we twist and cringe like worms in a paper bag, huddled away from the daylight. Pale and white and awful. He shuddered. —Shuddered, and saw, once more, his compartment with its tiny bed, washstand, desk, kitchen stove … and, in slumped, inert heaps, the empty husks of Tod and Helen, Morris, Fran and Norm Schein, his own wife Mary; their eyes stared emptily and he looked away, appalled. On the floor between them was his layout; he looked down and saw the dolls, Walt and Pat, placed at the edge of the ocean, near the parked Jaguar. Sure enough, Perky Pat had on the near-invisible Swedish swimsuit, and next to them reposed a tiny picnic basket. And, by the layout, a plain brown wrapper that had contained Can-D; the five of them had chewed it out of existence, and even now as he looked—against his will—he saw a thin trickle of shiny brown syrup emerge from their slack, will-less mouths.
>
> Dick 1991: 48

Can-D's main weakness as a drug is that its influence is so fleeting. The initial euphoria of the Perky Pat experience all too quickly turns to disappointment and disgust as the colonists return to their hardscrabble lives of farming and mining on alien worlds.

Pharmatopia

It would be easy at first glance to read into the novel's squalid scene of Can-D use as a disillusioned critique of 1960s drug culture. As a drug, Can-D seems to combine and amplify the hallucinogenic powers of LSD with the addictive qualities of heroin. Dick himself was both a connoisseur of hallucinogens and critic of the dangers they could potentially unleash. Shortly after finishing the Palmer Eldritch novel, the author reportedly curtailed his own drug use because of the "awful landscapes" revealed by "certain chemicals" (Dick 1996: 58–9). Can-D is not simply a drug, however. It also serves as an allegory for consumerism and the culture industry at large. The drug is secretly farmed on Venus by Bulero's organization and sold to Martian and Lunar colonists on the black market at the same time as the legal branch of the Perky Pat corporation relentlessly markets dollhouse miniatures by buying up ad time on radio stations staffed by orbital disc jockeys. In Bulero's business model, Can-D is quite literally produced and marketed as an "opiate of the masses" for the colonists living in off-world labor camps. "One plug of it wouzled for fifteen minutes," he says, and "no more hovel. No more frozen methane. It provides a reason for living" (Dick 1991: 24). But the consolations it provides are ephemeral and only increase the colonists' dependance on a product that will never provide them with lasting satisfaction. Adorno and Horkheimer famously end their essay on the culture industry with the observation that "the triumph of advertising in the culture industry is that consumers feel compelled to buy and use its products even though they see through them" (1969: 167). Dick illustrates this point quite directly with Can-D. The colonists know that the drug dream is false; they know that every high leads to an even deeper low, but they continue to buy the layouts because Perky Pat is the only show in town.[3] This begins to change with the arrival of Palmer Eldritch.

At the start of the novel, Eldritch and his aims are a mystery to the reader. Through overheard conversations, we learn that a ship has recently crash-landed on Pluto, and that UN authorities believe it might belong to Palmer Eldritch—an industrialist who left the solar system years ago to visit the alien Proxima system. Although extra-solar life is known to exist, most humans regard it with fear and suspicion. Lifeforms from Proxima are considered grisly things, and there is a law against any of them entering human-occupied areas. Even before we meet him, Eldritch is marked as a character who has gone beyond the pale and been transformed by a disturbing otherness from outside the human experience. His motivations for doing so appear to be a personal ambition that goes well beyond simple greed. Eldritch is considered both brilliant and reckless. We learn that:

> Eldritch was too wild and dazzling a solo pro; he had accomplished miracles in getting autofac production started on the colony planets, but—as always he had gone too far, schemed too much. Consumer goods had piled up in unlikely places where no colonists existed to make use of them. Mountains of debris, they had become, as the weather corroded them bit by bit, inexorably.
>
> Dick 1991: 13

Eldritch is an enigmatic and perhaps unhinged businessman—part Richard Branson and part Howard Hughes. His character also suggests Joseph Conrad's Kurtz, whose huge stockpile of ivory at the Inner Station resembles the mountains of useless consumer goods piled up by Eldritch on the outer worlds. Like Kurtz, Eldritch also seems to be thoroughly alienated from his peers and even the human world in general—an impression that is enhanced by his cyborg features: a robot hand, metal teeth, and artificial eyes. There is even some question of whether or not the person who landed on Pluto is Eldritch at all, or an alien entity that has taken his place.

Eldritch's plans only become clear once reports leak out that his crashed ship contained a cargo of alien lichens with hallucinogenic properties superior to those of Can-D. Word on the street is that he plans to brand the new drug "Chew-Z" and openly market it to off-world colonists. The new drug does not require any doll layouts to work, and unlike Can-D, Eldritch's Chew-Z will be sold legally with the official backing of UN officials who have been mysteriously convinced that it is harmless. As the P.P. Layouts CEO and an unofficial drug kingpin, Leo Bulero is understandably alarmed by these developments. Chew-Z could ruin his monopoly. He consults with his "precog" marketing advisers, Barney Mayerson and Barney's new assistant and lover, Roni Fugate, and asks them to look into the future of the business. Both Fugate and Barney have precognitive visions that Bulero will murder Eldritch in the not too distant future. Bulero is disturbed by this. He has never had to get his hands dirty in the past, but he has also never had any real competition before.

Convinced that inaction will mean defeat, Leo resolves that the best path forward is to confront Eldritch at his private Lunar estate. He attempts to infiltrate Eldritch's compound disguised as a reporter attending a press conference. The plan fails miserably. Eldritch's staff immediately recognizes Bulero, takes him into custody at an unknown location and gives him a dose of the mind-bending drug Chew-Z. At this point in the novel, both the imprisoned CEO and the reader lose the thread of reality and can only speculate about what is real and what is illusion. We are made to lose confidence in the consistency of Dick's fictional world, and are forced to regard every future character and narrative development with suspicion.

Bulero awakens to find himself standing on a grassy embankment in an alien world in the company of a young girl with a yo-yo. The girl calls herself Monica, but she might be an embodiment of Eldritch's daughter Zoe, she might even be Eldritch himself, she might be an alien consciousness, or she might be a product of Leo's imagination. Bulero cannot know, and neither can the reader. Speaking through the girl, or whatever she is, Eldritch (or what is assumed to be Eldritch) explains to Bulero that he is experiencing a drug trial designed to demonstrate the amazing powers of Chew-Z. With this new drug, "one can pass from life to life, be a bug, a physics teacher, a hawk, a protozoan, a slime mold, a streetwalker in Paris in 1904" (1991: 88). With Can-D, users have their options strictly limited by the P.P. Layout merchandize empire: women become Perky Pat and men become Walt Essex. However, "choosers" (Chew-Z users) can create whatever worlds they want and become who or whatever they want. It is presented as an ultimate freedom contained only by the horizon of the users' imaginations.

Bulero objects by saying that unlimited options are overwhelming, and that people are really much more comfortable when they are told what to want—a common defense of the culture industry. Eldritch counters by explaining that the colonists have grown tired of temporary and unfulfilling fantasies, their bodies wasting away in squalid hovels while their minds play beach blanket bingo with Pat and Walt. With Chew-Z, time and space are altered so that no time passes while the user is on the drug. Chew-Z freezes time and gives the users a measure of immortality. The trip lasts a long time, perhaps even forever, and the universe it creates is genuine. The users find that the new world is as real as the world they previously occupied. Bulero is initially unconvinced by this claim, but he gradually comes to believe it as he notices that he seems to be trapped in a nesting doll of alternate realities, unable to return to a world that is unpolluted by different manifestations of Eldritch.

There is one other important distinction between Can-D and Chew-Z that deserves mention. Can-D use is basically a communal experience. Users gather round a Perky Pat layout and take the drug together. The pleasure of the activity comes partly from the shared experience and the opportunities it creates—group sex, etc. It is like playing a board game with your friends or dropping acid with your swinging neighbors. Taking Can-D by yourself rather is like trying to play a board game when you are home alone. Not very much fun. Chew-Z, on the other hand, is a highly individualized experience. Users create their own discrete worlds and it is unclear whether or not they can share them with others. You can populate the Chew-Z world with the objects of your desires, but they appear as your playthings rather than as separate subjects with their own powers of creation. The one exception here is Eldritch himself, who seems to move in and out of every Chew-Z world. Though Palmer Eldritch claims that his new drug will provide a liberating alternative to the empty, mass-produced fantasies of the Perky Pat Corporation and its narco-capitalist empire, Chew-Z actually intensifies the social atomization brought about by the logic of late capitalism. Its consumers get to have whatever they want, whenever they want it, in a world that they create themselves and can never escape. It is the mental equivalent of the mountains of unwanted consumer goods the young Eldritch once piled on the outer worlds. By taking the logic of individual consumerism and personal gratification to an extreme level, Eldritch has turned desire into a wasteland. A Chew-Z trip is a frictionless dream in which things and people once desperately wanted are constantly conjured and discarded, hollow shells devoid of real meaning, drifting through consciousness like the immense vortex of discarded plastic slowly rotating in the North Pacific.

Eldritch simulates the outward forms of late capitalism without really adhering to its rules. He appears as an investor and businessman, but he does not seem to care about creating profits or maintaining a functional business model. While Leo Bulero is obsessively concerned with accumulating truffle skins (the fanciful currency of inter-planetary trade), predicting consumer trends, building a dependent customer base, and outfoxing the competition, Eldritch produces a product that has no meaningful connection to a system of supply and demand. Chew-Z gives its users everything they think they want, forever, at no cost other than the unsettling presence of Eldritch and his stigmata. Choosers may pay for the drug initially, but they seem to stay in its grip ever after. Eldritch basically bottles and disseminates the delirium of capitalism without the mechanism of capital itself.

His motivations for doing all of this are hazy to begin with and become even more questionable as the novel progresses. At times, it seems like Eldritch is on a religious mission to bring enlightenment and immortality to humanity. "God, Eldritch said, promises eternal life. I can do better; I can deliver it" (Dick 1991: 86). At other points in the novel, it is suggested that Eldritch is actually a pawn of the Proxian aliens and that Chew-Z will help them invade the solar system. We are also told that the global warming on Earth might also be part of their plan, forcing people to migrate to unpleasant locations where alien drug use becomes more appealing. Toward the end of the novel, Barney Mayerson, now on Mars and no longer employed by P.P. Layouts, encounters a hologram of Eldritch, who reluctantly reveals that he is actually an interstellar entity (neither Proxian nor Terran) who possessed Eldritch's body when the industrialist voyaged between the stars. Chew-Z, it says, is simply the way that it reproduces itself. Everybody who has taken the drug becomes the offspring of this god-like alien, allowing it to perpetuate itself across time and space. As Jameson explains, Eldritch should not be understood as "an exclusively and implacably evil force (whatever kind of alien he may be beneath his human disguise): indeed, like Stanisław Lem's sentient ocean in *Solaris,* he would like to do something beneficial for human beings, only he does not understand what that might be or how to go about it" (2007: 370). In this final version of events, the Eldritch god simply uses familiar human social arrangements—consumer capitalism, drug use, religion—to reward us for our unwitting participation in its reproductive process.

In the end, however, it is unclear which of these versions of the story is accurate. It may be that none of them are. We are told that Bulero eventually escapes the Lunar compound and cooperates with the UN to shoot down Eldritch's ship before it reaches Earth. Eldritch is supposedly dead, and Leo even sees a vision of a future monument built to commemorate his successful defeat of the alien invader. This development feels like wishful thinking and a convenient *deus ex machina,* however, and Bulero wonders if it is just another drug vision. Indeed, he and everybody else continue to see ghostly traces of Eldritch's stigmata wherever they go. This is where the novel ends. Everyday life on Earth and in the colonies seems to go on as before, but it is now haunted by the possibility that none of it is real and that nothing really matters. There is still a sliver of hope, however. It seems that the stigmata can be ignored by a determined mind. A meaningful future is still possible, but if it is to have any weight and purpose, it is up to people to make it matter through concentration and force of will.

Ontological uncertainty, politics, and global warming

The uncertain conclusion of *The Three Stigmata of Palmer Eldritch* is consistent with the reality-bending motifs of many of Dick's later novels. In his detailed work of literary criticism, *The Twisted Worlds of Philip K. Dick,* Umberto Rossi observes that Dick's writings are often distinguished by what he calls their "ontological uncertainty"—their "critical meditation on the nature of being, existence or reality, as well as the basic categories of being and their relations, *as they are found in a piece of fiction*" (2011: 10, emphasis in the original). As described by Stanisław Lem, "Dick seems to foresee a future in which abstract and highbrow dilemmas of academic philosophy will descend into the street so that every pedestrian will have to decide for himself such contradictory problems as 'objectivity' or 'subjectivity,' because his life will depend on the result" (1986: 79). Dick's focus on reality and its effacement is certainly part of what made his work a point of fascination for poststructuralist thinkers such as Jean Baudrillard.[4] However, it is important to note that Dick always anchors his ontologically uncertain stories in the material world. Jameson explains it best when he observes that

> [t]he causal attribution, then, of the hallucinatory experiences to drugs, [or] to schizophrenia [. . .] is not so much a concession to the demands of the older kind of reading or explanation as it is a refusal of that first, now archaic solution of symbolism and modernism: the sheer fantasy and dream narrative. To attribute his nightmares to drugs, [or] schizophrenia [. . .] is thus a way of affirming their reality and rescuing their intolerable experiences from being defused as an unthreatening surrealism.
>
> Jameson 2007: 350–1

Jameson goes on to claim Dick's maintenance of the tension between the objective and the subjective fits our "fragmented existence under capitalism; it dramatizes our simultaneous presence in the separate compartments of private and public worlds, our twin condemnation to both history and psychology in scandalous concurrence" (2007: 351). Though his stories may be fanciful and uncertain, Dick ensures that the alienation of his characters is governed by historical forces connected with their employment, family, and social life. This attention to social detail is what gives *The Three Stigmata of Palmer Eldritch* ongoing political relevance to our twenty-first-century world, even if, as early Dick critic Darko Suvin points out, the arrival of the titular Eldritch entity causes "the political theme and horizon [. . .] to give way to the ontological" (1975: 9).

One common complaint about Dick's writings is that he imagines politically charged worlds shaped by corporate greed, class conflict, and rampant consumerism without offering readers any political alternatives to these worlds. The pseudo-religious ending of *The Three Stigmata of Palmer Eldritch* is no exception to this. Dick's novel purposely avoids both the moralism of Ray Bradbury, for example, and the principled utopianism of his contemporary and former high-school classmate Ursula K. Le Guin.[5] Part of this is due to his approach to the craft of writing. In a 1974 essay titled "Who is an SF Writer?," Dick asserts that his primary goal is to create imaginative worlds and sympathetic characters rather than "to be manning the barricades, to be out on the street waving a banner" (1996: 77). The author's avoidance of direct politics is also likely due to his often tenuous work situation. As Rossi explains:

> We should not forget that Dick was a pro writer who had to earn a living and pay alimony to his former wives, unable to escape the ghetto of sf and its scanty remunerations—this brought him to produce as much as he could, using

amphetamines to write novel after novel. Such a situation sentenced him to frantic hyper-production (between 1963 and 1964 Dick completed nine novels, among which at least four of his most famous ones), which in turn did not always allow him to chisel and polish his sentences.

Rossi 2001: 4

The Three Stigmata of Palmer Eldritch was written during a period of frenzied productivity when the author was trying to please his publishers and support multiple households. Though his interviews and nonfiction writings indicate that Dick was critical of many social features of American life in the mid-1960s, especially the excesses of consumerism and the horrors of the Vietnam War, it seems safe to say that the author lacked both the time and the inclination to build direct political engagement into his novel.

Elysium

The absence of politics becomes especially clear if one compares *The Three Stigmata of Palmer Eldritch* to a more recent work that covers similar ground— the 2013 film *Elysium* by South African-Canadian writer and director Neill Blomkamp. Blomkamp's science fiction films are overtly political and allegorical. His highly successful 2009 film *District 9* is an allegory for apartheid told through the story of a race of intelligent but dispossessed alien arthropods stranded in South Africa and quarantined/imprisoned in an internment camp. *Elysium* addresses similar themes of inequality and xenophobia in its story of an over-populated and ecologically devastated Earth where the poor live in vast slums and work in unsafe robot manufacturing facilities while the rich escape to luxurious suburban estates on an orbiting satellite rather grandiosely named "Elysium." This satellite resembles Leo Bulero's orbiting estate—"Winnie-the-Pooh Acres" (where he keeps his mistresses), but where Dick's novel displays wordplay and whimsy in its mockery of the infantilizing decadence of the rich, Blomkamp's *Elysium* takes itself very seriously.

The symbolism of the film is not subtle. The inhabitants of Elysium frolic in a lush country-club setting where they speak French and listen to chamber music while the Earth-bound population toils in a radioactive ghetto, a sprawling dysto-pian version of Los Angeles, and speaks Spanish while gazing longingly at the shining platform in the sky. The residents of Elysium also enjoy advanced futur-istic medical care, not unlike the expensive e-therapy of Dick's novel, while the slum dwellers endure squalid clinics staffed by unsympathetic robots dispensing ineffective pills. The whole system comes crashing down when a working-class hero played by Matt Damon receives a fatal dose of radiation poisoning at the factory, and with nothing to lose and only days left to live, decides to infiltrate the orbiting gated community to obtain the medical care he feels he deserves. With the help of some cybernetic weaponry and a team of slum-rat hackers, he outmaneuvers Elysium's heartless defense minister, played by Jodie Foster, and her team of international mercenaries. The gated community in the sky is invaded by the downtrodden masses and its central computer is reprogramed to give high-quality healthcare to everyone. Justice and socialized medicine win the day!

The comparison between this explicitly political film and the *Three Stigmata of Palmer Eldritch* is instructive because it illustrates both the strengths and weaknesses of Dick's dystopia. For example, though Dick's novel describes a world wracked by global warming and forced migration, its view of the situation is narrowly American and there is little if any mention of the global poor that feature so prominently in Blomkamp's movie. Dick's planetary migration is forced not by hunger and poverty but by the assignment of mandatory coloniza-tion cards that resemble the draft notices of the Vietnam Era in the US. The people who receive these notices then try to beat the draft by convincing the colonization authorities that they are too mentally unstable to be useful colo-nists. And while both Blomkamp's film and Dick's novel present stories of rapa-cious capitalism and stark income inequality, they also both fall short of offering a plausible explanation of how this economy actually works. Dick's novel never really explains how a system of advanced inter-planetary consumer capitalism can be maintained by a customer base of poor subsistence farmers on the outer worlds. If their farms are as sad and failing as the ones presented in the novel, how can they afford their drugs and their designer layouts? Similarly, *Elysium* imagines an industrial capitalist dystopia where millions of enfeebled and seemingly unnecessary human workers are used to manufacture advanced robots that seem far more capable of just manufacturing themselves.

In pointing this out, the goal is not to evaluate the realism of these science fiction stories. That would be a fruitless project. However, it is worth noting that science fiction dystopias typically depend more on emotional truths rather than technological or social facts, and that their economic visions are sometimes out of step with the levels of development they imagine. Science fiction is often more about the past and present than about the future. For example, Bradbury explores the nineteenth-century American frontier on Mars and Asimov revisits the rise and fall of the Roman Empire in his *Foundation* books. In the case of Dick and Blomkamp, both dystopias attempt to tell a story about the dysfunctions of late capitalism while imagining social arrangements that belong to an earlier stage of industrial capitalism. They contain non-synchronous elements. Blomkamp's film resurrects visions of laboring masses that do not fit with the high-tech features of our world, and the economy of the Palmer Eldritch story is based on a currency of rare truffle skins that brings a taste of *haute cuisine* to the world of *haute finance*. Though the latter is a whimsical detail sprung from the author's abundant imagination, in economic terms truffles would serve as a de facto "gold standard" that belongs more to nineteenth-century national economies than to the multinational and multi-planetary economy Dick envisions—a sprawling system that would likely depend on fiat currency rather than hard-to-come-by trade items harvested from the natural world. The complex movements of capital through mechanisms of credit and debt, and the multinational financial institutions required to maintain these systems, are central to the unequal distribution of wealth and the migrations of labor that define our dystopian present, but they do not lend themselves to compelling fiction. So, it is no surprise that Dick and others bypass them in search of simpler times and simpler truths.

In the final analysis, however, it might be more fruitful to see the novel's truffles as more than just imaginative trifles or anachronistic mistakes. Though it may be objectively true that a limited truffle-skin currency would be poorly suited to an advanced capitalist economy of the sort imagined in *The Three Stigmata of Palmer Eldritch*, there is nevertheless something both quaint and unaffected about the author's vision of a transactional system based on something as basic and natural as a woodland fungus. This desire for the earthy and organic in a world of synthetic simulations is also found in bounty hunter Rick Deckard's yearning for a living (non-electric) animal in Dick's *Do Androids Dream of Electric Sheep?* (1968). Dick's impersonal commercial landscapes often contain remnants of things that do not really belong to (plants, animals, artisanal objects), and serve as reminders of, a world outside the logic of the corporation and its consumerist fantasies. As a fungus of the forest floor, the truffle is also an organism that thrives and builds a home for itself in conditions of decay. This, in the end, is also what most of Dick's protagonists want for themselves—to live and find meaning among the disintegrating ruins of a world past saving. Seen from this perspective, it makes perfect sense to find value in a truffle. For unlike the dead politicians and tomb-like monuments that decorate our present currency, it represents future life and some small hope for the future.

Notes

1   Although only *Blade Runner* (1982) was in production in Dick's lifetime, many of
    his novels and short stories have been adapted for Hollywood. The most famous
    examples include *Total Recall* (1990), *Screamers* (1995), *Minority Report* (2002),
    Paycheck (2003), *A Scanner Darkly* (2006), *Next* (2007), *The Adjustment Bureau*
    (2011), and the *Total Recall* reboot of 2012. To date, nobody has attempted to
    create a screen version of *The Three Stigmata of Palmer Eldritch*.

2   Science fiction writers often imagine and revisit social landscapes that they find
    compelling. For example, many of Ray Bradbury's stories are directly or indirectly
    set in small Midwestern towns, though they are sometimes located on Mars.
    Ursula Le Guin repeatedly imagines extraterrestrial neo-tribal communities
    loosely based on Native American cultures. Though his worlds are frequently
    urban, industrial, and post-industrial dystopias, Philip K. Dick's character selection
    seems to be influenced by what Fredric Jameson calls the "university town"—"a
    community of small businesses, used record shops, artists, drug users, attractive
    young women and ordinary folk that avoids the provincialism and claustrophobia
    of the classical Main Streets of the American Middle West" (2007: 361–2).

3   Jameson provides a similar reading of the novel when he observes that the Perky
    Pat experience is rather like watching a TV show, and that Dick's work suggests a
    close relationship between the products of the culture industry (TV in particular)
    and drug use. According to Jameson, "[t]elevision is [. . .] another one of those
    contextual 1950s themes and current-event references which we have observed
    Dick's works to soak up (as with the dramatization of the then novel Barbie dolls);
    and it may be suggested that in Dick drugs and schizophrenia are bad, not because
    they provide hallucinations, but because those hallucinations are too closely
    related to television" (2007: 371). Looked at from this angle, the glassy-eyed,
    drooling addicts in Sam Regan's Martian hovel resemble a TV audience camped in
    front of the "boob tube." And like a TV show, Can-D visions usually last only
    twenty or thirty minutes.

4   See, for example, Baudrillard's "Simulacra and Science Fiction," *Science Fiction
    Studies*, 18.3, 1991.

5   For more on the Dick and Le Guin connection, see John Wray's recent "Ursula K.
    Le Guin, The Art of Fiction" in *The Paris Review*, 206 (2013). As for Ray Bradbury,
    The Three Stigmata of Palmer Eldritch could be read as a partial response to
    Bradbury's own *The Martian Chronicles*. Bradbury frequently uses Mars
    colonization as a moral allegory for American Westward expansion, frontier
    politics and the extermination of indigenous populations. In contrast, Dick
    populates Mars with listless farmers seeking solace from hallucinogenic drugs.

They are refugees rather than intrepid pioneers, and their lives communicate no particular moral message. Their existence seems purposeless, a slow spiral into decay mirrored by the steady disintegration of their sandy gardens and malfunctioning farm equipment.

References

Adorno, T. and Horkheimer H. (1969), *Dialectic of Enlightenment,* J. Cummings (trans.), New York: Continuum.

Bradbury, R. (2012), *The Martian Chronicles,* New York: Simon & Schuster.

Dick, P. K. (1991), *The Three Stigmata of Palmer Eldritch,* New York: Vintage Books.

Dick, P. K. (1996), *The Shifting Realities of Philip K. Dick: Selected Literary and Philosophical Writings,* L. Sutin (ed.), New York: Vintage.

Jameson, F. (2007), *Archeologies of the Future: The Desire Called Utopia and Other Science Fictions,* New York: Verso.

Lem, S. (1986), *Microworlds,* New York: Mariner Books.

Rossi, U. (2011), *The Twisted Worlds of Philip K. Dick: A Reading of Twenty Ontologically Uncertain Novels,* Jefferson: McFarland and Company.

Suvin, D. (1975), "P.K. Dick's Opus: Artifice as Refuge and World View," *Science Fiction Studies,* 2.1, www.depauw.edu/sfs/backissues/5/suvin5art.htm, accessed 6 July 2014.

Wray, J. (2013), "Interview: Ursula K. LeGuin, The Art of Fiction," *The Paris Review,* 206.

Filmography

Elysium (2013), directed by Neill Blomkamp, Los Angeles: Sony Pictures, 2013, DVD.

7

Migrants and the Dystopian State

Matthew Goodwin

University of Massachusetts Amherst, USA

The citizens of Utopia in Thomas More's *Utopia* (1516) are strictly controlled in their ability to travel within their country, as the character Raphael Hythloday reports: "Anyone who takes upon himself to leave his district without permission, and is caught without the governor's letter, is treated with contempt, brought back as a runaway, and severely punished" (2011: 53). Since this beginning of the utopian and dystopian tradition, the restriction on migration has been a constant fixture. Dystopian fiction, in particular, commonly depicts a government that keeps control of its citizens by restricting migration, so that leaving the state or just traveling within one's own state becomes a challenge. At times, this means the use of natural barriers such as an island or the construction of an immense wall. In Yevgeny Zamyatin's *We* (1921), for example, the Green Wall serves to keep its inhabitants locked within their rationalized society, as the narrator D-503 gushes: "Oh, great, divinely bounding wisdom of walls and barriers! They are, perhaps, the greatest of man's inventions [...] Man ceased to be a savage only when we had built the Green Wall, when we had isolated our perfect mechanical world from the irrational, hideous world of trees, birds, animals" (1999: 93). At other times, it means instituting a bureaucracy that can be used to limit freedom of movement. In George Orwell's *Nineteen Eighty-Four* citizens need to have their passport endorsed just to travel 100 kilometers outside of the city, and "sometimes there were patrols hanging about the railway stations, who examine the papers of any Party member they found there and asked awkward questions" (1949: 117). And in Neal Stephenson's *Snow Crash* (1992) the protagonists must continuously use their passports to make their way through the border patrols of the many small city-states that make up the former United States. These brief examples show that when we imagine terrible societies, they are terrible in part because the state migration system (walls and borders, border patrol, and bureaucracy) has proliferated.

This essay looks at two Mexican short stories, José Luis Alverdi's "Azúcar en los Labios" ("Sugar on the Lips," 1994) and Gabriel Trujillo Muñoz's "Cajunia" (1994), and one Chicano/a play, Cherrie Moraga's *The Hungry Woman: A Mexican Medea* (2001), which develop this tradition of heightened control of migration to express the experience of contemporary migration.[1] In these stories, the experiences of the fictional migrants are analogous to the way that the majority of Mexican migrants to the United States are treated in real life, especially undocumented migrants. They are regulated by oppressive bureaucracies, their movements are monitored, and they confront guarded walls and borders. What is unique about these stories is that they are less extrapolative in regard to migration than mimetic. The equation between fictional and real-life migrants in these stories creates a frightening logic. Migrants in real life are treated the same as migrants living in a fictional dystopian society, therefore, migrants in real life face a dystopia. The term, coined by Maria Varsam, to refer to such real-life dystopias is "concrete dystopia," which she defines as "those events that form the *material* basis for the content of dystopian fiction which have *inspired* the writer to warn of the potential of history to repeat itself" (2003: 209, emphases in the original). The concrete dystopia at the heart of the dystopian works by Alverdi, Trujillo Muñoz, and Moraga is the state migration system of the United States.

On this foundation of a concrete dystopia, these stories create a set of role reversals. In "Azúcar en los Labios," it is not the government of the United States that restricts the movement of Mexican migrants, but the government of Mexico. The Mexican government takes on the role that the United States has in real life, that is, they organize the restrictive official body that controls migration across the Mexico-US border. In "Cajunia," migrants are trying to flee the United States, not enter it. It is the Mexican government that is now in the position of guarding the border and of making ethical decisions about who to let in and how. And in *The Hungry Woman: A Mexican Medea*, the Chicanos/as in the fictional nation of Aztlán are the group that deports another group, in this case, the gay and lesbian citizens who are subject to tougher state control. The role reversals in these stories result not only in critiques of the state migration system but are also the expression of a fear, and the potential asserted, that Mexico or the Chicano/a nationalist movement can become a dystopia. At the same time, there are significant utopian elements in these dystopian stories and they can be understood as being a part of the resurgence of dystopian fiction in the 1980s and 1990s, which Lyman Tower Sargent calls "critical dystopias." Referring to the work of authors such as Octavia Butler, he defines critical dystopias as: "a non-existent society described in considerable detail and normally located in time and space that the author intended a contemporaneous reader to view as worse than contemporary society but that normally includes at least one eutopian enclave or holds out hope that the dystopia can be overcome and replaced with a eutopia" (quoted in Baccolini and Moylan 2003: 7). Like other critical dystopias of the time period, the three works explored in this essay contain an element of hope in the dreams of migrants for a better life and the growing possibility of multi-ethnic collaboration.

Dystopia at the Mexico-US border

José Luis Alverdi's short story "Azúcar en los Labios" gives a snapshot of one person's experience in line at the Mexican emigration office, "la Secretaría Nacional de Expulsión Social" (The Ministry of Social Expulsion) or as it is nick-named "la Secretaría del Déjame Salir" (The Ministry of Let Me Go). In the narrative, following a period of economic instability, a major crisis ensues and a repressive government is instituted in Mexico. Many citizens want to leave because of poverty, and head north to where they can make better wages in the United States. The Mexican government, however, restricts those who can leave, issuing an "expulsion permit" only to the select. The real-life migration pattern of Mexicans leaving for the United States is kept intact in the short story. The reversal is that it is the Mexican government that makes it difficult for people to leave, instead of the reality of the border situation where it is the United States' government which makes it difficult for people to enter.

According to the scene described in the story, the chance of a successful crossing depends on how one approaches the official at the window and the reasons that one gives for leaving. While standing in line, the unnamed narrator observes that the emigration official rejects the application of a man because of his response to the question of why he wants to leave. She stamps his papers with a rejection "Por desagradecido" ("For being ungrateful", Alverdi 1994: 59). Presumably he had told the official something along the lines of wanting to help his family. The narrator waits while the emigration official chats with her co-workers until he is finally able to hand in his application. The official asks: "¿Por qué quiere dejar el país?" ("Why do you want to leave the country?", 61).

The truth of the matter is that the narrator is an engineer who wants to leave Mexico in order to take care of his family, in particular his sister who is in debt. While, in fact, he has the same reason as the poor man, he tells the official what she wants to hear and gives a memorized speech that praises the nation and graciously asks to leave in order to reduce the overpopulation. His lie is accepted.

The central organizing image of the story, sugar on the lips, becomes a symbolic means to understand the political and economic dynamics at the border—that the people are going north to avoid poverty while luxury goods go south to be sold for profit. The official is eating donuts while interviewing applicants and the donuts have left a sugar mustache on her upper lip. That the narrator observes this detail makes it an apt metaphor because it demonstrates the kind of mentality produced by standing in line, that one's world shrinks and one focuses on small details. The narrator observes:

> Desde mi sitio pude distinguir cómo la empleada, además de su deslavado uniforme, lucía una capa de azúcar en el labor superior; un dulce bigote dejando ahí al saborear las antojables donas importadas, que acompañaban su taza de café y el montón de documentos migratorios desparramados sobre la fórmica blanca de la cubierta del mueble.

> (From my place I was able to see that the employee, in addition to her unkempt uniform, wore a layer of sugar on the upper lip; a sweet mustache left there as she enjoyed the delectable imported donuts that accompanied her cup of coffee and the mountain of migration documents strewn about on the white formica of the desk cover.)

> Alverdi 1994: 59

The sugar mustache is correlated with the careless attitude and lack of respect that the official has for the people whose documents lie on her desk. What is of importance to her are the little luxuries of her work, not the work itself nor the people that she is serving. That the donuts are imported donuts shows that the official is connected to the source of power, the source of this luxury in the United States. The narrator continues:

> Se veía devorar el panecillo más con gula que con hambre, como si el sólo saborear el azúcar procesada en una sociedad avanzada ratificaba la importancia que sentía tener por su cargo, frente a todos los que esperábamos cruzar la frontera y viajar al tan cercano y a la vez lejano país del norte.

> (She seemed to devour the bread roll more with gluttony than hunger, as if to only taste the sugar processed in an advanced society confirmed the importance

that she felt for her position compared to those who waited to cross the border and travel to the so close and at once distant country of the north.)

Alverdi 1994: 60

The narrator interprets the manner in which the official eats as expressing something about her self-understanding, that she is more valuable and so merits certain luxuries simply because she is connected to the United States through the political and legal systems of both nations. While the citizens of Mexico suffer from poverty, her position allows her to live a life of some luxury. The sugar on the lips then displays the imbalance of wealth and power that is driving emigration towards the United States. At the end of the story, the narrator gives his thanks to her for accepting his application, which is unsurprisingly followed by her vapid response of taking another bite of her donut.

But while the narrator is critical of the official's greed, he himself has sugar on the lips, metaphorically speaking that is, as he is caught up in the desire for power. This is clear in that he uses his position as a professional to help him enter, and even seems to look down upon the official, fantasizing that he himself is the boss of the office, ordering her to do her job well. Nevertheless, while bowing to the power behind this dystopian scenario, the narrator retains the utopian impulse of migration: "Cruce la línea divisoria para adentrarme en un lugar extraño, donde podrían vivir mis hijos, cuando los tuviera, sin tantas deudas y pesares" ("I crossed the dividing line to get ahead in a strange place, where my children could live, when I have them, without so many debts and difficulties," 62). Even within an absurd and corrupt system that accepts lies over truth, where everyone is subject to the attractions of wealth, a basic hope remains. The desire, however, is not exactly a positive one for the United States, but just to be somewhere that seems better than Mexico. This in the end is the indomitable spirit of those who cross the real-life border, that even though the system is dystopian, the hope of migrants for a better life continues. It is a small hope, but one that has moved millions.

As "Azúcar en los Labios," Gabriel Trujillo Muñoz's short story "Cajunia" is set at the Mexico-US border, but in this story the border has moved north to the Mississippi River. The back story is that white supremacist groups have taken control of the United States and have formed the Aryan Confederation. Non-Aryans are enslaved, concentration camps are built, and the border patrol begins to stop people from leaving. In conflict with the Aryan Confederation is the state of Cajunia, also known as the "hermandad Afro-Mexico-Americana"

(AMA), which is described as being below the Mississippi and above the Papaloapan river in central eastern Mexico (Trujillo Muñoz 1994: 28–9). In this story, the border is at every level turned upside down through role reversals. Instead of people having to sneak into the United States, the characters have to sneak out. And so, instead of the United States trying to keep people out, the Aryan Confederation is trying to keep people in, using drones and the military to stop them. Coyotes, who in actuality work outside the law assisting migrants crossing into the United States, are helping people get out of the Aryan Confederation and into Cajunia. Under current laws, acting as a coyote is a federally punishable crime in the United States, and yet the coyote is a revered and often feared figure, especially as depicted in the border folk songs, the *corridos*. In this story, they are a group of official government border patrol agents.

The protagonist in the story is Teresa Caborca, a young Cajunian coyote who is being trained by her *tio* Harry "Buscabullas" Laredo.[2] Teresa, being of Mexican descent, had previously lived as a slave in the Aryan Confederation. Like the refugees she now helps, Teresa crossed the river into Cajunia, and so now she is giving back to the nation that accepted her. The plot begins as Teresa and Harry are on a mission to help ferry a group of refugees across the Mississippi and into the south. Traveling with the group of refugees is Gregorio Salas who is in possession of the formula for a vaccine that can protect against a biological weapon that the Aryans are planning to use against Cajunia. Because of Gregorio, Aryan soldiers follow the group into Cajunian territory but the coyotes are able to finally save the majority of the refugees, including Gregorio.

Cajunia is described, from the point of view of Teresa, as a racial paradise where "los mexicanos, los anglos, los indios y los negros vivían en paz, gozosa y pacíficamente entremezclados" ("the mexicans, anglos, indians and blacks lived in peace, joyfully and peacefully intermixed," 27–8). On the issue of race, the Aryan Confederation and Cajunia stand as a clear cut dystopia and a utopia. Nevertheless, the possibility that Cajunia could become a dystopia one day is expressed at the heart of the story when Teresa fires upon Carl Young, a young Aryan soldier, and wounds him. Because he is a young boy, and because of some level of attraction, Teresa saves him and takes him along with the refugee group. The group initially is resistant but Teresa orders them at gun-point to accept him as a member of the refugees. Once Teresa reaches the safe zone protected by the Cajunian military, the soldiers are likewise shown to be resistant, noting the illegality of helping an enemy and a white supremacist at that, and want to simply shoot him. "Tio Harry," however, trusts her judgment and defends Carl in a speech given to the soldiers:

> soy hijo de Cajunia, un hombre libre. Y por esa única razón me puedo cagar en todas las ordenanzas habidas y por haber. Por eso me caen de a madre los pinches arios y los nazis y los cabezas cuadradas [...] si ustedes siguen tan estirados e inflexible van a terminar siendo igualitos que los Nazis, van a creer que primero es una ley que un ser humano.

> (I am a son of Cajunia, a free man. And for this very reason I can shit on all present and future laws. For that reason I hate the fucking Aryans and Nazis and the square heads [...]. If you keep being uptight and inflexible you're going to end up the same as the Nazis, you're going to believe that laws come before humans.)
>
> Trujillo Muñoz 1994: 41–2

Harry stands on the ideals of his own nation and asserts that the threat to the nation is to become like the Aryan Confederation, to become racist and intolerant. While Cajunia is set up as a kind of utopia to the dystopia of the Aryan Confederation, Harry is keenly aware of the possibility that even their utopian hope may at any moment become itself another dystopia, and so he urges them to resist the dystopian threat that always circles around utopias.

A Chicano/a dystopia

Built up from the same concrete dystopia of the United States migration system, the previous two stories both focus their plots on the moment of crossing the Mexico-US border. This section explores Cherrie Moraga's *The Hungry Woman: A Mexican Medea*, which, while also built of the United States migration system, moves the conflict away from the border and into the interior of the nation, to the American Southwest. In this story, the fear is not that Mexico becomes a dystopia as in the previous two stories, but that the Chicano/a nationalist movement develops into a dystopia with its own state migration system.

The Hungry Woman is set in the second decade of the twenty-first century after an ethnic civil war has divided the United States into a number of smaller nation-states: Africa-America in the South, Aztlán in the Southwest, the Union of Indian Nations, Hawai'i, and Alaska. The protagonist, Medea, is a war hero living in the Chicano/a state of Aztlán, and married to Jasón. Jasón discovers that Medea is having a lesbian affair with her lover Luna, and so Medea is expelled along with her son Chac-Mool to Phoenix. Years later, Jasón wants Chac-Mool and Medea to return to Aztlán, but only because he does not have enough indigenous blood to fulfill the requirement for owning land in Aztlán. Similar to her literary ancestors in Euripides' *Medea* and *La Llorona*, the original Mexican Medea of folklore, Medea kills her son rather than lose him to a treacherous husband and an oppressive state.

Before the ethnic civil war, the United States underwent a period of anti-migrant sentiment, or as one character describes it: "Wetback go home" (Moraga 2001: 22). This system of deportation was then passed on to the smaller states and used for a new purpose. Medea's mother, Mama Sal, explains the way this happened: "Just like the Gringo and Gachupín before them, and then en masse, all the colored countries threw out their jotería, queers of every color and shade and definition. Y los homos became peregrinos, como nomads, just like our Aztec ancestors a thousand years ago" (24). This aspect of the story is a rich metaphor for the exclusion that Chicano/a gays and lesbians experienced from the Chicano/a nationalist movement, and so, Aztlán in the story may be a utopia for some Chicano/a nationalists, but for the Chicano/a queers it is a nightmare dystopia. Chicano/a nationalism mimics United States' imperialism with the result that the queers are deported just as Mexicans were deported. This phrase "los homos became peregrinos" (the homos became pilgrims) connects queers to the multiple migrations that are referred to in Chicano/a thinking: the original journey of the Aztecs from North America to the South, the journey of Chicanos/as back to Mexico, and contemporary Mexican migration. In this sense, the connection between being a migrant with being queer, roots queers in the Chicano/a community. The Chicano/a border patrol plays an important symbolic role in the play as well. When Chac-Mool goes to the border to get his migration documents to re-enter Aztlán and try to change it into a queer-friendly state, the border guard demands that he give his loyalty to the new anti-queer state. The border guard describes herself as his "revolutionary conscience"—the state co-opts his loyalty to the revolution, asking him to transfer that loyalty to the counter-revolution and the state itself. The play suggests that any utopian construction such as Aztlán can turn dystopian as soon as it is intent on restricting the movement of some of its citizens.

The Hungry Woman has some of its roots in the complex conversations about Chicano/a nationalism and the utopian formulation of the nation of Aztlán. It was conceived as originally referring to the legendary homeland of the Aztecs in the north; however, it also referred to the area of the Southwest United States that was taken from Mexico in the Treaty of Guadalupe Hidalgo in 1848. Since the 1960s the term has taken on many different configurations, often referring to the Chicano/a spirit as much as to a geographical location and a political project. In her theoretical essays, particularly "Queer Aztlán: The Re-formation of the Chicano Tribe" (1993), Moraga worked at reimagining the nation so that it was inclusive of all sexualities. *The Hungry Woman* is an attempt to work out some of the challenges of this stance.

Patricia Ybarra, in her essay "The Revolution Fails Here," argues that "*The Hungry Woman* is a meditation on the failure of the 'Queer Aztlán' project articulated in 1993" (2008: 63). She continues: "Medea's refusal to let him try [Chac-Mool to change the policies of Aztlán] marks the failure of the possibility of a non-marginalized queer Aztlán within the frame of the play" (75). While this is certainly true in the sense that Aztlán is not reformed from within, Medea and Chac-Mool's failure to change Aztlán is not a failure of Queer Aztlán as such, but a failure of homonormative politics. The idea of Queer Aztlán is not just to reform Aztlán so that it is queer friendly. As Moraga explains in "Queer Aztlán: The Re-formation of the Chicano Tribe": "Chicana lesbians and gay men do not merely seek inclusion in the Chicano nation; we seek a nation strong enough to embrace a full range of racial diversities, human sexualities, and expressions of gender" (1993: 164). Queer Aztlán was never identical to Aztlán, as if Queer Aztlán were simply Aztlán plus the queers. A reformed Aztlán does not fully represent Moraga's vision of a Queer Aztlán and so does not indicate a failure of that vision; that is, Moraga does not envision a liberal Aztlán but a radical Aztlán.

The community of Phoenix, in fact, displays some of the characteristics of a Queer Aztlán in the sense that Medea is able to live freely with a supportive and extended family, including her lover, Luna. And yet, the city is clearly not a utopian alternative to the dystopia of Aztlán. The play is after all a tragedy: Medea is an alcoholic, kills her son, and goes insane. That Phoenix is not conceived of as a utopia or a powerful Queer Aztlán, but as a community full of human frailty, is significant because Queer Aztlán is not conceived of as a nation-state. Moraga's Queer Aztlán is constructed in *The Hungry Woman* as an ambiguous and imperfect community, between tradition and revolution, without a flag or state, but formed by a utopian impulse that takes the dystopian threat seriously. Furthermore, while Queer Aztlán is based in a nationalist construction, it is not the concept of a fixed nationality that defines the new community of queers, but their exile, as described in this conversation between Mama Sal and Luna's friend Savannah:

SAVANNAH: And we made a kind of gypsy ghetto for ourselves in what was
    once a thriving desert.
MAMA SAL: They call it "Phoenix," pero entrenos, we name it "Tamoanchán,"
    which means—
CHAC-MOOL: "We seek our home."
MAMA SAL: And the seeking itself became home.

                                                                   Moraga 2001: 24

In a community formed on the concept of migration, as opposed to nationality,
there would be no border and no border guard, and so there is little chance that
a dystopia can be formed.

It is crucial, finally, in understanding Moraga's vision of the community in
Phoenix to point to the fact that it is devised with a science fiction background.
The stage directions describe Phoenix this way: "Phoenix is represented by the
ceaseless racket of a city out of control (constant traffic, low-flying jet planes,
hawkers squawking their wares, muy 'Blade Runner-esque'). The lighting is
urban neon. Most people look lousy in it" (7). *Bladerunner* (Ridley Scott, 1982)
is often seen as representing the paradigm of the dystopian city, nevertheless, it
is significant to note the presence of Chicano/a actor Edward James Olmos in
the film. Olmos, who had shortly before the filming of *Bladerunner* portrayed a
classic Chicano/a character in the film *Zoot Suit* (Luis Valdez, 1981), reprised a
futuristic version of this role for *Bladerunner*. It is in the multi-ethnic Los
Angeles of *Bladerunner* that Olmos' character Gaff, who is himself a multi-ethnic
mix, is comfortable. And so, there is a utopian element here in imagining Phoenix
as the place where Gaff can flourish. The community of Phoenix is not imagined
as a complete utopia nor dystopia, but as an imaginative space, and a Chicano/a
science fiction space.

Conclusion

As of the writing of this essay, some 11 million migrants remain undocumented
in the United States, living in the dystopia of the state migration system. Of
course, for the majority of people living in the United States, this situation is not
experienced as a dystopia at all, and may even be seen as utopian in its avail-
ability of cheap labor. As Keith Booker observes: "what one person considers
an ideal dream might to another person seem a nightmare" (1994: 3). For the
Mexican and Chicano/a authors discussed in this essay, it is not a question—it is

assumed that the state migration system is a dystopia. The state migration system is the material that constructs their fictional dystopias. No extrapolation is needed, just representation. Beyond that, they seek to make their own nations responsible for avoiding becoming such a dystopia. And the utopian hopes they express are powerful yet so cautious because the stakes are so high: the survival and flourishing of the migrant community in the United States.

Notes

1   All translations of Alverdi and Trujillo Muñoz are my own.
2   *Buscabullas* can be roughly translated as "troublemaker."

References

Alverdi, J. L. (1994), "Azúcar en los labios," in F. Schaffler González (ed.), *Más allá de lo imaginado III: Antología de ciencia ficción Mexicana*, Fondo Editorial Terra Adentro, 4, Mexico City: Consejo Nacional para la Cultura y las Artes.

Baccolini, R. and Moylan, T. (2003), *Dark Horizons: Science Fiction and the Dystopian Imagination*, New York: Routledge.

Booker, K. (1994), *The Dystopian Impulse in Modern Literature*, Westport, CT: Greenwood Press.

Moraga, C. (1993), *The Last Generation: Prose and Poetry*, Boston, MA: South End Press.

Moraga, C. (2001), *The Hungry Woman: A Mexican Medea*, Albuquerque, NM: West End Press.

More, T. ([1516] 2011), *Utopia*, New York: W. W. Norton & Company.

Orwell, G. (1949), *Nineteen Eighty-Four*, London: Signet Classics.

Stephenson, N. ([1992] 2008), *Snow Crash*, New York: Bantam Books.

Trujillo Muñoz, G. (1994), "Cajunia," in P. I. Taibo (ed.), *Frontera de espejos rotos*, México: Roca.

Varsam, M. (2003), "Concrete Dystopias: Slavery and Its Others," in R. Baccolini and T. Moylan (eds), *Dark Horizons: Science Fiction and the Dystopian Imagination*, New York: Routledge.

Ybarra, P. A. (2008), "The Revolution Fails Here: Cherrie Moraga's 'The Hungry Woman' as a Mexican Medea," *Aztlán: A Journal of Chicano Studies*, 33.1: 63–88.

Zamyatin, Y. ([1921] 1999), *We*, M. Ginsburg (trans.), New York: EOS HarperCollins Publishers.

8

Meeting the Other:
Cyborgs, Aliens, and Beyond[1]

Bianca Westermann

Ruhr Universität Bochum, Germany

This essay aims to contextualize hybrid figures in contemporary cinema as indicators of broader cultural anxieties and concerns. Central to this project are two films from 2009, *Avatar* (James Cameron) and *District 9* (Neil Blomkamp), that contain human-alien genetic hybrids whose unique feature is to resolve the ambiguity that has been traditionally associated with fantastic images of hybridity. These transitory forms allow us to question why it is that our contemporary culture is eager to dissolve and absorb ambiguities. That is to say: why is there a desire to resolve such ambivalences rather than keep them alive, especially as ambivalence and hybridity have been key features of the postmodern era? To extend the scope of this question, this essay contextualizes these transitory hybrids in two different but entangled lineages. The first sees transitory hybrids as descendants of the most prevalent hybrid of the late twentieth century: the cyborg, who has always been a figure of undisclosed identity as well as of liminal space. The second is the figure of the stranger living as a liminal being at (cultural) borders, who raises the question of what it means to be an alien in a transnational world.

Avatar (2009) and *District 9* (2009), two blockbuster films, both feature a clash of cultures. Each film presents a familiar plot in Western cinema: *Avatar* depicts the conquest of an unknown planet, while *District 9* portrays an alien migration that is met by intolerance and segregation. The common ground of these two films is a well-known narrative structure: a dramatic bodily change. A comparison of these two films with earlier presentations of their motifs highlights certain developments within the culture of cinema: Kevin Costner's revival of the Western genre, *Dances with Wolves* (1990), is centered around an encounter with the alien other and aims to teach the audience to respect the other as equal; and David Cronenberg's *The Fly* (1986) illustrates the horror of an involuntary body-transformation that transgresses the fleshy borderlines of the human body and alters the human self.[2]

The fact that *Avatar* as well as *District 9* rework key elements of previous films is counterbalanced by visual strategies and effects that create novel and updated messages. Although their specific plots could not differ more, in both cases the aim is to immerse the audience in a cinematic environment. *Avatar*'s fame is due to it being one of the first 3D films of the twenty-first century, presenting a beautiful and visually stunning alien moon which offers audiences an immersive environment. *District 9* presents the alien slum as a dirty, unfriendly, and dangerous place. The film begins and ends as a mockumentary, a fictional movie mimicking a documentary style by imitating news footage and using staged TV interviews and recordings from security cameras (see Sisco King 2013: 80ff.). The middle of the film, however, relies on visual strategies known from other films and genres (see 93f.).

The transitory hybrid, which mediates the cultural contact with the alien others, is the figure that connects both films and upon which this essay will focus. Hybrid figures are well known in science fiction where they often retain their ambivalences. In these films, however, the transitory figures eventually aim at resolving their ambiguity.

Jake Sully (Sam Worthington), the paraplegic protagonist in *Avatar*, is an accidental test subject to link his mind to a biotechnologically developed avatar that merges human and alien DNA. Originally, the hybrid-body was created to serve Jake Sully's twin brother Tom, a well-known scientist, as a second body that would have enabled him to explore Pandora in order to gain mining rights. However, when Tom Sully dies, Jake is asked to take over his assignment and avatar. These avatars are built after the visual model of the native residents of the alien moon Pandora: the Na'vi, who are blue-skinned, ideally proportioned creatures. Their bodies are almost twice the size of an average human, with long limbs and strong but fluid movements and cat-like faces.

Sully steps literally into the shoes of his brother when uplinked to his brother's avatar for the first test drive of this "remotely controlled" body. His way of talking about it shows the distance between him and the artificial avatar body. But this changes immediately when he does not only operate but also feels his new body for the first time: against the scientists' advice he jumps up and starts running. His new, strong legs carry him on a track metaphorically summarizing his life and the plot of the film: he passes a military obstacle course presenting his old life before he runs into Grace Augustine (Sigourney Weaver), the leading scientist of the Avatar Program, representing his new life. Enjoying the ability to feel again, he digs his toes into the soil of Pandora almost like a tree striking root—a gesture that seems to anticipate his final decision to stay on Pandora and become part of the native culture.

Compared to Jake Sully, Wikus van de Merwe (Sharlto Copley), the lead character of *District 9*, experiences a piecemeal transformation of his body into that of an alien in which he loses his body and, potentially his identity. After being accidentally exposed to a mysterious alien fluid, van de Merwe's mutation is, at first, unnoticed as it is hidden under a bandage: step by step his body turns into an insectoid creature with pincer-like hands and a wasp-like mouth. The "prawns," as the aliens are pejoratively called, are bigger and stronger than humans, but their exterior, their odd movements, their grunting tongue and their strange behaviors mark them as radically different. When van de Merwe's mutation is noticed his only shelter is among them in District 9, a slum where the aliens have lived for twenty years.

His left hand thus acts as a *pars pro toto* for his bodily change as well as for his desperate struggle to cope with it. This struggle is made manifest in a frenzied attempt at self-amputation: a handy-cam shot shows him hiding in the bushes and placing his alien hand on a cinder block. The following close-up depicts a sweaty van de Merwe squinting and turning his head away. The cut contrasts his mutated hand with the desperate expression on his face as he repeatedly tries to amputate his hand with a stolen meat cleaver. He does not have the nerve to do so, but, finally, he manages to cut off one of his alien fingers. As he screams in pain, the scenery is immediately shown in a long shot, indicating his loneliness and special status before cutting back again to a close-up on his face grimacing with pain. Van de Merwe is thus cursed with a body that, at once, belongs to him and does not belong to him.

This first look at the two films reveals that, despite their focus on transitory hybrid forms, they differ a good deal in how they draft their narratives: in one narrative the aliens are stranded on Earth possibly seeking asylum, whereas in the other, humans are invading an alien planet. While one film centers on a complete bodily change, in the other a human body mutates. Described in terms of the familiar and the alien, two different developments are at work: in *Avatar* the attribution of what is familiar and what is alien is inverted; when Sully embraces his avatar body as his real body, it is presented as a reconnection with himself. In contrast, *District 9* reinforces the perception of what is alien and what is familiar even more. So how is the alien constructed as the perfect stranger in these films?

From strangers to the other

Modern culture knows two variations of foreignness: an eerie and threatening dystopia, as presented in *District 9*, or a paradisiacal utopia, as presented in *Avatar* (see Giesen 1993: 92). Both variations are hypothetical attempts to understand the impossibility of the perfect and absolute alien, as we cannot step beyond the boundaries of our own experiences (see Malmgren 1993: 17). Portraying aliens as insectoid creatures, as in *District 9*, is therefore a visual transfer of the already known to the realm of the unexpected, creating the impression of the unknown: an almost human form combined with insect-like features. A closer examination reveals that the visual design of the alien creatures on Pandora employs a similar strategy: those creatures are combinations of diverse features from animals we already know.

It is only in the very moment of the first encounter—when the stranger is an absolute stranger we know nothing about—that it is possible to experience an entity as utterly and absolutely alien. This is why both films center on the encounter with an extraterrestrial race to portray the alien. And this is why in the beginning of both films—as a generalization of the human perspective—the aliens are described as non-humans, wild and brute beings. The transformation of the leading characters from a human being to a human-alien hybrid to an (almost) alien illustrates the process not only of getting to know the alien (culture) but also of learning to respect the aliens as some kind of humanlike beings. With these individual transformations the narrations begin to focus on the view of the protagonists, thus establishing characters with whom the audience can identify.

With the advent of modernity, the encounter with the alien has informed the figure of the stranger as a "sociological form" (Simmel 1950: 402). The German sociologist Dirk Baecker points out the process of transformation that the figure of the stranger is subjected to in the course of time. In the premodern period, he describes the stranger as an occasional softening of a strict border separating one's own culture from the uncultured barbarians (see Baecker 2003: 12f.). Though the stranger stayed alien, his accepted presence implied an initial questioning of one's own lifestyle (Baecker 2003: 13). With the advent of the modern world, comparison became the leading cultural skill (see 65f.). In a globalized society cultural contacts are common. Only if one culture observes and perceives the other culture on equal terms (that is, as a viable alternative set of different values and behaviors) will the characteristics of the observing culture become transparent to itself. Concurrently, contingency, as an awareness of alternatives and different options, became a characteristic of modernity. In postmodernity this development increases and the reflexivity of culture becomes self-reflexive (see 71).

Against this background Baecker diagnoses the reduction of the barbarian to a mere dramatization, while the alien, as a category, was transformed into the difference between one's own and the other (see 13). In every cultural contact we search, at once, for commonalities and differences. Therefore, as soon as we start to learn about the stranger s/he becomes the other: someone, who is different, but (almost) equal and is therefore able to challenge or establish our identity. The important question from the viewpoint of cultural science is how the other is formed in different contexts.

In the case of both films, the representation of the encounter with the alien as a meeting of joint partners is no longer applicable. In fact, the alien becomes part of the most familiar, the bodies of the protagonists. Notably this hybridization challenges bodily integrity, but it does not radically transform identity. The ambivalence between the familiar and the alien is, of course, not new to science fiction. It is the key feature of one of its leading figures: the cyborg, who embodies this ambivalence.

From cyborgs to transitory hybrids

Being a hybrid of technological and biological parts, cyborg figures undermine a differentiation between the familiar and the alien. In pointing to this constitutive ambivalence over and over again, the cyborg emphasizes it in order to open it for constant negotiation. As a hypothetical figure, although potentially realized in the culture of the Cold War and the Space Race, the cyborg was born in the 1950s. Created by Manfred E. Clynes, an engineer, and Nathan S. Kline, a psychiatrist, the cyborg sought to alter human bodies to fit possible conditions on alien planets, instead of building starships to provide a liveable biosphere. Becoming a cyborg should allow (former)[3] human beings to conquer outer space. The central feature of their conception of the cyborg was to create a "self-regulating man-machine [system]," that functions without conscious control "in order to cooperate with the body's own autonomous homeostatic controls" (Clynes and Kline 1995: 30). The cyborg is a liminal being on the outside, as s/he is designed to discover foreign spaces, and as on the inside, as a cyborg is commonly understood as a human-machine hybrid. This ambivalence is the key quality of the cyborg on a cultural level: a cyborg is always both—man and machine, biological flesh and technological steel, animate and inanimate. The core issue of who or what the cyborg is needs to stay contingent to retain its cultural attractiveness.

Donna Haraway reshaped the cyborg as a cultural metaphor in her famous manifesto. She sought to understand the entanglement between humans and technologies in our everyday lives in the early 1980s as well as to analyze current social structures of this period from a feminist point of view: "I am making an argument for the cyborg as a fiction mapping our social and bodily reality and as an imaginative resource suggesting some very fruitful couplings" (Haraway 1991: 150). Her assessment of contemporary culture aims to overcome gender, race, and class as social dominating constitutives (see 157). She diagnoses three collapsing borders: first "the boundary between human and animal," second the "leaky distinction [...] between animal-human (organism) and machine," and, third, "the boundary between physical and non-physical" (151–3). These conceptual macerations question not only what it means to be human, but also how we understand our machines. Haraway positions the cyborg as an ambivalent figure denying consistency and a holistic identity, while embracing wisely chosen elective affinity and willful fragmentation (155). Haraway does not seek unrestricted freedom (111); rather she asks for a conscious, responsible deconstruction of dominant dualisms that constitute the other as an inferior, defining and conserving structure of power (177): "So my cyborg myth is about transgressed boundaries, potent fusions, and dangerous possibilities which progressive people might explore as one part of needed political work" (154). Postcolonial and feminist studies point out that the other is not only the representation of an alternative, but a counterpart proving and consolidating already existing structures of control.

Understanding the cyborg as a figure that keeps ambivalences and contingency alive, it is especially interesting to take a closer look at how and why the transitory hybrids Jake Sully and Wikus van de Merwe, who strive for unambiguousness, evoke the cyborg.[4] The striking fact as to why both transitory hybrids cannot be considered cyborgs is that both are in no way human-machine hybrids and therefore lack the defining symbiosis with technology. Instead, both become genetic hybrids between human and alien. However, the common ground of all reminiscences of the cyborg is a general reference to technology. Hence a closer look at how each film describes technology would be illustrative.

In *Avatar* we see a confrontation between an older concept of technology, linked to a technophile industrialized society like the twentieth century, and a more contemporary one, based on networks as associated with twenty-first-century technology. The old human technology is represented in a nutshell by Colonel Miles Quaritch (Stephen Lang) who offers to give Sully back his "real legs" while driving an "Amplified Mobility Platform," a human-operated battle-robot. The new form of technology is best represented by a biological port every living being on Pandora has, and which enables direct connections to any other living being: "there is some kind of electrochemical communication between the roots of the trees, like the synapses between neurons. [...] Get it? It's a network. It's a global network and the Na'vi can access it. They can upload and download data. Memories."

Hence the Na'vi, as a hunter-gatherer society, could be understood as an allegory of a network society (see Castells 2000) with a swarm memory. And even this could be understood as a resemblance to a key trait of the cyborg: the implantation of a chip that allows the cyborg to connect directly with computers and virtual worlds might be considered *the* defining feature of the cyborg. Sully's final decision to abandon his human body can therefore not only be read as an opting for the new networked technology but also as a reference to the cyborg as Clynes and Kline have articulated it: after all, his new body not only seems to be more adapted to the environment of the alien planet, it also seems to be the superior one.

In *District 9* the main human interest in the alien refugees is based on a desire to utilize their advanced weapons technology, which can only be accessed with their genetic signature. Van de Merwe becomes, then, the central object of a test series by the Multi-National Unit (MNU), a private business group he works for, as soon as his mutation is discovered. After realizing that his transformation has reached the "key stage in the metamorphosis" when his "DNA is in perfect balance between alien and human," the corporation is only interested in one thing: if he can use the alien technology and how this ability can, in turn, be weaponized. An intense scene within the overall narrative shows van de Merwe at the mercy of the scientists and, simultaneously, the loss of control of his body that he experiences because of his mutation. Shot with a shaky hand-held camera, we see a quivering and sweaty van de Merwe, who is bound upright and forced with electroshocks to use alien weapons. The cut alternates between medium shots and close-ups of the prisoner and medium-long shots of his changing targets. This shot-reverse-shot is also intercut with images of the weapons. The scene is marked by poor quality imagery that suggests a surveillance or security camera as a diegetic documentation of the tests. Shots showing a control center in which the MNU directors watch the experiment confirm this impression. In the course of the test the camera draws nearer and nearer to van de Merwe, creating a strong feeling of getting too close, which, in turn, culminates in images of van de Merwe forced to kill a living alien with an alien weapon fired with his human hand.

Although there is a desire for technology portrayed in both films, there is a shift in how this technology works as part of the narration when compared to typical science fiction stories of the twentieth century. In both films there are two kinds of technology. We see the first kind as one that may be modernized, but is clearly rooted in an understanding of it as it was shaped by industrialization. This technology is presented as the human technology. The second kind of technology is associated with fluidity and networking. This kind is clearly shown as the technology of aliens and holds promise for the humans who encounter it: it is the alien technology that promises van de Merwe a reversion of his mutation and it is the networking nature-technology in *Avatar* that enables Sully to abandon his human body and to live permanently as Na'vi. Although technology still plays a major part in the narration, its potential to solve problems has changed. Technology has become a means to an end. Only the alien technology is credited with some kind of faith in its functional potential. There seems to be a search for a new kind or a new understanding of technology at work, that is not only informed by the age of information and cross-linking but also by an aspiration for permeable borders between long established and ever since scrutinized oppositional concepts, like nature and technology, reality and virtuality.

In comparison to the cyborg, the transitory hybrid that Sully becomes can be read as a replacement focusing on the positive aspects of the cyborg: his avatar is an optimized body that adapts to new environments and tasks. Van de Merwe's transitory nature can be read as focusing on the negative aspects of his metamorphosis: by becoming a "prawn," he loses his bodily integrity. Still, the question remains as to why resolving the ambivalence manifest in the hybrid appears to be more attractive than the ambivalence that we see in the figure of the cyborg. An answer might not only work on the level of the individual narrations but also refer to our contemporary moment.

A desire for decidedness?

To extend this question, a comparison of *Avatar* and *District 9* with Kevin Costner's *Dances with Wolves* and David Cronenberg's *The Fly*, focusing on the development of the protagonists, promises to highlight important changes in the presentation of the related tropes in recent cinema. Both *Avatar* and *Dances with Wolves* tell the story of a white conqueror, who learns to see the natives as a morally superior culture and decides to change allegiance and fight alongside the noble savage. Similarly, *District 9* as well as *The Fly* center on the radical mutation of their leading character's body which forces him to question his identity.

At first sight, *Dances with Wolves* tells a similar story to that of *Avatar*. There are, however, fundamental differences between both narrations.[5] The first and most important one is a much more differentiated picture of the encounter with the alien in *Dances with Wolves*. The film aims to paint a realistic portrayal that will help to overcome old prejudices against the Native Americans: "Nothing I have been told about these people is correct," says Costner as First Lieutenant John J. Dunbar, "[t]hey are not beggars and thieves. They are not the bogeymen they've been made out to be. On the contrary, they are polite guests and have a familiar humor I enjoy" (Dunbar; see Prats 1998: 7 and 3).

Though he desires to experience borderlands in the first place, Dunbar does not foresee that the borderlands he will explore are not only spatial but cultural ones (see Ahmed 1999: 58). Arriving in his abandoned post, Fort Sedgwick, he enjoys the unbound beauty of the prairies and embraces his isolation. The visual language of *Dances with Wolves* is characterized by extreme long shots capturing this overwhelming landscape. To intensify the visual impression of the openness of the prairie, these extreme long shots are consistently contrasted with close-ups drawing the viewer into the scene. Despite aiming at an authentic and impartial picture of the Native Americans, *Dances with Wolves* is a declaration of love to the nature of the West.

His first encounter with the Natives changes Dunbar's feelings: now desiring their companionship he starts to feel not only "alone [...] but [...] completely lonely" (Dunbar; see Ahmed 1999: 58). Two sequenced scenes portraying Dunbar dancing sum up his transformation from enjoying being "alone" to being "lonely" to becoming part of a social group. The first scene shows Dunbar dancing around his fire at night imitating the Native dance. More important than his imitation of their culture is whom the cut establishes as observing this dancing: close-ups on their eyes make his animal companions— Two-Socks, the half-tamed wolf, and Cisco, his horse—witnesses to his desire for human companionship. Here, the animal witnesses indicate a lack in his life as both are mute companions.[6] The next day Dunbar dances again, but this time he is witnessed by the Sioux. When Dunbar goes to visit, in turn, the Sioux, he tries to send Two-Socks, who is following him, away. This almost playful interaction between wolf and man is interpreted by the Natives as a dance. The moment he sends his wolf companion away he is invited into the social group of the Sioux as they choose to derive his Native name from their misinterpreted observation: Dances-with-Wolves.

Dances with Wolves and *Avatar* share the notion that living with the original inhabitants[7] and sharing (literally and figuratively) their horizon allow both Dunbar's and Sully's understanding of their way of life to develop. This empathetic transformation ultimately forces them to confront their traditional system of allegiances, while it establishes their identities which have been, up to that point, marked by injury and loss. In the end Dances-with-Wolves becomes Dunbar's real identity: "I felt a pride I never felt before. I've never really known who John Dunbar was. Perhaps the name itself had no meaning. But as I heard my Sioux name being called over and over I knew for the first time who I really was." In a similar way, Sully's worldview changes: "Everything is backwards now. Like out there is the true world and in here is the dream." From the viewpoint of the Na'vi, Jakesully's, as they call him, arrival tells the story of a liberator who has to find himself before he can rescue "the people." Unlike Dunbar, Sully has to experience a second coming of age, which includes rites of passage to become a part of the Na'vi. By teaching him their way of living, the Na'vi seek to get to know the alien Jakesully. But Sully's journey is just an amplification of who he has always been, which is—ironically but not unexpectedly—an idolization of the marine: what, in the beginning, appeared as an identification with the alien turns out to be the idolization of Western, human traits.

The main difference between Sully and Dunbar/Dances-with-Wolves manifests itself in the ending of each film. Taking George Simmel's definition of the stranger into account, the difference between them becomes apparent. Simmel, who created the stranger as a figure of social critique, defines it as a liminal being in a spatial context:

> The stranger is [...] the person who comes today and stays tomorrow. He is, so to speak, the *potential* wanderer: although he has not moved on, he has not quite overcome the freedom of coming and going. He is fixed within a particular spatial group, or within a group whose boundaries are similar to spatial boundaries. But his position in this group is determined, essentially, by the fact that he has not belonged to it from the beginning, that he imports qualities into it, which do not and cannot stem from the group itself.
>
> Simmel 1950: 402, emphasis in the original

Following this definition, it becomes obvious that Dunbar/Dances-with-Wolves not only stays a stranger amongst the Sioux—someone who is potentially on the move and who remembers his ways as a white soldier—but is equally a stranger to the Americans, as he accepts the ways of the Natives and treats them as equals. In the end, he is a stranger to both cultures (see Ahmed 1999: 59), who cannot be a complete part of either one. It becomes obvious that the hybridity of Dunbar/ Dances-with-Wolves does not come from within, but is ascribed to him by the awareness of others. These others are not only the Natives, who accept him as a friend and a liminal being, but also the Whites, who do not accept him at the border of both cultures, as they do not accept the Native culture. Jakesully, on the contrary, resolves his hybridity not only corporeally, but conceptually as well. He does not end up between the cultures but chooses one. Whereas *Dances with Wolves* is a story of becoming a cultural hybrid, *Avatar* is a story of closing cultural hybridity and becoming an entity again—at least on the layer of visual appearance. Whereas Dunbar/Dances-with-Wolves loses his place in society realizing his ambivalent status, Jakesully finds his place, reducing his ambivalence to a hidden minimum. Jakesully's lack of ambiguity is made possible by a body that could be seen as a social prosthesis (see Westermann 2012b: 186f.).

Sully's decision to abandon his human body invites a comparison between the Na'vi's form of society and a postmodern one. In this perspective Sully's transformation into Jakesully could be clearly described in terms of regressions: he leaves behind not only the complexity of a postmodern world, but also many of its problems, such as environmental devastation or the negative aspects of industrialization. By depicting a return to simpler times, *Dances with Wolves* could also be considered as regressive, but only superficially so. The narration, however, focuses on postmodern issues of identity as Dances-with-Wolves/Dunbar realizes the incoherency and indissolubility of his fragmented self. Furthermore, the film points allusively to postmodern problems, for example in portraying an untouched nature and creating an empathetic relationship between the viewer and the environment.

Strange bodies

To cast a critical eye upon the changing and mutating body, Sara Ahmed's approach to "strangerness" (2000b: 51), which is informed by embodiment as well as feminist and postcolonial studies and focuses on the sociospatial dimension of encountering the alien, is helpful: "Through strange encounters, the figure of the 'stranger' is produced, not as that which we fail to recognize, but as that which we have already recognized as 'a stranger'" (2000a: 3). By not thinking explicitly of the alien in terms of an extraterrestrial encounter, her definition of the stranger suggests a change of perspective: in understanding the stranger as a product of knowledge (2000b: 49) she shifts the focus onto how this knowledge is produced on a sociopolitical level, thereby creating (social) hierarchies (2000a: 6). Her attention to the actual spatial encounter as the social moment, in which frontier crossings create the stranger, directs the focus back onto the encountering bodies (39). Strangerness is no inherent attribute of any body but the product of relations between bodies (44). Despite postmodern contingency, Ahmed's notion points to the critical potential of comparison: the strange body is observed "*as the body out of place*" (39, emphases in the original), marked by difference:

> Strange bodies are precisely those bodies that are temporarily assimilated *as* the unassimilable within the encounter: they function as the border that defines both the space into which the familiar body—the body which is unmarked by strangeness as its mark of privilege—cannot cross, and the space in which such a body constitutes itself as (at) home. The strange body is constructed through a process of incorporation and expulsion—a movement between inside and outside, which renders that the stranger's body has already touched the surface of the skin that appears to contain the body-at-home.
>
> Ahmed 2000a: 54

With Ahmed's perspective in mind, a closer look at how the bodily transformations are inscribed in the protagonist's bodies is called for. Depicting the encounter with the alien as a negotiation of hybridity on a social level, *Dances with Wolves* as well as *Avatar* inscribe the effects of their orientation onto the skin of their leading man's body. Dances-with-Wolves/Dunbar's change of appearance symbolizes his growing inclusion: the more he is accepted and accepts the Sioux culture the more native pieces of clothing he wears while taking off his uniform piece by piece. Simultaneously, he starts to trim his beard before he shaves it off and starts to grow his hair, which is later decorated with a small braid. A similar change of the outer appearance can be observed in *Avatar* but is intensified by the body change: Sully not only starts to shape his avatar body—changing his haircut—but at the same time begins to disregard his human body—he neither wants to eat nor to shave.

In *District 9* and David Cronenberg's *The Fly*, the encounter with the alien is depicted as an intra-corporeal experience. These films amplify the effect of strangeness as they increase the proximity beyond the skin-formed borders of the body: the strangeness literally infiltrates the body. Both portray the ongoing process of the mutation of their leading character into an insectoid creature, calling into question the impact on their identity of the metamorphosis. What is interesting here is the time pattern portraying each individual mutation. While testing his new invention, a teleportation pod, for the first time on himself, Seth Brundle (Jeff Goldblum) accidentally and unknowingly splices his own DNA with that of a fly. His transformation picks up pace and intensity as it proceeds: a tri-phase pupation starts, in which fascination and fear constantly alternate. At first, the change affects only his personality as he starts to feel more energetic and powerful. His growing appetite for sugar and his increasing strength are forerunners of his visible corporeal mutation, which—after a fluent passage—brutally alters his outward appearance in the second stage of his transformation. He not only develops new abilities such as crawling on the ceiling like a fly, but also begins to digest like one. His flesh forces open the cutaneous border of his body, turning him inside out. When he starts to feel the insect within take control, Brundle realizes the mutation has not only affected his body: "I—I'm an insect who dreamt he was a man and loved it. But now the dream is over—and the insect is awake."

His desperate attempts to become human again are met with an exponential increase of hybridity: Brundle's solution to his mutation is another fusion. Abandoning the hope of "defusing" himself and reversing his mutation, he aims for a more complex fusion with the other as a way of gaining control. The other that he has in mind is the mother of his unborn child, Veronica Quaife (Geena

Davis), a scientific journalist writing about his experiments. Brundle believes that the fusion with Veronica and the fetus should increase the percentage of the human DNA and make him more human—although not human again. Just when he begins to put this plan into action, his pupation reaches its final stage. During his fight with Veronica, she accidently breaks off his jaw, which signals the start of the next stage of his transformation: this time the expanded boundaries of his flesh are violently forced open, giving birth to his new body. In the end a second, failed teleportation fuses the "Brundlefly" with the telepod itself and adds a fourth stage of mutation: instead of creating the "ultimate family [...] joined together in one body" (Brundle), a second-order hybrid is generated, merging man, fly, and machine. Once the mutation has started it cannot stop and affects every aspect of his being, his body, and his self. Ultimately, only death can stop the hybridization of this ultimate stranger, who involuntarily becomes an inoperable nightmare as a cyborg.

In contrast, the mutation of van de Merwe changes its speed during the narration. While the transformation of his hand happens rather quickly in only a few hours, almost three days after the exposure his body is still mostly human, though the mutation has visibly spread to his left eye and parts of his upper left torso. After establishing his hybridity, this ambivalence is kept alive until the very end of the narration. Only then a full transformation is implied: staged as an open ending, it questions the whereabouts of van de Merwe as it gives—within the diegesis—hope for sanctuary among the aliens, who have accepted him. At this point van de Merwe's transformation produces a body which could be considered a social prostheses as well (see Westermann 2012b: 186f.). At the end of his process of mutation, van de Merwe becomes one among a million: he may feel lost as a former human body whose still human self is trapped in an alien body, but for the distant viewer he does not stand out of the approximately 2.5 million aliens living in District 10. He becomes the ultimate other, establishing the social hierarchies not only between humans and aliens but also affecting the social hierarchies within the human race by giving the (former) oppressed others—women, people of color, and others—an other to feel superior to. But Claire Sisco King has a point in highlighting how the film ultimately reinforces established hegemonies (2013: 95). Despite its intended mass audience, Blomkamp's *District 9* could be read as a plea against social segregation and oppression.

Challenging the postmodern?

Being aware that a corpus of four films is in no way representative, this essay concludes by turning to the intriguing development indicated by the comparison of *The Fly* and *Dances with Wolves* with *Avatar* and *District 9*. This comparison may not point to a total loss of interest in the category of the hybrid, but it could certainly imply a reshaping of the expectations that audiences bring and that genres offer. The later films portray the hybrid as something that needs to be resolved in the very ending—at least, on the (visual) surface. It may be a simplified generalization to see *The Fly* and *Dances with Wolves* as examples of a general cultural fascination with hybridity while *District 9* and *Avatar* stand for the exact opposite as they hold out the possibility of a complete transformation that negates the power of ambiguity. But reading hybridity as a prominent feature of the postmodern allows for a contextualization of all four films as variations of the question of how to cope with a fragmented identity.

The German cultural theorist Andreas Reckwitz offers an interesting definition of hybridity. He provides a theory of Western modernity that is at the same time a theory of the subject and of culture. He sets any separation of culture and subject aside, for a subject is always a product of its culture as it produces its culture. To Reckwitz every modern subject is already a hybrid (see Reckwitz 2010: 19). Not necessarily by means of an interconnection of different materials or bodies, such as genetic hybrids or the cyborg, but because of the different cultural codes rooted in different orders of subjectivity ("*Subjektordnungen*") which inform the subject. Reckwitz distinguishes three different hegemonic orders of subjectivity: first, a morally sovereign subject ("*moralisch-souveränes, respektables Subjekt*") of bourgeois modernity (in the eighteenth and nineteenth century); second, an employee-subject ("*extrovertiertes Angestelltensubjekt*") of organized modernity (since the 1920s); and, third, the creative, consuming subject ("*kreativ-konsumtorisches*" *Subjekt*) of postmodernity (since the 1980s) (15f., emphases in the original).

Reckwitz's understanding of subjectivity does not suggest the need for a different interpretation of the portrayal of hybridity in *The Fly* and *Dances with Wolves* and in *District 9* and *Avatar*, as the latter solve cultural, as well as bodily, hybridity. But as his approach is based on the change in the dominant order of subjectivity, the transitional periods in between become relevant. These transitional periods are marked by the rise of new practices and new discourses building new formations (see Reckwitz 2010: 76). Though, in retrospect, they are easily distinguishable, according to Reckwitz, when witnessed from within these periods they appear to be defined by an undisclosed and ambiguous future. Perhaps the comparison of these four films indicates such a transitory period? Are we tired of ambivalence and contingency? After all, postmodernity has persisted—following Reckwitz—since the 1980s. Maybe it is time for a new age?

Then again, what possibilities are left after the postmodern? Maybe all its horizons are open and explored and we are stuck within the postmodern, forced to decline its potentials over and over again. Following this argument, all four films are equal realizations of narrations considering the encounter with the perfect alien as a questioning of postmodern concepts of identity. But, at this point we may only be able to raise this question as we are not yet prepared to determine which perspective describes our actual situation.

Notes

1 A German version of this essay is published in Spangenberg and Westermann (2012: 161–92). Compared to this version, the German essay focuses on questions of (bodily) identity raised by the transitory hybrids in *Avatar* and *District 9*.
2 This comparison, of course, is based on the assumption that, on the one hand, blockbusters can be considered as easygoing entertainment while, on the other hand, the escapism they are portraying may allow them to mirror cultural needs, at least to a certain degree.
3 Clynes and Kline never viewed their optimization of the body as an overcoming of the human but an improvement upon it.
4 I broach the issue of the changes in fictional cyborgs in the twenty-first century based on a comparison of *I'm a Cyborg but that's Okay* (Park Chan-wook, 2006) and *Cyborg She* (Kwak Jae-yong, 2008) elsewhere as well: Westermann (2012a).
5 Both of my analyses are based on the director's cut of each film as published in the German DVDs. For a detailed comparison between the American theatrical release of *Dances with Wolves* and the "five-hour miniseries" on ABC, which seems to be a little shorter but still quite similar to the German DVD's director's cut, see Prats (1998).
6 Not without reason every film refers to animals in one way or another. Donna Haraway's approach to the animal as the other is especially interesting here: "Instead of thinking about what separates our species from all others, ask how the entities in any encounter make us all the things we are" (Haraway in Else 2008: 50). In her book *When Species Meet* (2008) Haraway questions the idea of human

exceptionalism by analyzing our entanglement with non-human others. With the concept of companion species she focuses on the ever ongoing process of meeting with different kinds of others, in which "we shape and reshape each other into what we are" (Haraway in Else 2008: 51): there is a great difference between encountering a dog, a stranger, or a cyborg.

7   The Term "Na'vi" seems to be an acronym for Natives.

References

Ahmed, S. (1999), "Phantasies of becoming (the Other)," *European Journal of Cultural Studies*, 2.47: 47–63.

Ahmed, S. (2000a), *Strange Encounters: Embodied Others in Post-Coloniality*, New York and London: Routledge.

Ahmed, S. (2000b), "Who knows? Knowing Strangers and Strangerness," *Australian Feminist Studies*, 15.31: 49–68.

Baecker, D. (2003), *Wozu Kultur?* Berlin: Cadmos.

Castells, M. (2000), *The Rise of the Network Society, The Information Age: Economy, Society and Culture*, Cambridge and Oxford: Blackwell.

Clynes, M. E. and Kline, N. S. (1995), "Cyborgs and Space," in C. H. Gray (ed.), *The Cyborg Handbook*, New York and London: Routledge, 29–33.

Else, L. (2008), "Interview: the age of entanglement," *New Scientist*, 198.2661, 21 June 2014.

Giesen, B. (1993), *Die Intellektuellen und die Nation*, Frankfurt am Main: Suhrkamp.

Haraway, D. (1991), "A Cyborg Manifesto: Science, Technology, and Socialist-Feminism in the Late Twentieth Century," in *Simians, Cyborgs and Women. The Reinvention of Nature*, New York and London: Routledge, 149–81.

Haraway, D. (2008), *When Species Meet*, Minneapolis, MN: University of Minnesota Press.

Malmgren, C. D. (1993), "Self and Other in SF: Alien Encounters," *Science Fiction Studies*, 20.1: 15–33.

Prats, A. J. (1998), "The image of the other and the other Dances with Wolves: The Refigured Indian and the Textual Supplement," *Journal of Film and Video*, 50.1: 3–19.

Reckwitz, A. (2010), *Das hybride Subjekt. Eine Theorie der Subjektkulturen von der bürgerlichen Moderne zur Postmoderne*, Weilerswist: Velbrück Wissenschaft.

Simmel, G. ([1908] 1950), "The Stranger," *The Sociology of George Simmel*, K. H. Wolf (ed. and trans.), Glencoe, IL: The Free Press, 402–8.

Sisco King, C. (2013), "A Gendered Shell Game: Masculinity and Race in *District 9*," in

R. L. Jackson II and J. E. Moshin (eds), *Communicating Marginalized Masculinities. Identity Politics in TV, Film, and New Media*, London: Routledge, 80–9.

Spangenberg, P. M. and Westermann, B. (eds) (2012), *Im Moment des Mehr. Mediale Prozesse jenseits des Funktionalen*, Münster: Lit Verlag, 161–92.

Westermann, B (2012a), "Dear Cyborg, what's next?" in A. Berti and A. Torrano (eds), *JGCinema, Dossier: Cyborgs*, www.jgcinema.com/single.php?sl=cyborg-she, accessed 21 June 2014.

Westermann, B. (2012b), "Transitorische Hybride—Über die Ruhigstellung ambivalenter Identiäten," in P. M. Spangenberg and B. Westermann (eds), *Im Moment des Mehr. Mediale Prozesse jenseits des Funktionalen*, Münster: Lit Verlag, 161–92.

Filmography

Avatar (2009), directed by James Cameron, Los Angeles, CA: 20th Century Fox, 2010, DVD.

Der mit dem Wolf tanzt (*Dances with Wolves*) (1990), directed by Kevin Costner, Berlin: Studiocanal, 2004, DVD.

District 9 (2009), directed by Neill Blomkamp, Culver City, CA: Sony Pictures Home Entertainment, 2010, DVD.

The Fly (1986), directed by David Cronenberg, Los Angeles, CA: 20th Century Fox, 2005, DVD.

Part Three

Alien Identities

9

Space: The Final (Queer) Frontier—The Sexual Other in Eleanor Arnason's *Ring of Swords*

Emilie McCabe

University of Toronto, Canada

From H. G. Wells' *War of the Worlds* (1898), to Robert Heinlein's *Starship Troopers* (1959), to Ursula K. Le Guin's *The Left Hand of Darkness* (1969), alien-encounter narratives have been a staple of the science fiction genre.[1] In an article entitled "Self and Other in SF: Alien Encounters," Carl Malmgren describes alien-encounter narratives as "fictions [that] explore the nature of selfhood from the vantage point of alterity" (1993: 16); that is, these narratives provide a critical distance for readers to examine the discourses that inform human subjectivity.[2] This type of narrative can be an effective tool for dealing with issues of subjectivity because, as Pamela Annas notes in her article, "New Worlds, New Words: Androgyny in Feminist Science Fiction": "[science fiction] allows ideas to become flesh, abstraction to become concrete, imaginative extrapolation to become aesthetic reality" (Annas 1978). In other words, the amorphous concept of the alien other can be "embodied" in order to articulate the social and cultural concerns that arise out of contact with the other. The tools that alien-encounter narratives offer—critical distance and concrete expressions of abstract notions— are particularly useful when discussing human sexuality.

Eleanor Arnason's 1993 novel *Ring of Swords* uses the genre's ability to make "idea become flesh" by imagining an alien species, the *hwarhath*,[3] as furry grey bipeds whose entire society is homonormative,[4] in order to explore the discourse of sexuality. In the novel the contact between the two ideologically opposed species, the heteronormative humans and the homonormative *hwarhath*, provides an opportunity to examine some of the ways in which cultural produc- tions, such as literature and drama, can facilitate a nuanced understanding of those that are considered as 'other,' to lay bare the constructed nature of sexuality and to explore what it means to be 'queer.' My aim for this essay, then, is first to explore some of the ways that cultural productions, such as literature and drama, are able to shape subjectivity. The second objective is to provide a glimpse of the work that *Ring of Swords*, and science fiction in general, can do to "make visible to us the unthinking assumptions that limit human potentiality" (Pearson 2003: 159); that is, science fiction can expose the discourses that are often taken for granted but that dictate human behavior. Science fiction narratives are littered with images such as aliens and cyborgs that allow for an examination and critical analysis of the discourses that underpin human subjectivity. Despite its populist reputation, the intrinsic aspects of the genre—escaping old norms, imagining new material situations that bring about new subject positions, and its metaphors and concepts—offer ways of thinking differently about the subject. These inherent elements provide the opportunity to circumvent the normative discourses that shape subject formation in order to imagine as yet impossible subject positions that might have the possibility of influencing what is understood as an intelligible human subject.

Cultural productions and subjectivity

Cultural productions such as visual art and literature have traditionally been an arena where subject positions, both those that are socially intelligible and those that are not, have been depicted and as a result transmitted throughout human society. In her essay, "The Technology of Gender" (1987) and her earlier work, *Alice Doesn't: Feminism, Semiotics, Cinema* (1984), Teresa de Lauretis explores the ways in which cultural productions such as theory[5] and cinema guide prevailing understandings of gender. While her work focuses specifically on the discourse of gender, her observations about the impact that these cultural productions have on human subjectivity are applicable to other discourses. In her essay, she writes: "*The construction of gender goes on today through the various technologies of gender (e.g. cinema) and institutional discourses (e.g. theory) with power to control the field of social meaning and thus produce, promote, and 'implant' representations of gender*" (de Lauretis 1987: 18, emphasis in the original). In this instance, de Lauretis equates the influence of cinema—or any artistic production—with that of theory to "produce, promote, and 'implant' representations of gender." This statement is important because it highlights the role that artistic productions can play in subject formation; that is, depictions of subject positions in works of art can be a means of influencing and disseminating ideas about what constitutes an intelligible subject. Thus, science fiction's ability to imagine as yet impossible subject positions is a way of thinking differently about the human subject and can be a way of effecting change in the current norms of behavior because science fiction, "like all cultural production, forms a part of the world of available subject positions, of possible models for identification" (Vint 2007: 20).

De Lauretis goes on to observe that the role of art does not stop there: "the terms of a different construction of gender also exist, in the margin of hegemonic discourses. [...] [T]hese terms can also have a part in the construction of gender" (1987: 18). For de Lauretis, the "margins of hegemonic discourses" are the "blind spots, or space-off, of its [hegemonic discourse's] representations" (25).[6] These marginal spaces afford the opportunity to critique dominant discourses as well as to propose alternatives that challenge them. As de Lauretis notes, despite their marginal status, these depictions have the ability to influence change in the general understanding of a specific discourse. Works of art, whether they are mainstream or not, can be both a means of implementing cultural norms and a way of undermining or challenging them. As cultural productions, then, science fiction works contribute at either end of the spectrum—from pulp to literary productions—to the conception of the human subject through their representations of subject-positions both normative and those outside current cultural norms.[7]

Thinking differently about alien encounters

Narratives of alien encounters are often ones of paranoia that describe a fundamental fear of infiltration, contamination, and extermination perpetrated by the other. Science-fictional alien-encounter narratives are a perfect forum in which to express the fears that arise when encountering the alien other, since the other is fully embodied as an, often dehumanized, alien being.[8] As an alien-encounter narrative, *Ring of Swords* does not conform to genre expectations. Instead of depicting epic battles, the novel takes place over the course of two sets of diplomatic negotiations between the humans and the alien species, the *hwarhath*. The aliens in the novel are intelligent and militarily aggressive, and their society is entirely homonormative; that is, there is absolutely no form of heterosexual interaction between males and females since the sexes are segregated as soon as they reach sexual maturity.[9] The narrative is focalized through two characters: the first is Anna Perez, a human biologist whose specialty is non-human intelligence, while the second perspective is that of Nicholas Sanders, a human

military intelligence officer who was captured by the aliens and has lived behind
enemy lines for over twenty years The entire novel is devoted to themes of
communication and trust, and in particular, how to nurture that trust so that it
does not break under the inevitable strain that will arise when two different
cultures clash. These themes play out at two levels in the narrative, between the
two species, as well as in the personal relationship of Nicholas and his *hwarhath*
male lover, Gwarha.

Although the negotiations between the humans and the *hwarhath* provide
the framework for the alien encounter, the narrative's tension is created by the
hwarhath's dilemma about whether to consider humans as people. Within the
hwarhath culture, people are defined as intelligent and moral beings, which for
the aliens means that people do not behave like animals by reproducing sexually.
This decision is important because the outcome will determine how the aliens
will engage in war should this come to pass. The *hwarhath* have very rigid rules
of engagement that they must follow when they go to war that forbid them from
attacking civilian targets. Thus, if the *hwarhath* decide that humans are people,
these rules place the *hwarhath* at a distinct disadvantage since humans would
have no difficulties attacking the *hwarhath* home-world while the aliens would
not be able to attack Earth. If, however, the *hwarhath* decide that humans are
animals then they will no longer be bound by their rules of war and, as a result,
would be able to slaughter all humans regardless of their sex or civilian status.

While this second outcome is catastrophic for humans, it also implies dire
consequences for the *hwarhath*: if the *hwarhath* come to the conclusion that
humans are animals then the *hwarhath* will no longer have a worthy enemy to
fight. In a discussion with Anna, Nicholas explains why having an enemy is so
imperative to the *hwarhath* social structure and, in particular, the male sense of
identity.

> I told you that their history is long and bloody. It led to the creation of the
> Weaving, which became a world government. There are obvious benefits to
> world peace, and they don't really want to give it up. But they don't know what to
> do with their men. They think, and they are almost certainly right, that they can't
> maintain their society the way it is without an enemy. What is going to happen
> when the young men stop believing in war? What if men begin to say, There is no
> point in training for battle and no point in living on the perimeter? Jesus Christ,
> they might even want to come home and not just for a visit. A frightening idea.
> It certainly frightens the *hwarhath*.
>
> Arnason 1993: 284

The *hwarhath* find the prospect of the males returning home frightening because then the males who are "innately violent" (Arnason 1993: 283) would bring that violence into the female sphere. Not only does the male presence on the home-world present a danger to the world peace that exists but it would also entail a disruption of the existing power structure, which could potentially result in the collapse of the entire social system. Eh Matsehar, a playwright and friend of Nicholas, clarifies the dilemma when he explains that since the *hwarhath* males have left the home-world and especially since they have encountered humans "everything has changed but we continue as before. This is not the plain of Eh or the hills that belong to Ettin. This is space, and the enemy we fight is nothing like us. We will be destroyed if we do not learn new ways of thinking" (1993: 194). This situation draws attention to the danger of basing one's identity solely in relation to an other, since without that other a sense of self crumbles. This observation holds true for any subject position: for instance, if humans persist in understanding sexuality as a simple binary between homo- and heterosexuality there will never be an opportunity to imagine sexuality as something more complex while simultaneously consigning those who do not conform to remain a marginalized group of individuals. It is important, then, to learn "new ways of thinking" so that the subject positions we imagine exist outside of the restrictive confines of binary identity. *Ring of Swords* challenges genre expectations by presenting an alien-encounter narrative that focuses on building trust rather than annihilating the alien other, while also laying bare the underlying danger of constructing subject positions that rely on an external other in order to be intelligible.

Cultural productions and identity in *Ring of Swords*

Another way that *Ring of Swords* addresses the question of how to understand subject formation is its exploration of some of the ways that cultural productions, specifically plays, are repositories of representations of normative subject positions that contribute to their production and promotion. Each species uses the subject positions represented in cultural productions as a means of understanding the other: Nicholas uses *hwarhath* plays in order to better comprehend the alien social norms, while the *hwarhath* use translations of various works of art to understand humans, the most important of these being Shakespeare's *Macbeth*. This choice appears to be random, however its central themes of the power struggle between a man and a woman and the risks involved in grasping for power are particularly relatable to a *hwarhath* audience. For instance, Matsehar uses *Macbeth* in an attempt to explain to Anna some of the political machinations that are taking place amongst the *hwarhath* during the second set of negotiations (Arnason 1993: 239–40).[10]

Nicholas's situation is quite odd: he is the only human living among the *hwarhath*. Once Nicholas was no longer a prisoner of war, but not able to return home, he assimilated himself into the male *hwarhath* social order. He has managed to integrate into the alien society to such an extent that he has a job and is the lover of one of the *hwarhath* generals, Ettin Gwarha. When Nicholas first started to participate in *hwarhath* society, he understood the basic principle that the sexes did not mix but he had no idea how or why that social structure had come about. In his journal, he explains that his interest in *hwarhath* dramas (64–5) stems from the fact that this art form facilitates his understanding of the nuances of the alien society as well as provides a way for him to better comprehend his lover, Gwarha. As Nicholas explains in his journal, there are several types of dramas that the *hwarhath* enjoy, all of which he likens to Japanese Noh plays: "The costumes are always splendid, and the works themselves can have the spare beauty of a Noh play" (64). By placing the *hwarhath* works within a human context, the subject positions represented in the alien plays become more intelligible to Nicholas. And, as a result, the alien art and the species as a whole seem less foreign to him, thus facilitating his integration into their society.[11]

There is one type of play that particularly fascinates Nicholas because of its usefulness in understanding Gwarha's motivations. "There is one final kind of hero play, which does (I guess) still interest me. The plays about the *rahaka*: the men who will not die, who keep on living when any normal person would have chosen the option" (65). To understand Nicholas' statement it is important to know that suicide, "the option," is often the way that individuals remove the stain of dishonor left by any shameful act from themselves and their family. A *rahaka*, then, is someone who does not subscribe to the dominant discourse of *hwarhath* society, and therefore lives as an outcast. This information is important because both Gwarha and Nicholas think of themselves as *rahaka*, as men who are outsiders because they refuse to conform. During the negotiations with the humans, Gwarha refuses to act aggressively like the other males because he is acutely aware that if the negotiations were to fail there would be dire consequences for his species—either complete annihilation at the hands of the humans or the devastating loss of identity the *hwarhath* would suffer if they were to wipe out the human species. Gwarha is therefore willing to be scorned in order to avoid either outcome for his species.

While the traditional understanding of the *rahaka* seems somehow an act of cowardice, Gwarha thinks of it differently, especially when it comes to Nicholas. When Nicholas was captured and interrogated by the *hwarhath*, Gwarha was an observer and saw how Nicholas reacted when he was tortured. "[He] never gives up," says Gwarha. "When you think he is retreating, he is only moving to a new position to rest or to find a new way to resist or attack. I saw this in the interrogation room. If there is a good form of *rahaka* this is it" (Arnason 1993: 304). In this instance, Gwarha uses his understanding of what it means to be *rahaka* as a way of understanding Nicholas' motivations. Gwarha's ability to map a *hwarhath* subject position onto a non-*hwarhath* allows Gwarha to see Nicholas as a person instead of as an alien. The figure of the *rahaka*, then, is for each lover a way of understanding someone who is alien by providing a context that helps to explain what motivates each of these two very different individuals.

Until the humans and the *hwarhath* enter into negotiations, the cultural exchange between the two species is fairly limited due to the hostility that exists between them and, in particular, the *hwarhath*'s repugnance for human heteronormativity. Nicholas' playwright friend, Eh Matsehar, is interested in human productions of dramatic arts. In an attempt to learn more, Matsehar reads Shakespeare's *Macbeth* and finds it compelling, so much so that he writes a target-oriented translation of the play into the *hwarhath* main language.[12] Matsehar meets Anna at the second set of negotiations, which take place on a space station that the *hwarharth* have constructed specifically to hold the talks with the humans. "I had to compress it," Matsehar explains to Anna. "Your plays are so long! I tried to make it simple. There is power in simplicity and the play is about power" (333). Anna reads Matsehar's version of the play, which he translates back into English for her, and she describes it as "a familiar object seen through water or in a distorting mirror" (333). Anna notes that the content is necessarily transformed in order to accommodate the shorter length of the play, however, the most noticeable transformation is that Matsehar changes the primary relationship between Macbeth and Lady Macbeth from husband and wife, a concept that is not only unintelligible to the *hwarhath* but also repugnant, to that of a male and his mother. Although Matsehar's version of *Macbeth* is very different from Shakespeare's, Matsehar is able to keep the central themes of the play intact while depicting a social context that is intelligible to his audience.

Over the course of the second set of negotiations, it becomes evident to Gwarha's female relatives that in order for the negotiations to continue it must be decided whether or not humans are people. " 'The question of what humans are has to be resolved,' said Ettin Per. 'And it is not a question for men. They have never decided who is a person and who isn't. The task has always belonged to women'" (Arnason 1993: 314). In order to convince the females, who control all foreign and domestic policy (314), that humans are people, Matsehar and Nicholas are sent to the *hwarhath* home-world to present the play to them. Nicholas returns to the station to tell Anna, the only other human who knows what has taken place on the *hwarhath* home-world, what the females have decided: "Humans are people but not the same kind of people as the *hwarath*. We [humans] have our own moral system, which is—the Weaving says—almost impossible for them to understand. We can't be judged by the standards which the People [this is what the *hwarhath* call themselves] apply to one another" (345). Since the human diplomats are not even aware that their personhood is in doubt, human cultural productions must act as ambassadors for all of humankind. While *Macbeth* may not be the work that humans might have selected to represent themselves, it nonetheless succeeds in providing a framework for the *hwarhath* to understand human social norms and motivations, thereby making humankind less alien to the *hwarhath*.

The representations of subject positions in both the *hwarhath* and human plays that fall within the norm achieve two objectives. First, the subject positions represented in cultural productions are often guides to normative forms of behavior and as such are important social touchstones as they can illustrate some of the motivations that prompt certain kinds of behaviors or attitudes. Second, these representations of various subject positions create contexts in which the alien other becomes less foreign and therefore gains a measure of personhood (humanity is perhaps not the right word here). The role that cultural productions play in subject formation is considerable since these productions are a repository of, and a means of disseminating, models of normative behavior.

The discourse of sexuality and science fiction

The cultural productions discussed above are used as a means of creating a sense of identity and understanding behavioral norms. One of the benefits of science fiction is that it is able to question and even undermine current subject positions by laying bare the discourses that inform them and by presenting new and different subject positions that do not necessarily conform to the norm. This ability to question the norm is particularly useful when examining the discourses that inform human sexuality, as they are so often accepted without question as 'natural.'

The common understanding of subjectivity, which in this postmodern era is one of a multifaceted and unresolved subject (Hall 2004: 118), has become increasingly enmeshed with concepts of sexuality. Indeed, it seems that often one's entire sense of identity hinges on one's sexuality. In his work *Sexuality* (1997), Joseph Bristow addresses the complexity of this issue. "The term sexuality," he writes, "is historically contingent, coming to prominence [in the nineteenth century] when detailed attention was increasingly turned to classifying, determining, and even producing assorted sexual desires" (5). There are two points that should be highlighted in Bristow's remark. First, sexuality is historically contingent, which means that "the normality or abnormality of a particular sexual behavior, identity, or style depends largely on the interpretive lens through which it is observed" (17). Thus, any attempt to define sexuality will necessarily reflect a discourse, whether it is scientific, religious, or political, thereby establishing the parameters for normative behavior to suit that discourse. The second point is that the very act of categorizing behavior can actually produce that behavior.

Despite the fact that science fiction has traditionally taken for granted "the continued prevalence of heteronormative institutional practices—dating, marriage, the nuclear family and so on" (Pearson 2003: 150) when it imagines future societies, there is still an enormous potential within the genre to consider different forms of sexuality. This exploration of new and different subject positions is possible because of the sense of estrangement produced by science fiction texts that arises out of the disparity between the readers' empirical reality and the fictional reality of the work. The concept of estrangement and how to define it within the science fiction community—including authors, critics, fans, and scholars—has been debated since the genre's inception;[13] however, most agree that the sense of estrangement produced by science fiction texts arises out of the disparity between the readers' empirical reality and the fictional reality of the work. In *The Seven Beauties of Science Fiction*, Istvan Csicsery-Ronay explains how this effect occurs:

This alternative world is a model that readers make sense of by constantly, though not always consciously, comparing it with the familiar world. All fiction works this way, to some degree. [...] The novum[14] establishes a distance from which reality can be seen with fresh eyes, a distance that the regime enforcing the reader's consensus reality strives to suppress. The [science fiction] reader shuttles back and forth over this gap, comparing the imaginary model with the ideological one, the process or feed-back oscillation that Suvin calls *cognitive estrangement*.

Csicsery-Ronay 2008: 50

This sense of estrangement provides an unparalleled opportunity in which to think differently and critically about the discourses that govern human behavior. The potential, then, for critique of the readers' present exists within science fiction works since the estrangement that readers experience allows them to perceive their reality in new, and possibly critical, ways.[15] When discussing human sexuality, this sense of estrangement is useful since, as Wendy Pearson observes, "for many people [...] sexuality—and particularly heterosexuality— can be envisioned only within the category of the 'natural'" (2003: 149). In other words, sexuality is often understood as instinctual and innate and therefore beyond question.

Homonormativity in *Ring of Swords*

Although it is impossible to catalogue and dissect every aspect of human sexuality, it is nevertheless important to acknowledge and question some of the more entrenched discourses that inform it. By using a homonormative society as a way of estranging the current understanding of human sexuality, *Ring of Swords* is able to expose some of the discourses that underpin the general understanding of sexuality and subjectivity in Western culture, such as the concept of a gender core and 'natural' sexuality.

In order to maintain their social ideal of homonormativity, the female *hwarhath* live on the home-world while the males, once they have reached adolescence, are sent to outer space. Nicholas explains to Anna why these intelligent beings have chosen to live this way:

The People believe that men are innately violent and innately [...] hierarchical. [...] Left to their own devices, they will try to dominate every situation. They will do physical harm. I have to say, I think this is a crock; but there is no question that *hwarhath* males are socialized to be intensely competitive and to think that violence is no big deal. [...] The People try, as much as possible, to keep men away from home. They don't want their children or the women to be afraid. They don't think continual fear is healthy, even continual fear at a low level—for example, never knowing when someone in the family, Uncle or Elder Brother or whoever, is going to blow up and strike out. [...] *Hwarhath* males are sent to the edges of their society, where their violence is useful and where they'll only kill other adult men.

Arnason 1993: 283-4, emphases in the original

There is an implicit criticism of human heteronormativity here as one of the drawbacks of having men and women live together is "continual fear at a low level." In order to remove that fear, the *hwarhath* have removed what they perceive to be the source of the violence: the males. It is important to note, however, that the *hwarhath* are not concerned if the males engage in violent behavior with one another, instead they simply want that behavior to be away from the females and children and, if possible, used to benefit the group by focusing that violent behavior on a potential enemy.

Nicholas' comments also explain how the males understand their role in society: *hwarhath* male identity is based on fighting the enemy, whoever that may be, in order to protect the females and the offspring. While this may be a preferable way to organize a society so as to avoid violence and conflict, it assumes that there are innate gender cores that cannot be changed, an idea that is neatly undercut when Nicholas utters the words "I think this is a crock" (283). Nicholas' insight highlights the arbitrary and learned aspects of gendered behaviors by foregrounding the fact that the male *hwarhath* are socialized to behave in certain ways and, as a result, the discourse that the males are innately violent and hierarchical is perpetuated because the males do act that way. Nicholas' comments are equally applicable to human understandings of gender and gender identities. In other words, there are no identities, either human or *hwarhath*, based on a gender core, but rather, gender is performative;[16] that is, gender is a learned behavior instead of an expression of something innate.

Ring of Swords also works to challenge the accepted concept of gender by depicting the male aliens as fierce warriors bent on the domination of humankind on the one hand, while on the other hand, they are homosexuals. This representation of the male *hwarhath* undermines two different discourses: the genre expectation of the invading, inseminating alien[17] by making the *hwarhath*; homosexuals and, more importantly, the human stereotype of the 'sissy' or 'fey' homosexual by making the aliens tough and competent soldiers without falling into the cliché of turning them into butch supermen. By disrupting the link between gender and sexuality the novel discredits the idea that biological sex and gender are inextricably linked, which also calls into question the assumption that sex and gender must necessarily dictate sexuality.

The reader's assumptions about gender and sexuality continue to be challenged once Anna meets the female *hwarhath* who have come to the second set of negotiations to find out more about humanity. Since the female *hwarhath* are the policy-makers, they are interested in learning more about human social structures. The females are specifically interested in how heterosexuality affects social organization since the *hwarhath* believe that all intelligent animals would, upon reflection, abandon heterosexual behaviors. Here is how one of the females explains their logic to Anna:

> We thought it was natural and inevitable. Once an animal has intelligence and is able to make choices, it will not continue to live as its ancestors did, mixing everything together—fighting and breeding and raising children and seeking love all in one place. [...] Now we have found creatures with a language and a material culture, who can travel through space, and they behave toward one another in a way that we thought was impossible once intelligence was achieved.
>
> Arnason 1993: 249

During their discussions with Anna, the female *hwarhath* are quite open about the fact that their social structure has been constructed to accommodate their goal of removing male violence from the center by moving the males to the periphery of the territory where their violent tendencies can be useful. Moreover, they are not bothered by the resulting homonormativity. It seems that the *hwarhath* envision sexuality as a product of discourse rather than as the expression of an essential self, meaning that sexuality can be manipulated in order to suit specific social needs.

When the *hwarhath* ask Anna to explain human sexual habits, this is her reply: "We always thought that heterosexuality was natural. It's what all the other kinds of animals on our planet did. We thought it was natural for men and women to live together and raise children together. That also was done by many kinds of animals" (250). Both the *hwarhath* and Anna use the term "natural" to describe their respective species' sexual norms; however, for the *hwarhath*, "natural" means not behaving like animals, while for humans "natural" means behaving as all other animals do. Although Anna's description of hetero-normativity is valid, the premise that humans are like all other animals is faulty, something that Nicholas points out to Anna:

> But humans don't have a mating season and neither do the People. We are sexually active and sexually interested all the time. I figure there is an evolutionary benefit to being horny all the time. It keeps you intensely interested in other people, and it gives you a reason to stay on good terms. It holds us together. We have to get along with one another, if we are going to get laid.
>
> Arnason 1993: 210

So, if humans are not like animals who have mating seasons, why do humans think that it is "natural" to maintain a heterosexual norm? Nicholas' observations foreground the fact that humans are, indeed, different from animals and, surprisingly, have more in common with the *hwarhath* than it would first appear.

It is important to recognize that the sexuality of both species is shaped by a specific discourse. Anna's description of heteronormativity is just as much a narrative as the one that the *hwarhath* use to account for their sexual norms, however, unlike the *hwarhath*, humans seem oblivious to the implications of their heteronormativity.[18] The fact that the *hwarhath* appear to be conscious of the way in which their sexuality has been manipulated only serves to emphasize how the human use of the term "natural" is a way of occluding the constructed nature of heteronormativity.

Since the *hwarhath* so confidently manipulate their sexuality to suit their ideology, it would appear that the novel advocates the idea of sexuality as completely pliable. However, the novel troubles that position by depicting a character who contradicts that notion. The playwright Eh Matsehar comes to Nicholas with a problem: Matsehar is heterosexual. "He had never had any interest in men, Matsehar said. As far back as he could remember, all of his sexual fantasies had been about women. There was despair in his voice. [. . .] 'You under-stand, don't you Nicky? You come from a society where this kind of thing is normal. I would not be a pervert there'" (202). Matsehar is stuck in a system of compulsory homosexuality but even though he attempts to conform he cannot. In this instance, Matsehar's inability to adhere to the social norm troubles the idea that desire can be compelled.

Queer: The final frontier

Matsehar's suffering is due to the rigid structure of *hwarhath* society. As Nicholas explains: "The two sides of *hwarhath* culture were too widely separated. There was no way for a man to meet a woman, except those in his lineage, and the People regard incest with profound horror. [...] There was no heterosexual subculture, no underclass of men and women who made love together" (Arnason 1993: 203). This situation draws attention to the idea of what it means to be queer by reversing the human norm: here it is the hetero-sexual who is queer. As David Halperin writes: "'Queer,' then, is not a positivity but a positionality *vis-à-vis* the normative" (1995: 62). Since it is possible for humans to enter into sexual relationships that do not conform to the norm, human society seems to be a better place to be queer. Yet the vocabulary that Nicholas unconsciously uses to describe queer culture—"subculture" and "underclass"—is evidence that while human society may be more permissive of "abnormal" sexual behavior, to be queer means to be relegated to the margins of society. Finally, the conversation between Nicholas and Matsehar is highly ironic because Matsehar comes to Nicholas as a fellow heterosexual, but, in fact, Nicholas is the biggest queer in the novel: he has sex with furry grey aliens. So, Nicholas is able to relate to Matsehar, not as a heterosexual, but as a queer. The novel exposes sexuality as a discourse that creates specific subject positions; however, Matsehar's situation makes it clear that those subject positions cannot necessarily regulate desire.

Nicholas and Gwarha's relationship is an example of a relationship that exists outside of all of the norms of either species, making it entirely queer. Their relationship is simultaneously an example and a challenge since it is an example of how two species can get along and a challenge to both the humans and the *hwarhath* to do so. Although this relationship can be used as a model for interspecies harmony, Nicholas and Gwarha have had to cultivate their relationship in order to make it viable. Despite some ups and downs, these two individuals manage to work through their differences because they are willing to think differently. In their personal relationship things go awry when Nicholas thinks like a human by telling Anna about the *hwarhath* rules of war and when Gwarha thinks like a *hwarhath* and expects Nicholas to be unquestionably loyal to Gwarha as his commanding officer. The relationship works best when both Nicholas and Gwarha discard their respective worldviews and try to figure out a solution together. In a conversation with Nicholas,

Matsehar captures the essence of this ability to think differently when he says: "Ettin Gwarha is more remarkable than I had realized. He can look at you and see a man. When I look at Perez Anna, I see an alien. [...] That is a great gift, Nicky, to look at people and find them loveable" (Arnason 1993: 190–1). Matsehar understands the benefit of Gwarha's ability to think outside the norm—that is, to think and to act "queerly" allows Gwarha to accept an alien other as a person.

Thinking differently, thinking queerly

Arnason's novel is a fascinating work because it manages to accomplish two goals that appear to be at odds: demonstrating how cultural productions can be used as a way of promoting and preserving normative subject positions, while imagining an entire social structure that challenges the discourse of heteronormativity. The way that the characters in *Ring of Swords* consistently use cultural productions in order to create a sense of identity and to understand those around them highlights the role that fictional representations of normative subject positions have in subject formation. Arnason pushes the argument further by demonstrating that consuming foreign cultural productions can be one of the ways of making the other less alien. This familiarization of the other is achieved by integrating and assimilating the subject positions in the foreign works of art, thereby transforming alien subject positions into intelligible ones.

By demonstrating the ability of cultural productions, and in particular literature, to affect subject formation, Arnason implicitly bolsters the other project of the novel, which is to challenge and undermine current understandings of human sexuality by representing subject positions that do not conform to the norm, because she has just demonstrated that subject positions represented in cultural productions can affect subject formation. Therefore, the representations of queer subject positions have the potential not only to be models of behavior but also to disrupt and modify the way that the norm is generally understood. The value of *Ring of Swords*, and science fiction in general, is that it provides a way of thinking differently, or thinking queerly, with the goal of estranging and thus disrupting the dominant discourse in order to pave the way for new and different ways of being. As a result of this estranging process, discourses no longer appear to be natural, given, or immanent, thereby creating the necessary distance to evaluate whether there is an ongoing benefit of constructing subjectivity according to those parameters. Once free of the influence of these discourses, it is possible to explore the as yet impossible subject positions and what might be required in order to bring them about. The ultimate benefit to this approach is that it creates a "readiness for new norms of reality" (Suvin 1979: 84) since by introducing these fictional subject positions into the cultural lexicon they not only lose their strange and potentially threatening quality but they also become catalysts for discussions about current subject positions as well as models for future behaviors.

Notes

1 Since alien-encounter tales are a central aspect of all types of science fiction narratives regardless of the medium in which they appear—text, film, graphic novel, or game scenario—I have limited my comments to textual versions of these types of narratives.

2 Donald Hall defines subjectivity as: "our social constructs and consciousness of identity. We commonly speak of identity as a flat, one-dimensional concept, but subjectivity is much broader and more multifaceted; it is social and personal being that exists in negotiation with broad cultural definitions and our own ideals. We may have numerous discrete identities [subject positions] of race, class, gender, sexual orientation, etc., and a subjectivity is comprised of all of these facets, as well as our own imperfect awareness of ourselves" (2004: 134).

3 Arnason italicizes *hwarhath* throughout the novel and so I am following her convention.

4 I use the term "homonormative" as the complementary term to "heteronormative"; thus, "homonormative" denotes a society in which homosexuality is the norm.

5 De Lauretis uses the term "theory" as a "generic term for any theoretical discourse seeking to account for a particular object of knowledge, and in effect constructing that object in a field of meaning as its proper domain of knowledge, the domain being often called 'discipline'" (1987: 19).

6 De Lauretis borrows the term "space-off" from film theory and it is defined as "the space not visible in the frame but inferable from what the frame makes visible" (1987: 26).

7 When Darko Suvin wrote his seminal work, *Metamorphoses of Science Fiction: On the Poetics and History of a Literary Genre* in 1987, science fiction was considered a marginal genre. However, since then science fiction has not only grown in popularity with the general public—populating book shelves, television series,

films and video games—but it has also become a topic of serious academic research due in large part to its potential to question normative discourses and to propose new ways of thinking and of being. Nonetheless, it should be noted that although this potential exists within the genre, the majority of texts do not take advantage of this potential and unthinkingly reproduce societal norms (Hollinger 1999).

8 For example, the aliens in H. G. Wells' *War of the Worlds* or Robert Heinlein's *Starship Troopers* are monstrous and less-than-human because they have none of the attributes that we value as human such as honor, empathy, and compassion.

9 I use the terms "male" and "female" to refer to the aliens because the terms "men" and "women" have gendered connotations that I do not think apply to them.

10 In addition to the overt presence of *Macbeth*, there are several allusions in the novel to *Hamlet* and *Othello*. These plays provide contexts for the characters' actions such as Nicholas' struggle with his decision whether or not to act, which echoes Hamlet's struggle, while Gwarha's jealousy echoes Othello's possessiveness.

11 Although Nicholas has gained a general acceptance in the male social structure, there are still many *hwarhath* who regard him as an animal rather than as a person. And so, despite his own excellent understanding of *hwarhath* society, he has not gained full membership in the alien society.

12 A "target-oriented translation" is a concept used in translation theory to explain that translations are not simply a direct translation from one language into another. In this type of translation, not only has a text been translated into a different language but it has also been slightly altered, that is targeted, in order to make sense within a specific cultural context.

13 The inability to conceive a coherent definition for the genre and the role of estrangement therein is a long-standing dilemma within the field of science fiction study. The difficulty arises because science fiction is an extremely heterogeneous genre. In the introduction to his cultural history of science fiction, Roger Luckhurst explains how science fiction has come to be this way: first, because it is "part of a network that ties together science, technology, social history and cultural expression with different emphases at different times" (2005: 6); and second, because science fiction "emerged as a hybrid form in the nineteenth century and has remained one, interweaving with strands of Gothic, Realist, fantasy and utopian writing" (11). Due to its hybrid nature, the way that estrangement features in science fiction works varies greatly thus making it difficult to provide a description of the precise role of estrangement in these narratives.

14 In 1978, Darko Suvin was the first to introduce the concept of the novum "as the defining trope of the genre" (Csicsery-Ronay 2008: 47), which has since then

become an influential critical concept in science fiction theory. For Suvin, then, "a novum or cognitive innovation is a totalizing phenomenon or relationship deviating from the author's and implied reader's norm of reality" (1978: 64).

15 It is important to note that although estrangement may be present in science fiction works, its presence does not necessarily guarantee that the overall critique presented in the text will be a liberal or leftist one. As Wendy Pearson discusses in her essay, "Science Fiction and Queer Theory," estrangement is used by both conservative and radical texts alike when she points out that a heteronormative agenda is at work even in those texts that depict alternative forms of sexuality. Pearson uses Heinlein's novel *The Moon is a Harsh Mistress* (1966) as an example of this conservative bent: "Lunar society permits a variety of options for marriage beyond the basic one-male-one-female model that is acceptable in most contemporary Western cultures—but only so long as these arrangements, whether between three people or twenty, remain exclusively heterosexual" (2003: 150–1). Although the sexual arrangement in this situation is putatively "liberating" because it removes the monogamy taboo, it expressly upholds heterosexuality as the only "correct" form of sexual congress.

16 In her seminal work, *Gender Trouble: Feminism and the Subversion of Identity*, Judith Butler proposes that gender be understood as performative: "acts and gestures, articulated and enacted desires create the illusion of an interior and organized gender core" (1999: 173). While this proposition may seem liberating, Butler points out that gender performativity is compelled because it is "a strategy of survival within compulsory systems, gender is a performance with clearly punitive consequences. Discrete genders are part of what 'humanizes' individuals within contemporary culture; indeed, we regularly punish those who fail to do their gender right" (178). There is, however, still the possibility of agency within this mode. Butler explains that even though gender is "a forcible production" (1993: 231) that the performance "is never quite carried out to expectation, whose addressee never quite inhabits the ideal s/he is compelled to approximate" (231). Thus, agency may be found in the failure to properly perform gender.

17 The figure of the alien is one of the oldest metaphors of the science fiction genre and as such "the career of 'aliens' in [science fiction] has reflected (as all science fiction concepts must) changes and developments in the real world" (Jones 2009: 34). Over time aliens have represented imperial colonizers, cold war invaders, and migrant workers. These representations of invading aliens carry with them the obvious fear of being conquered either physically or ideologically. There is a correlative fear of the inseminating alien who co-opts the "purity" of humankind; in other words a fear of miscegenation. This "interbreeding" carries with it the tacit

threat of physical and ideological domination of humans through their human-alien offspring. Octavia Butler's *Xenogenesis* trilogy is a nuanced and extensive examination of this fear of the inseminating alien.

18 In the first volume of *The History of Sexuality*, Michel Foucault (1990) discusses at length how the discourse of heteronormativity induces specific types of behavior in order to create productive and docile bodies. One of the benefits of this discourse is that it produces a large workforce in a capitalist-industrial economic system.

References

Annas, P. J. (1978), "New Worlds, New Words: Androgyny in Feminist Science Fiction," *Science Fiction Studies*, 9.2, www.depauw.edu/sfs/backissues/15/annas15art.htm, accessed 22 June 2014.

Arnason, E. (1993), *Ring of Swords*, New York: Tor.

Bristow, J. (1997), *Sexuality*, London and New York: Routledge.

Butler, J. (1993), *Bodies That Matter: On the Discursive Limits of Sex*, New York and London: Routledge.

Butler, J. (1999), *Gender Trouble: Feminism and the Subversion of Identity*, New York and London: Routledge.

Csicsery-Ronay, Jr., I. (2008), *The Seven Beauties of Science Fiction*, Middletown, CN: Wesleyan University Press.

de Lauretis, T. (1984), *Alice Doesn't: Feminism, Semiotics, Cinema*, Bloomington, IN: Indiana University Press.

de Lauretis, T. (1987), "The Technology of Gender," in *Technologies of Gender: Essays on Theory, Film and Fiction*, Bloomington, IN: Indiana University Press.

Foucault, M. (1990), *The History of Sexuality: An Introduction*, R. Hurley (trans.), New York: Vintage Books.

Hall, D. E. (2004), *Subjectivity*, London: Routledge.

Halperin, D. M. (1995), *Saint Foucault: Towards a Gay Hagiography*, New York: Oxford University Press.

Hollinger, V. (1999), "(Re)reading Queerly: Science Fiction, Feminism and the Defamiliarization of Gender," *Science Fiction Studies*, 26.1 (March), www.depauw.edu/sfs/backissues/77/hollinger77.htm, accessed 21 June 2014.

Jones, G. (2009), *Imagination/Space: Essays and Talks on Fiction, Feminism, Technology, and Politics*, Seattle, WA: Aqueduct Press.

Luckhurst, R. (2005), *Science Fiction*, Cambridge: Polity.

Malmgren, C. D. (1993), "Self and Other in SF: Alien Encounters," *Science Fiction Studies*, 20.59: 15–33.

Pearson, W. (2003), "Science Fiction and Queer Theory," in E. James and F. Mendlesohn (eds), *The Cambridge Companion to Science Fiction,* Cambridge: Cambridge University Press.

Suvin, D. (1978), *Metamorphoses of Science Fiction: On the Poetics and History of a Literary Genre,* New Haven, CT and London: Yale University Press.

Vint, S. (2007), *Bodies of Tomorrow: Technology, Subjectivity, Science Fiction,* Toronto: University of Toronto Press.

10

Alienation, Hybridity, and Liminality in Ray Bradbury and Archie Weller

Célia Guimarães Helene
Universidade Presbiteriana Mackenzie, Brazil

The question of identity is, and has been, a central motif within the literatures of science fiction and post-coloniality. Here, identity is central to both characters and authors who find themselves transplanted to another country than that of their origin and, in order to survive, must adapt to the new environment and adopt new ways of life and, frequently, new worldviews. In this process, shedding their "old" identities in order to construct a "new" one brings the migrant or refugee to a state of liminality, of being at the border between two cultures which, in many cases, might be incompatible. According to Stuart Hall, "identities are never unified and, in late modern times, increasingly fragmented and fractured; never singular but multiply constructed across different, often intersecting and antagonistic, discourses, practices and positions" (2008: 4).

In a different way, colonized people also suffered a kind of displacement as they were and still are forced to adjust to the culture of the colonizers, who imposed their lifestyles upon them, making the subaltern individuals feel ashamed of their own ways and traditions. Being alienated from their own culture but never able to shed it completely, they find themselves in a state of hybridization, in which, similar to what happens to migrants, at least two identities merge and contend with one another. In this case, the position of the subaltern is not of his/her own choice but rather assigned to him/her by the colonizers who, in the process of subjugating the native inhabitants of the land, convert them into the diasporic subjects. As Avtar Brah points out in *Cartographies of Diaspora*:

> The ways in which indigenous peoples are discursively constituted is, of course, highly variable and context-specific. During imperial conquests the term "native" came to be associated with pejorative connotations. In the British Empire the

transformation of the colonized from native peoples into "the Native" implicated a variety of structural, political and cultural processes of domination, with the effect that the word Native became a code for subordination [...] as the term "British" assumed a positionality of superiority with respect to the Native. The Native became the Other. In the colonies, the Natives were excluded from "Britishness" by being subjected as natives.

Brah 2003: 190–1

In this essay, I compare and contrast two works which, in spite of their differences, have in common the themes of alienation, assimilation, hybridity, and liminality. One of these is Ray Bradbury's science fiction story "Dark They Were, and Golden-Eyed" (1949), in which Terran refugees on Mars at first resist assimilation but eventually become "Martians," apparently forgetting their "earthly" identity. The other story is Australian Aboriginal writer Archie Weller's "Going Home" first published in 1986. In this story, the protagonist's efforts to shed his Aboriginal identity in order to become part of the mainstream culture, in spite of an apparently successful integration, are eventually revealed to be a failure. He cannot escape the condition of hybridity and liminality, which is the inevitable lot of the colonized, who, according to Avtar Brah (2003: 190–1) are ironically assigned the position of the "other" by the self-appointed "superior" colonizers.

Hybridization—'the same but different'

In his poetic short story "Dark They Were, and Golden-Eyed," Ray Bradbury metaphorically discusses the issue of alienation versus assimilation as experienced by a group of migrants to another planet. These "Earthmen," as the narrator calls them, have escaped the threat of nuclear war by flying to Mars on a rocket and, upon arriving, try to establish a colony there, in which they still preserve their old ways. This is not difficult in the beginning since they have brought food and other goods from Earth and communication with their planet is not yet interrupted. The story centers around one family, the Bitterings, composed of the father Harry, his wife Cora, and their three children Dan, Laura, and David. However, one day, the war on Earth begins and all contact ceases, making the Bitterings, as well as the other refugees, adopt "Martian" ways. Although they do not see any Martians around, they feel a presence that threatens them but, at the same time, they gradually begin to change to what, presumably, is the Martian appearance and lifestyle. At the end of the story, the assimilation is so complete that they do not remember ever being different—they have, for all purposes, become "real Martians."

Although Bradbury's story can certainly be regarded as both utopian (complete assimilation to a new environment) and dystopian (being stranded in a new and hostile planet with no hope of ever coming back home), one of the possible alternative readings that it can yield consists in finding in it allegorical parallels to the condition of the migrant or refugee who tries to preserve the customs and traditions of his/her original culture out of a fear that integration could lead to a loss of identity. Thus, we see the Bittering family, upon arrival on Mars, resist adopting ways different from those they had brought with them from their planet, fearing that the new air might erase their original identity,[1] to which they still want to adhere: "The wind blew as if to flake away their identities. At any moment the Martian air might draw his [Mr. Bittering's] soul from him, as marrow comes from a white bone. He felt submerged in a chemical that could dissolve his intellect and burn away his past" (Bradbury 2010: 567).

In the inhospitable environment in which they find themselves ("There was no answer but the racing hiss of wind through the stiff grass," 567), the refugees are taken by fear and a sense of displacement that refuses to leave them, even after they settle in the new world:

> They built a small white cottage and ate good breakfasts there, but the fear was never gone. It lay with Mr. Bittering and Mrs. Bittering, a third unbidden partner at every midnight talk, at every dawn awakening.
>
> "I feel like a salt crystal," he said, "in a mountain stream, being washed away. We don't belong here. We're Earth people. This is Mars. It was meant for Martians."
>
> Bradbury 2010: 567–8

In spite of the fact that the new arrivals do not see any Martians around, there is the implication that a presence can be felt and that the natives of the planet cannot be seen or understood because they are completely different from Earth people and they will never be able to co-exist:

> "I don't know," said David. "Maybe there are Martians around we don't see. Some nights I think I hear 'em. I hear the wind. The sand hits my window. I get scared. And I see those towns way up in the mountains where the Martians lived a long time ago. And I think I see things moving around those towns, Papa. And I wonder if those Martians *mind* us living here. I wonder if they won't do something to us for coming here."
>
> Bradbury 2010: 568, emphasis in the original

In this quotation it is possible to see the expectation of rejection that accompanies every refugee, every migrant, in short, every displaced person, especially when, as in Bradbury's story, there is little or no hope of ever going back to the country of their roots: " 'We're stranded on Mars, forever and ever!' " (569), says Laura, the Bitterings' daughter, when she learns that communication with Earth has been interrupted, at least temporarily.

However, the need for adaptation soon appears. To one of the children's questions: " 'Father, what will we do?' " (569) Mr. Bittering replies: " 'Go about our business, of course. Raise crops and children. Wait. Keep things going until the war ends and the rockets come again.' " At this point, the adaptation still consists in keeping their old ways, for instance planting Earth flowers and eating the food they had brought from Earth and have kept in a deep-freeze, for, as Mr. Bittering states, eating Martian stuff would make them change— " 'who knows to what? I can't let it happen' " (571).

But inevitably, assimilation begins to take place and the refugees find themselves in a state of hybridization, which is expressed in the story by means of beautifully paradoxical images of what is and, at the same time, is not. The following passage reveals the perplexity that this awareness causes in the hybrid subject. When he touches some peach blossoms, Mr. Bittering tells his wife that they look different and that they are " '[. . .] *wrong*! I can't tell how. An extra petal, a leaf, something, the color, the smell!' " (570, emphasis in the original), although to Mrs. Bittering they seem to be all right. Afterwards,

> The children ran out in time to see their father hurrying about the garden, pulling up radishes, onions, and carrots from their beds.
> "Cora, come look!"
> They handled the onions, the radishes, the carrots among them.
> "Do they look like carrots?"
> "Yes . . . no." She hesitated. "I don't know."
> "They're changed."
> "Perhaps."
> "You know they have! Onions but not onions, carrots but not carrots. Taste: the same but different. Smell: not like it used to be."
>
> Bradbury 2010: 571

This quite poetic description illustrates what Homi Bhabha, commenting on T. S. Eliot's ideas in *Notes Towards a Definition of Culture*,[2] claims about hybridization: "This part culture, this *partial* culture, is the contaminated yet connective tissue between cultures—at once the impossibility of culture's containedness and the boundary between. It is indeed like culture's 'in-between', bafflingly both alike and different" (Bhabha 2008b: 167, emphasis in the original).

The image of the vegetable garden is an appropriate one since the term "hybrid-ization" derives from biology and agriculture, where different species are combined to form a new one. The hybrid subject, likewise, becomes a new being, forged in the encounter of two different configurations, retaining some characteristics of each, thus resembling and not resembling at the same time. Seeds brought from Earth germinating in the Martian soil, in the Martian atmosphere, sprout as plants which are like the ones grown on Earth but not quite. This is what Bhabha, resorting to a Freudian figure, says of "the form of difference that is mimicry— *almost the same but not quite*," or, if one talks of mixed ethnicities, "*Almost the same but not white*" (2008b: 127–8, emphases in the original).[3]

The modified vegetables function as a metonym for the family's physical and, later, psychological transformation. The Martian sun burns their skins and makes their eyes turn golden and the air they breathe whispers new words in their ears as if to make them aware that a change of identity is occurring. As things gradually transform, as the migrants begin to accept the new environ-ment and incorporate its ways, the process of assimilation begins, symbolically represented by the roses that turn green, the cow that grows a third horn, the purpling lawn, the house warped out of shape. Such assimilation is resisted at the start, with Mr. Bittering desiring to return to Earth, for which purpose he sets out to build a rocket, especially when they notice that their very appearance is undergoing a transformation—as shown above, their eyes change from gray or blue to yellow, they become taller and thinner and their skins turn a dark color. Mr. Bittering rebels against the change, a rebellion that is symbolized by his breaking the mirror when he first sees "little, very dim flecks of new gold captured in the blue of his eyes" (Bradbury 2010: 573). Foucault's discussion of the mirror as utopia and heterotopia applies here, since Mr. Bittering sees himself where he is not (i.e. in the looking-glass) but is shocked because he does not see his reflec-tion as he would like it to be, to wit, as his old self, or else, he sees it in the mirror held to him by his original culture.[4]

However, resistance cannot last. Even living in the settlement, which is reminis-cent of the ghetto in which migrants are frequently segregated in a foreign country, the refugees from Earth start, in spite of themselves, to utter strange words, Martian words, hitherto unknown to them but whose meanings, somewhat mysteriously, dawn on them. The uttering of Martian words is followed by the changing of their own names to Martian ones, signaling that their fear of losing their identity is replaced by the acceptance of a new identity, forged in the process of coming to grips with their new situation. It is emblematic of this new identity that Sam, another refugee, when asked by Mr. Bittering if his eyes did not use to be gray, answers: "'Well now, I don't remember'" (Bradbury 2010: 572).

After this comes the decision to move to the Martian villas, which lie deserted, away from the Earth settlement. At first this is only for the summer, but they will eventually be converted into their permanent dwelling. Apparently, at this point, Mr. Bittering is the only one who still feels torn between two opposite forces: the need for assimilation and the desire to go back to Earth and, thus, to keep or recover his former identity, an impulse that is represented by his unwillingness to give up the rocket that could eventually take him back to his original environment. It is, however, necessary to emphasize that, upon moving to the Martian villas, the family leaves behind tokens of their former life: the furniture, books, and dresses, which do not seem to suit them any longer. Abandoning the furniture in the little white cottage, the mother says: "'It looked just fine in Boston [...] and here in the cottage. But up at the villa? No. We'll get it when we come back in the autumn'" (578).

It is at this moment that Mr. Bittering has an insight into the condition of the migrant as one who, in spite of not foregoing his original self and his original culture altogether, will never be able to recover them in their entirety: if something is gained by dislocation, something is also irretrievably lost. When he steers the truck towards the villas, Mr. Bittering, looking at the cottage, is "filled with a desire to rush to it, touch it, say good-bye to it, for he felt as if he were going away on a long journey, leaving something to which he could never quite return, never understand again" (578).

With the passing of time, the refugees start viewing their previous existence on Earth, or on Mars while they still kept to the Earth ways, with astonishment— as if it were something they would not like to be associated with:

> Mr. Bittering gazed at the Earth settlement far away in the low valley. "*Such odd, such ridiculous houses the Earth people built.*"
>
> "They didn't know any better," his wife mused. "*Such ugly people. I'm glad they've gone.*" [...]
>
> "We'll go back to town maybe next year, or the year after, or the year after that," he said, calmly. "Now—I'm warm. How about taking a swim?"
>
> *They turned their backs to the valley.* Arm in arm they walked silently down a path of clear-running spring water.
>
> Bradbury 2010: 579, emphasis mine

Although this alienation from feeling as Earthmen happens gradually, the moving to the villas can be seen as the definitive turning point, as the point of no return, when the Bitterings finally see themselves as "Martians" without any possibility of ever coming back to their old ways.

The assimilation is so complete that, five years later, when, after the end of the war on Earth, men arrive on a rocket to rescue the refugees, nobody from Earth could be found: there were only "Martians," former Earth people turned Martians. As the newly arrived lieutenant tells his captain:

> "The town's empty, but we found native life in the hills, sir. Dark people. Yellow eyes. Martians. Very friendly. We talked a bit, not much. They learn English fast. I'm sure our relations will be most friendly with them, sir."
>
> "Dark, eh?" mused the captain. "How many?"
>
> "Six, eight hundred, I'd say, living in those marble ruins in the hills, sir. Tall, healthy. Beautiful women."
>
> "Did they tell you what became of the men and women who built this Earth settlement, Lieutenant?"
>
> *"They hadn't the foggiest notion of what happened to this town or its people."*
>
> Bradbury 2010: 580, emphasis mine

Liminality—"lost in a sea of brownness"

In "Going Home," we meet the protagonist, Billy Woodward, "a handsome youth, with the features of his white grandfather and the quietness of his Aboriginal forebears" (Weller 1994: 56). Having left his home to go to university five years before the story begins, he has become a successful football player and painter. He is described as standing "tall and proud, with the sensitive lips of a dreamer and a faraway look in his serene amber eyes" (56), because, as we soon learn, he has left the home of his origins (the poor district in which his Aboriginal family lives) to become a successful athlete and artist.

Living now in the white community, where he apparently enjoys recognition of his success and social ascension, he has partially forgotten or rejected his origins and his own people, as can be seen in several passages of the story. Right at the beginning, after many years of distancing from his family, he decides to pay them a visit but, when he is on the way, the narrator, giving voice to what goes on in Billy's mind, says: "The man doesn't know that world. His is the world of the sleek new Kingswood that speeds down the never-ending highway. [...]

For five years he has worked hard and saved and sacrificed. Now, on his twenty-first birthday, he is going home. New car, new clothes, new life" (Weller 1994: 53).

Here one can already notice the situation of the hybrid subject, whose origin is elsewhere and somehow calls him back but who sees himself as belonging to another social class, another culture, and even to another ethnic group. "New car, new clothes, new life" echoes the feeling that the Bitterings, in "Dark They Were, and Golden-Eyed," had when leaving their settlement behind (inadequate houses, ugly people) to live in the better villas of the Martians.

As Ania Loomba points out in *Colonialism/Postcolonialism*, Frantz Fanon suggests that "liminality and hybridity are necessary attributes of 'the' colonial condition" (2002: 176) and are, therefore, inevitable. For Fanon, "psychic trauma results when the colonised subject realises that he can never attain the whiteness he has been taught to desire, or shed the blackness he has learnt to devalue" (176).

Billy Woodward contrasts himself with those of his own ethnicity, a comparison which shows his estrangement from those who are, supposedly, like him. "His movements are elegant and delicate. His hair is well-groomed, and his clothes are clean. Billy Woodward is coming home in all his might, *in his shining armour*" (Weller 1994: 53ff., emphasis mine).[5] The "shining armour," like the Earthmen's physical transformation, is what would prevent him from being seen as a young man of Aboriginal descent. Like the Bitterings, he has left behind his previous life and, together with it, his previous identity: "no one can stop him now. He forgets about the river of his Dreaming and the people of his blood and the girl in his heart" (55). After becoming a famed player and artist, he "never went out to the park at Guildford, so he never saw his people: his dark, silent staring people, his rowdy, brawling, drunk people. *He* was white now" (55, emphasis mine).

The image that Billy Woodward has of himself as "white," belonging to the mainstream, dominant culture, echoes the physical transformation that the characters in "Dark They Were" symbolically undergo. The need to be an object of consideration for the dominant community leads Weller's protagonist to reject his own people, again echoing Mrs. Bittering's " 'Such ugly people. I'm glad they've gone'" (Bradbury 2010: 579). This can be seen in his reaction when he meets first his uncle and, afterwards, his aunt.

Once, in the middle of the night, one of his uncles had crept around to the house he rented and fallen asleep on the verandah. *A dirty painful carcass, encased in a black greatcoat that had smelt of stale drink and lonely, violent places.* A withered black hand had clutched an almost empty metho[6] bottle.

In the morning, Billy had shouted at the old man and pushed him down the steps, where he stumbled and fell without pride. The old man had limped out of the creaking gate, not understanding.

Weller 1994: 55, emphases mine

Not satisfied with expelling his uncle from his house and, hopefully for him, from his life, Billy moves on the next day since his white neighbors had seen the scene and might connect him with the drunk old man. When, on another day, he meets a middle-aged Aboriginal woman, his aunt, who "grinned up at him like the Gorgon" (56), the following encounter unfolds:

"Billy! Ya Billy Woodward, unna?"

"Yes. What of it?" he snapped.

"Ya dunno me? I'm ya Aunty Rose, from down Koodup."

She cackled then. *Ugly, oh, so ugly. Yellow and red eyes and broken teeth and a long, crooked, white scar across her temple. Dirty grey hair all awry.*

His people.

His eyes clouded over in revulsion. He shoved her away and walked off quickly.

He remembered her face for many days afterwards whenever he tried to paint a picture. *He felt ashamed to be related to a thing like that. He was bitter that she was of his blood.*

Weller 1994: 56, emphases mine

In the same way that the "Earthmen," on leaving their settlement, avoid looking behind to what they do not see as belonging to them anymore, namely, the cottages in which they had lived for years, Billy Woodward sees grotesquerie and strangeness in the landscape of his old life:

Grotesque trees twist in the half-light. Black tortured figures, with shaggy heads and pleading arms. Ancestors crying for remembrance. Voices shriek or whisper in tired chants: tired from the countless warnings that have not been heeded.

They twirl around the man, like the lights of the city he knows. *But he cannot understand the trees.* They drag him onwards, even when he thinks of turning back and not going on to where he vowed he would never go again.

Weller 1994: 57, emphases mine

The threshold between cultures can be considered the space of transition or, in Avtar Brah's words, the "diaspora space" (2003: 190–1).

In Bradbury's story, it is possible for the refugees to assimilate to the new culture, attaining a total forgetfulness of their origins and their former ways. In the fictional world of Archie Weller's story, which purports to reflect reality, however, no matter how hard the protagonist wants to leave behind his previous life (to the point of breaking ties with his family in such a way that he did not even know that his father had died), he is inescapably placed in the in-betweenness of the two cultures he has in different ways belonged to: "His people [he thinks when asked if he is eager to see his family again]: ugly Aunty Rose, the metho-drinking Uncle, his dead forgotten father, his wild brother and cousin. [...] They are all his people. *He can never escape*" (1994: 58, emphasis mine).

It is ironic that Billy represents the liminal subject, caught between two cultures, unable to feel comfortable in either, accepted by the whites when he is playing their game, viewed with suspicion by the white policemen when he is among the people of his own ethnicity when this very position was historically assigned to him by the colonizers who, in the process of subjugating the Aboriginal inhabitants of the land, converted them into diasporic subjects.

The emphasis on the contrasting spaces that Billy Woodward is connected with is, in Ashcroft et al.'s words, "a major feature of postcolonial literature with its preoccupation with place and displacement [...] It is here that the special postcolonial crisis of identity comes into being; the concern with the development or recovery of an effective identifying relationship between self and place (1991: 8–9)." For Billy, who finds himself alone and dislocated in both spaces, that of the whites and that of his own family, this identification becomes problematic. It is, perhaps, the result of the historical destruction of his native identity by "*cultural denigration*, the conscious and unconscious oppression of the indigenous personality and culture by a supposedly superior racial or cultural model" (Ashcroft et al. 1991: 9, emphasis in the original).

When the Bitterings, in Bradbury's story, move to the marble villas of the Martians, leaving behind their previous identity, one can see a utopian world in which total assimilation to the new environment is made possible. Billy Woodward, on the other hand, although he tries to negate his past and imagines himself as resembling the whites, is seen from the outside as an Aborigine. When he is in the reserve where his family still lives, he is mistaken for a robber and taken to prison. At this moment, his brother, who is being arrested with him says: "Welcome 'ome, brother" (Weller 1994: 64).

In his article "Identity and Cultural Studies: Is That All There Is?," Lawrence Grossberg (2008: 91) discusses the issue of fragmentation, emphasizing the "multiplicity of identities and of positions within any apparent identity" and "a particular concrete and lived identity" as, quoting Haraway, "a kind of disassembled and reassembled unity." Thus, "Identities are [...] always contradictory, made up of partial fragments." Billy Woodward will always be a composite of his native origin (blackness, dispossession) and his acquired "white" image (social ascension, wealth, success). As Freud says of the notion of origins in relation to the fantasy of the colonized: "Their mixed and split origin is what decides their fate. We may compare them with individuals of mixed race who taken all around resemble white men but who betray their coloured descent by some striking feature or other and on that account are excluded from society and enjoy none of its privileges" (quoted in Bhabha 2008b: 127). Despite his contact with the white society and culture, Billy Woodward, while "white" due to his education and social ascension, will always be physically black and considered as such by people who do not know that he is a successful footballer and painter. When, on his way home, he stops at a pub and asks for a drink, the white waiter, reacting to a somewhat rude remark of Billy's, calls him a "smart black bastard" (Weller 1994: 59). At this point, the narrator, again voicing the protagonist's feelings, states:

> He is black and the barman is white, and nothing can change that. All the time he had gulped in the wine and joy of the nightclubs and worn neat fashionable clothes and had white women admiring him, played the white man's game with more skill than most of the wadgulas[7] and painted his country in white man colours to be gabbled over by the wadgulas: all this time he has ignored his mumbling, stumbling tribe and thought he was someone better.
> Yet when it comes down to it all, he is just a black man.
>
> Weller 1994: 59

Conclusion

In spite of the similarities between the two stories, it must be said, before concluding, that they differ in some important aspects. The obvious one is that, from a generic perspective, Bradbury's "Dark They Were, and Golden-Eyed" is a work of science fiction whereas Weller's "Going Home" is a realist narrative that discusses the plight of the transnational, diasporic subject. By comparing the two works, the generic classification of Bradbury's story can be read as an allegorical investigation of identity that transcends the perceived "limitations" of science fiction. In a similar manner, Weller's must be read as a speculative, if not fantastical, investigation of a consciousness alienated from the cultures through which it moves.

Another aspect that sets the stories apart is the fact that in "Dark They Were" the "Earthmen"—both migrants and refugees to and from their "own planet"— forcibly had to leave behind their original culture and adapt to the new one since they had no other choice as there was little possibility of returning to their planet. Gradually breaking all the ties with their past existence made them adapt to the new environment to the point of forgetting who they had been before and acquiring a new identity, not without undergoing a state of hybridity, in which the two cultures co-existed and contended.

In Weller's "Going Home," Aborigine Billy Woodward believes he has attained an identification with the white community to the point of rejecting and forgetting his family and his roots. However, his people are still there, near him, and call him back, a summons that he tries to answer only to learn that, by accepting to play the white man's game, he is now in a state of in-betweenness, neither black nor white, neither completely part of the mainstream culture nor at home anymore in his own. Commenting on Gayatri Spivak's discussion of alienation, R. Radhakrishnan (1996: 167) states that, in a philosophical sense, that concept, "when understood deconstructively admits of no final correction" and asks if the subaltern subject will ever arrive at its true identity.

Although the story uses a strategy similar to the effacing of the "Earthmen" identity in "Dark They Were," which approaches what Homi Bhabha calls "mimicry,"[8] Billy Woodward's attempt at integration with the whites is not a successful one. As he is shown to think, looking at his brother and cousin, comfortable in the space assigned to them, he "is nowhere" (Weller 1994: 62); he is a displaced individual to a large extent deprived of his identity. As Ania Loomba (2002: 173) aptly states: "One of the striking contradictions about colonialism is that it both needs to 'civilize' its 'others,' and to fix them into perpetual 'otherness.'"

As to Billy Woodward's feeling that there is no place for him, one could again resort to Avtar Brah, who says:

> Where is home? On the one hand, "home" is a mythic place of desire in the diasporic imagination. In this sense it is a place of no return, even if it is possible to visit the geographical territory that is seen as the place of "origin." On the other hand, home is also the lived experience of a locality. Its sounds and smells,

its heat and dust, balmy summer evenings, sombre grey skies in the middle of the day [. . .] all this mediated by the historically specific everyday of social relations.

Brah 2003: 192

When he goes back "home" and talks to his relatives, for a brief moment, Billy feels that the happiness of his childhood and adolescence returns to him: "They chew on the sweet cud of their past. The memories seep through Billy's skin so he isn't William Woodward the talented football player and artist, but Billy the wild, half-naked boy, with his shock of hair and carefree grin and a covey of girls fluttering around his honey body" (Weller 1994: 62). Unfortunately, these are the memories of an idealized past to which Billy Woodward, caught in the entanglements of the post-colonial condition, will never be able to return.

Notes

1   Cf. Homi Bhabha's "fading of identity" (2008b: 80).
2   "The culture which develops on the new soil must therefore be bafflingly alike and different from the parent culture," quoted in Bhabha (2008a: 54).
3   This will also be valid, and even more so, for the discussion of Archie Weller's "Going Home," in which issues of ethnicity (Aboriginal versus White) will be in the foreground.
4   "The mirror is, after all, a utopia, since it is a placeless place. In the mirror, I see myself there where I am not, in an unreal, virtual space that opens up behind the surface; I am not over there, there where I am not, a sort of shadow that gives my own visibility to myself, that enables me to see myself there where I am absent: such is the utopia of the mirror. But it is also a heterotopia in so far as the mirror does exist in reality, where it exerts a sort of counteraction on the position that I occupy. From the standpoint of the mirror I discover my absence from the place where I am since I see myself over there. Starting from this gaze that is, as it were, directed toward me, from the ground of this virtual space that is on the other side of the glass, I come back toward myself; I begin again to direct my eyes toward myself and to reconstitute myself there where I am. The mirror functions as heterotopia in this respect: it makes this place that I occupy at the moment when I look at myself in the glass at once absolutely real, connected with all the space that surrounds it, and absolutely unreal, since in order to be perceived it has to pass through this virtual point which is over there" (Foucault 1984: 4).
5   The "*shining armour*" can be interpreted in the light of what Lacan, quoted by Bhabha in relation to the link between mask and identity, says: "In case of display

[...] the play of combat in the form of intimidation, the being gives of himself, or receives from the other, something that is like a mask, a double, *an envelope,* thrown off skin, thrown off in order to cover *the frame of a shield.* It is through this separated form of himself that the being comes into play in his effects of life and death" (quoted in Bhabha 2008b: 91, emphases mine).

6 Metho—methylated spirits, drunk as a cheap substitute for other forms of alcohol.

7 Wadgula: white people in the Aboriginal language of south-western Australia.

8 Homi Bhabha (2008b, 121–31) discusses mimicry as a strategy of the colonizers, imposed on the subalterns, but it certainly reverberates in the colonized individual's perception of himself/herself: "colonial mimicry is the desire for a reformed, recognizable Other [...] Which is to say, that the discourse of mimicry is constructed around an *ambivalence*; in order to be effective, mimicry must continually produce its slippage, its excess, its difference" (122, emphasis in the original).

References

Ashcroft, B., Griffiths, G., and Tiffin, H. (1991), *The Empire Writes Back: Theory and Practice in Post-Colonial Literatures,* London and New York: Routledge.

Bhabha, H. K. (2008a), "Culture's In-Between," in S. Hall and P. Du Gay (eds), *Questions of Cultural Identity,* Los Angeles: Sage Publications, 53–60.

Bhabha, H. K. (2008b), *The Location of Culture,* London and New York: Routledge.

Bradbury, R. ([1949] 2010), "Dark They Were and Golden-Eyed," in R. Bradbury, *The Stories of Ray Bradbury,* New York, London and Toronto: Alfred A. Knopf, 567–80.

Brah, A. (2003), *Cartographies of Diaspora: Contesting Identities,* London and New York: Routledge.

Foucault, M. (1984), "Of Other Spaces: Utopias and Heterotopias," www.web.mit.edu/allanmc/www/foucault1.pdf accessed 3 May 2014.

Grossberg, L. (2008), "Identity and Cultural Studies: Is That All There Is?," in S. Hall and P. Du Gay (eds), *Questions of Cultural Identity,* Los Angeles: Sage Publications, 87–107.

Hall, S. (2008), "Introduction: Who Needs 'Identity'?" in S. Hall and P. Du Gay (eds), *Questions of Cultural Identity,* Los Angeles: Sage Publications, 1–17.

Loomba, A. (2002), *Colonialism/Postcolonialism. The New Critical Idiom,* London and New York: Routledge.

Radhakrishnan, R. (1996), *Diasporic Mediations: Between Home and Location,* Minneapolis, MN and London: University of Minnesota Press.

Weller, A. (1994), "Going Home," in W. Morgan (ed.), *Figures in a Landscape: Writing from Australia,* Cambridge: Cambridge University Press, 53–64.

11

Case Histories: Alienated Labor in William Gibson's *Pattern Recognition* and *Zero History*

Jen Caruso

Minneapolis College of Art and Design, USA

If William Gibson's *Neuromancer* (1984) valorized the expert male hacker, for whom technology-enhanced cognition and the augmented reality of cyberspace promised a mode of overcoming the conditions of embodiment, derided as "meat" (Heise 2009: 211), Gibson's 2003 novel *Pattern Recognition* is more ambivalent, portraying "a more ordinary world in which the technological acceleration and global mobility of human bodies outpace the adaptation capabilities of the mind," but, more suggestively, produce marketable symptoms. This register shift, from male to female, describes a critical reworking of the figure of the global nomad, which John Marx recognizes as part of the "feminization of globalization" (2006: 1).

Pattern Recognition is the first of a trilogy sometimes termed the "Bigend" novels, which includes *Spook Country* (2006) and *Zero History* (2010). This grouping presents a shift in temporal locations for Gibson, who, until this point, had located his books in geographically recognizable futures, to that of the future-present, specifically, 2002, just after 9/11, and the transition to the new century. This is self-consciously referenced in a statement made by Hubertus Bigend, marketing, advertising, and media mogul, to his "cool hunter" under contract, Cayce Pollard, the protagonist. He says:

> Fully imagined cultural futures were the luxury of another day, one in which "now" was of some greater duration. For us, of course, things can change so abruptly, so violently, so profoundly that futures [...] have insufficient "now" to stand on. We have no future because our present is too volatile. We have only risk management. Pattern recognition.

> Gibson 2003: 57

A coolhunter or trendspotter, "a dowser in the world of global marketing," Cayce's expertise at pattern recognition, her "tame pathologies" are the result of a hypersensitivity which responds like "human litmus paper" to branding (Gibson 2003: 2, 13, 65). An analysis of her pathological behaviors—particularly, panic and hypervigilance—suggest these to be a response to the conditions of globalization, those same conditions into which she can subsequently market her skills. She is exemplum or herald, but not the exception. Gibson describes both the origin of, and the emergent conditions of, globalization and its effect on human subjectivity as embodied symptoms, skills which are readily commodified. Moving from contract to contract, city to city, Cayce experiences permanent "jet lag," which Ursula K. Heise has interpreted as a metaphor for alienation, inducing a state "as though she is inhabited by something single-minded, purposeful, yet has no idea what it plans or wants" (Gibson 2003: 25). The psychic dislocation provided by jet lag provides the conditions of possibility for a mode of embodied resistance, and the novel describes the journey through which she comes to realize that she has allowed pathology to define the nature of her life, engaged in primarily immaterial labor (94). Obsessed with identifying the maker of a cultural object called "the footage," she eventually discovers and witnesses "The Maker" at work, and finds her symptoms have abated. Cayce returns in *Zero History*, now a clothing designer for a "secret brand," Gabriel Hounds, an uneasy resolution to this potential for resistance.

The soul at work: Alienation

Pattern Recognition begins by describing Cayce, a New Yorker in London, suffering the effect of jet lag, a temporal dislocation into a "flat and spectral non-hour" (1): "Her mortal soul is leagues behind her, being reeled in on some ghostly umbilical down the vanished wake of the plane that brought her here, hundreds of thousands of feet above the Atlantic. Souls can't move that quickly, and are left behind, and must be awaited, upon arrival, like lost luggage."

Later, in the context of the exchange referred to previously with Bigend, she describes ordinary people as "actual living souls" (56), a word he repeats back to her, in a questioning tone, "Souls?" Later that same evening, speaking about her jet lag, he observes that the effect of jet lag has to do with permanent damage, the brain visibly "shrinking" which is "clearly visible on a scan" (60), something Cayce denies. " 'No,' she says, 'it's because the soul travels more slowly, and arrives late' " (60). This prompts the following exchange:

"You mentioned souls earlier."

"Did I?" She can't remember.

"Yes. Do you believe in them?"

"I don't know."

"Neither do I."

Gibson 2003: 60

Heise wonders about the curious metaphor suggested by this "comparison of the travelling soul to lost luggage", noting that it reflects a shift in Gibson's early valorization of cyberspace, and the premise that "the mind is detachable from the body and able to travel much more swiftly and flexibly without physical baggage" (2009: 211). Case's odd use of the term "soul" bears much in common with Franco Berardi's materialistic conception of the soul in his 2009 *The Soul at Work: From Alienation to Autonomy*. "Soul" is used "metaphorically and even a bit ironically" (2009: 22), but is key to his thinking about alienation. Not a reference to the "spirit," the idea of the soul, as Jason E. Smith explains in his preface, neither suggests exclusively "mind" nor the "capacity for cognition":

> It is an aesthetic organ as well, the exposure of thought to the contractions and dilations of space, to the quickening and lapsing of time [...] The soul is not simply the seat of intellectual operations, but the affective and libidinal forces that weave together a world: attentiveness, the ability to address, care for, and appeal to others.

Smith 2009: 9

In Gibson's text, jet lag is first a symptom and sign of a resistance of the body to the speed of globalization, described as "soul-delay." Jet lag experienced as "low-level dissonance" in response to shifts in location is a way to perceive "this eerie vacillation between similarity and difference" (Heise 2009: 229): "eerie mixtures of the familiar and the alien" against "the homogenizing force of global markets." In the context of *Semiocapitalism*, in which the "tools for the production of value" are the "mind, language, and creativity" (Berardi 2009: 21), the "new forms of alienation" must be identified as "the automatisms of mental reactivity, language, and imagination" (22). It might also describe a reactionary symptom; one's soul "delayed" results in an inability to "to address, care for, and appeal to others" experienced as "paranoia" and "panic" symptoms (9).

Cayce Pollard—"cool hunter"—suffers "a morbid and sometimes violent reactivity to the semiotics of the marketplace" (Gibson 2003: 2), but these have been harnessed into "tame pathologies." She does not "critique" nor offer "creative input." In her jobs, she is "there to serve as a very specialized piece of human litmus paper" and this is something that she specifies, in her contract, as "absolute" (Gibson 2003: 13). Faced with a brand logo, "[s]he knows immediately that it does not, by the opaque standards of her inner radar, work. She has no way of knowing how she knows" (12). She is, as Lauren Berlant has claimed, "distinguished not only by [her] acute intuition, but also by [her] *professionalization* of intuition" (2008: 846, emphasis mine):

> We see her go "sideways" falling apart at the force of the commoditized sign, and she, too, is never wrong (17). The very authenticity of her powerful nonsovereignty makes people want to hire her, to link their products to her nervous system. She markets her nerves as a freelancer, one of the sovereign figures of neoliberalism, the person on contract who makes short-term deals for limited obligation and thrives through the hustle over the long haul. However, she prefers precarity to the too-closeness of the world, and the novel is structured around her physical and affective migration from one place to another, a becoming found in becoming lost [...] in this, she is an extreme of exemplarity, not special.
>
> Berlant 2008: 855

When in "Immaterial Labor," Maurizio Lazzarato had identified "a pure virtuality," "an opening and a potentiality" in the "precarious worker" that had a historical origin in the "struggle against work," he had cautioned that this was not a "utopian vision" (1996: 135). But he did suggest that within the cycle of immaterial labor would emerge a "social labor power that is independent and able to organize both its own work and its relations with business entities" (135). This, identified as "a surplus in relation to collective cognitive mechanisms," he defines first as spatial: "at a territorial level, a space for a radical autonomy," but also as *temporal*. He suggests the emergence of "a kind of 'intellectual worker' who is him- or herself an entrepreneur, inserted within a market that is constantly shifting and within networks *that are changeable in time and space*" (139, emphasis mine). Writing in 2009, Berardi had noted a shift in conditions, and that the precarious worker would find no moment in space or time in which their cognition would not be fully engaged: "Putting the soul to work: this is the new form of alienation. Our desiring energy is trapped in the trick of self-enterprise, our libidinal investments are regulated according to economic rules, our attention is captured in the precariousness of virtual networks: every fragment of mental activity must be transformed into capital" (2009: 24). Berlant argues of Cayce's agency in *Pattern Recognition*:

whatever potentiality exists here is not about futures, in any real sense of world-changing. It is about alternative presents, interrupting what there is and world-making in the just now, the thick space of the present moment [...] People follow their intuitions and so change the shape of the present, which is not fleeting at all, but a zone of action in a transitioning space [...] a drama of adjustment, of intuitive retraining.

Berlant 2008: 856

This sets the conditions for what Gibson will, by the time of *Zero History*, describe as "atemporality."

Pattern Recognition is focalized through Cayce's experience, a quest narrative to identify "the Maker" of the "footage"— a sequence of virally distributed fragments of film footage, around which has coalesced a subculture of fans, the only cultural product that seems to have successfully represented the "polyphonic" sense of collective loneliness and isolation. This feeling of loneliness deepens over time, but is replaced, gradually, with "a sense that it's going somewhere, that something will happen. Will change" (Gibson 2003: 109). This footage sustains Cayce through both the personal and collectively experienced trauma of 9/11, in which her father, a security expert and consultant to the CIA, has disappeared. Cayce has become hypervigilant, and suffers extreme panic reactions, quelled only by exposure to the footage, which reveals to her "the extent of her present loneliness" (24) twinned with the reassurance of belonging to a collective and the "suggestion of just how many people might be following" it (52).

Cayce's experience of 9/11 and the particularities of her trauma are described in terms of what she had witnessed, not the event itself, but "a micro-event that seemed in retrospect to have announced [it] privately and secretly" (135). On her way to a client meeting, "[s]he had watched a single petal fall, from a dead rose, in the tiny display window of an eccentric Spring Street dealer in antiques." The window contains the following:

> [T]hree rusted cast-iron toy banks, each a different height but all representing the Empire State Building [...] The dead roses, arranged in an off-white Fiestaware vase, appeared to have been there for several months. They would have been white, when fresh, but now looked like parchment. This was a mysterious window, with a black-painted plywood backdrop revealing nothing of the establishment behind it. She had never been in to see what else was there, but the objects in the window seemed to change in accordance with some peculiar poetry of their own.

Gibson 2003: 135

She reads this configuration of objects, as well as the "micro-event" to which she is "sole witness" of the petal falling (coinciding as it does, with, she will only later realize, the sound of the first plane hitting the tower) as an expression of "the loneliness of objects" a sentiment with which she overidentifies: "Their secret lives. Like seeing something move in a Cornell box" (135). This mysterious window could be said to present a kind of skyline, an echo of the "window that frames the towers" (137). These mute objects stand in for the memory of people she must have seen falling, but does not retain in memory.

It is here we can see the origins of Cayce's sensitivity to objects, as the opening up to a liminal state, a hallucinatory world full of communicating things, whose "existential elegies, tug at her" (15). Walter Benjamin, writing in "The Image of Proust," had identified a similar threshold experience. Turning days into nights, Proust was able to extend, indefinitely, "the hour that was most his own"—"in such a way that everyone can find it in his own existence. We might almost call it an everyday hour; it comes with the night, a lost twittering of birds, or a breath drawn at the sill of an open window" (1968: 203). Benjamin had realized that Proust lived "not a model life" but an "exemplary" one (201). The word refers both to that which is the best of its kind, but also that which might serve as a warning. Proustian experience was identifiable to bourgeois readers because the extreme pathology under which he lived would become normalized. Benjamin identified in Proust the pathologies that have become our present moment— extreme wealth, obsession with purposeful activity; countered only by an abso- lute inability to be productive without pharmacology, manic consumption, panic disorder, and crushing depression. If Proust "finally turned his days into nights, devoting all his hours to undisturbed work in his darkened room with artificial illumination" in order to produce an "*image*" of his life that could be recognized by "everyone," it could only take the form of an image of "the most banal, most sentimental, weakest hour in the life to whom they pertain" (203).

Feeling not foreign, but alien

Pattern Recognition ends with Cayce strangely "cured" of her marketable skills, her sensitivity, registering all as "neutral." The conditions of this 'cure' may be caused either by "critical event stress" or inoculation with an unidentified drug, comprised of "industrial chemicals" unfit for "use on human beings" (quoted in Berlant 2008: 857; Gibson 2003: 354). She is "warmly socketed" into place, into bed, with a man (356). As Berlant, with a degree of ironic distance, concedes, "[s]till, even they need a vacation from it all, an impasse folded into the fold of the present" (2008: 857). Noting the ambivalent politics of this ending and questioning Cayce's autonomy, Berlant suggests only that the novel, as a whole, speaks of "the productivity of ordinary crisis that is also a potentiality that is accessible, at times, as a felt sense and structure of affinity and solidarity, a lived utopianism of *we*-are-thereness" (858). Further, Berlant argues that "crisis within the ordinary incites research projects, going to the library, to the internet, and to other humans to find out something not in the idiom of pasts and futures, no longer about the past's presence as *revenant* but about the present's ongoing condition [...] to cruise the situation and to redirect it toward a better here and now" (858). As John Marx presciently observes, "Cayce's retirement must be temporary" (2006: 16).

I would like to begin with the moment in *Pattern Recognition* that could be said to mark the place in which Cayce begins to question the precarious conditions under which she has come to labor and begins to strike out for herself. What does it mean that she does "not know where [she'll] be in a month or two"? (Gibson 2003: 88–9). Why does she have "fewer things in her apartment than anyone"? Much has been made of her relentless minimalism. A "side effect" of hypervigilance (8) and of "too much exposure to the reactor cores of fashion," her wardrobe consists only of objects "that could have been worn, to a general lack of comment, during any year between 1945 and 2000" (8). She reacts to objects that, as negatively described as fashionable commodities, are so far "removed from the source" they are "devoid of soul" (18). Less has been written about the qualities of objects to which she *is* attracted. What she likes is "evidence of long habitation, but nothing too personal" (90).

Her attention, for example, is caught by the bar patrons in a "less gentrified" neighborhood, the street, a market full of "dead men's clothes" and analog media. Her gaze is then caught by the way that "the wood of the bar is worn the way that old boats can be worn, virtually to splinters, held together by a thousand coats of coffin-colored varnish" (86), like the varnished floor in her own, nearly empty apartment that "seals the furry splinters of wear" and is painted in "an ancient tint" used for "centuries" by "peasants" (90). This group clings to the edges of gentrification, like the "homeless" who "however individually transitory" congregate, daily en masse, "defending" their Victorian doss-house shelter against the tide of the fashionable Children's Crusade (88). When she catches a young alcoholic boy's "ageless" eyes, she "shivers." She walks on, feeling not foreign but alien, made so by this latest advent of something that seems to be infecting everything.

Consider Cayce's original metaphor of alienation, a comparison of her soul to "lost luggage." Now consider the next moment in which she, walking, briefly, in synchronicity with another, smiles sideways, seeks to reassure her fellow pedestrian that she bears no threat, but he, frowning, falls out of step, "walks faster" (Gibson 2003: 94). Her attention switches focus onto what he carries, "a piece of vintage luggage":

> A very small suitcase, brown cowhide, that *someone* has waxed to a russet glow, reminding her of the shoes of the old men in the home in which her grandfather, Win's dad, had died. She looks after him, feeling a wave of longing, loneliness. Not sexual particularly, but having to do with the nature of cities, the thousands of strangers you pass in a day, probably never to see again. It's an emotion she experienced a very long time ago, and she guesses its coming up now because she's on the brink of something, some turning point, and she feels lost.
>
> Gibson 2003: 94, emphasis mine

What I want to suggest is that within Cayce's emerging aesthetic is a *displacement* of a desire for human connection, but at a distance, a taste for material things that bear evidence of human habitation, but barely, and a fragile sense of the power that holds it all together, just at the point where it might break apart. It is in these terms that we can begin to explore the ambiguity of such an aesthetic, which, having its origins in *atemporality*, a connection to a community of makers whose members communicate mainly through made objects, in the afterlife of things, uneasily slips back into a ritualized commodity fetishism.

Zero history, atemporality, dead men's clothes

Let's begin again with the image of the commodity against which Cayce's aesthetic is constructed. It is epitomized in *Pattern Recognition* as the clothing of Tommy Hilfiger, which represents a "null point, the black hole. There must be some Tommy Hilfiger event horizon, beyond which it is impossible to be more derivative, more removed from the source, more devoid of soul" (18). This temporal limit point had been, as Jason E. Smith in his introduction to *The Soul of Work* tells us, imagined by Marx as "the impossibility that capital might circulate 'without circulation *time*,' at an infinite velocity, such that the passage from one moment in the circulation of capital to the next would take place at 'the speed of thought.' Such a capital would return to itself even before taking leave of itself [...] a cycle contracting into a point" (Berardi 2009: 11). The impossible has occurred, and exposure to Tommy Hilfiger induces, in Cayce, a psychological response, a "slide" or "going sideways," a panicked, flight response.

In what way does this determine the aesthetic of her clothing brand, Gabriel Hounds? First, these objects must resist the gravitational pull of the black hole of commodification, the collapsing inward of the object, and must represent a fantastical excess of material as counterweight. Her clothing is uncannily dense: denim is described as "very heavy," "unusually heavy" (Gibson 2010: 334), or "brutal heavy" and always "slubby" (35). Indigo blue is described as "bordering on black" (31), while black denim is "black as ink" or "absolute black" and "[m]etal buttons" are "dead black, nonreflective." Indigo, "an earthy jungle scent" is always present, sometimes displayed in "bowls [...] shards of pure solidified indigo, like blue-black glass."

Cayce describes her origin as a maker, first, through picking and curation, using her "eye for detail" (118) to identify the well-made out of "thrift shops." Exploring the "ruins of American manufacturing" (336) from which had once come "beautifully made" products, she then activates a latent network: "I started bumping into people who remembered how to make things." She begins, "left alone," to "explore processes, learn" and to "experiment" (337).

How the desire to understand the process of making begins as a desire to create what once had been, but is no longer, is described by the vintage clothing dealer and shoe designer Meredith Overton, once foot soldier of the "grossly, baroquely dysfunctional" fashion industry, unable to produce a shoe for its "intensely nomadic" models who must "walk everywhere," unable to afford public transportation (117). Overton "imagines [shoes] that weren't ugly at all, that didn't fall apart. But somehow untainted by fashion" (118). She explains:

> I really wanted to understand shoes, their history, how they work, before I tried to do anything. Not that conscious a decision, but a decision. So I applied to Cordwainers, was accepted, moved to London. Or rather, simply stopped moving. In London. I may just have been enamored of the idea of waking up in the same town every day, but I had my mission, the mystery runners that I couldn't quite imagine.
>
> Gibson 2010: 119

Meredith concludes that she had been on the right track: "It's about atemporality. About opting out of the industrialization of novelty. It's about deeper code" (116).

Bruce Sterling (2010), in "Atemporality for the Creative Artist," describes atemporality as "about the nature of historical knowledge. What we can know about the past, and about the present, and about the future." In an atemporal situation, praxis, the making of the world, a problem that suggests itself, cannot be solved, cannot even be asked, but "a lot of work about its meaning and its value, its social framing" can be explored, through "database mining" and "collaboration":

> What we are facing over a decade is a decade of emergency rescue, of resiliency, of attempts at sustainability, rather than some kind of clear march toward advanced heights of civilization. We are into an era of decay and repurposing of broken structures, of new social inventions within networks, a world of "Gothic High-Tech" and "Favela Chic" (as I've called it), a crooked networked bazaar of history and futurity, rather than a cathedral of history, and a utopia of futurity. [...] We are living in an atemporal network culture, and I don't think that requires a moral panic. I think it ought to be regarded as something like moving into a new town. We've moved into a new town, and the first order of business is like: ok, what gives around here? Well, there seems to be this sort of decayed castle, and there's also a lot of slums [...].
>
> Sterling 2010

Of the aesthetics of the forms of cultural production that will come to fruition under these new conditions, Sterling speaks of two. The first, recognizable as "remix" or "mash-up" culture, is the "native expression" of these conditions:

> Well, the immediate impulse is going to be the "Frankenstein Mashup." Because that's the native expression of network culture. The "Frankenstein mashup" is to just take elements of past, present, and future and just collide 'em together, in sort of a collage. More or less semi-randomly, like a Surrealist "exquisite corpse."
>
> You can do useful and interesting things in that way, but I don't really think that offers us a great deal [...] The kind of thing is tragically easy to do, but not really very effective. It's cheap to do. It's very punk rock. It's very safety pins and plastic bags.
>
> Sterling 2010

What Sterling valorizes, in contrast, is that which expresses "an atemporal meaning of life": "High-art. And I would like to see some of that. I think there is a large hole there that could be filled, from an atemporal perspective. Not at the lowest end of artistic expression, but way up at the top philosophical end."

Following the logic of his metaphorical description, these would not be the "native" expressions of the inhabitants of such conditions, but ones that emerge from the sense that one is "moving into a new town." Interestingly, Richard Sennett, in his "Prologue" to *The Craftsman*, uses a similar metaphor to describe the mode of "self-critique" needed to challenge the sense of being "entitled to belong." We must all become "like immigrants thrust by chance or fate onto a territory not our own, foreigners in a place we cannot command as our own" (2008: 13). And Sterling, like Sennett, equates object making with material praxis, giving form to life.

Sennett argues for just this emergence of an atemporal "meaning of life," an ethics that emerges through a materialist aesthetics as an attentiveness to material culture, the making of, and the study of the making of, things as a form of embodied cognition. The things Sennett is speaking about—*made* things—include "cloth, circuit board [...] worthy of regard in themselves" (8). Making activates a mode of cognition: "Thinking and feeling are contained within the process of making" (7). "Learning from things requires us to care about the qualities of cloth ... fine cloth enables us to imagine larger categories of 'good.'" More ambiguously, deriving "pleasure" from "things in themselves" is said to be the mode through which these things "might generate religious, social, or political values" (8).

Considering that the history of material culture is, in the scale of geologic time, "a few seconds," we have in the things with which we are surrounded "a catalogue of experiments in making things" that is absolutely current (14). Sennett explains that given the brevity of human existence, little should be "alien to our understanding." But if material history is brief in the scale of geologic time, it is long in relationship to "biological life" (15). Sterling describes the potential in studying: "garbage [...] environmental damage, even corpses. You can look at what's been learned from the corpse of 'Otzi,' this Bronze-Age European. Fantastic things" (2010).

Further, reading material culture means reading for "deeper code" that is not primarily literary or linguistic (Gibson 2010: 116). In N. Katherine Hayles terms, "code is the unconscious of language" requiring a non-linguistic mode of cognition to understand it, like touch or sensation (2006: 137). Further, "nothing is more difficult than to decipher code someone else has written and insufficiently documented; for that matter, code one writes oneself can also become mysterious when enough time has passed."

Making is, inherently, a melancholic impulse, one that acknowledges that human lives are short, and object lives are long: "Objects do not inevitably decay from within like a human body" (Sennett 2008: 15). Sennett, in his description of the process of making, suggests that the maker holds "discussions mentally with materials rather than with other people," although "people working together certainly talk to one another about what they are doing" (7). But this conversation mainly takes place "through" the material as "anonymous workers," the nameless dead only "leave traces of themselves in inanimate things" (10). But this anonymity is true of all well-made things, which are "impersonal"; their makers share "a kindred impersonality" (27). It is this impersonal character that Sterling refers to when he says that we are at the point of developing a "potentially objective history" (2010): "All craftsmanship [...] has something of this impersonal character. That the quality of work is impersonal can make the practice of craftsmanship seem unforgiving: that you might have a neurotic relationship to your father won't excuse the fact that your mortise-and-tenon joint is loose [...] This blunt impersonality turns people outward." Cayce Pollard recognizes craft in works which do not bear the personal "mark" of a maker, and seeks to achieve it in her own designs. The realization of such objects seems to be an expression of a collectivity, within an open-knowledge system ("the creative process is no longer [...] contained within an individual skull") (Sennett 2008: 68). It is in these terms that we can then seek to understand what it means when she uses "we" instead of "I" when speaking of the brand's "coming out": "We're coming out. It's time" to stop or to take it to the next level (Gibson 2010: 337).

But Hollis Henry notes the way in which Bigend's values have in some way determined Cayce's aesthetic, about which her friend Garrett observes: "'Sufficiently perverse and titanic arseholes,' he said, 'can become religious objects. Negative saints. People who dislike them, with sufficient purity and fervor, well, they do *that*. Spend their lives lighting candles'" (Gibson 2010: 346). It is perhaps in these terms that we can see an implicit critique of Cayce's practice that troubles the ethical possibility of any collective action that might form around Cayce's secret brand, but also the bias implicit in Sterling's own belief that something "higher" should emerge from the conditions of atemporality.

"[P]eople who'll go to very considerable trouble to find" Gabriel Hounds (Gibson 2010: 46), are completely self-absorbed as they engage in this act of consumption, however ritualized as an act of worship. "Focused," as the musician Clammy has observed, himself one of the demographic. "No chatting. And they all see[m] to be alone" (78). Clammy, junk-sick (or, more likely, ill through work stress; the equivalent to being junk-sick in this new austerity economy), is *sick* for Hounds, and will do anything to get his "gear" (Gibson 2010: 33, 344). Shopping has become a religious ritual, the display counter, an altar:

> It smelled of vanilla and something else, masking jungle indigo. Candles pulsed in retail twilight, along the massive slab of polished wood that Hollis remembered from her previous visit. Aromatherapy candles, their complicated tallow poured into expensive-looking glasses with vertical sides, their wicks paper-thin slabs of wood, crackled softly as their flames pulsed. Faintly sandblasted on each glass, she saw, the Hounds logo. Between the candles were a folded pair of jeans, a folded pair of khaki pants, a folded chambray shirt, and a black ankle boot. The boot's smooth leather caught the candle-light. She touched it with a fingertip.
>
> Gibson 2010: 333–4

Are we to take seriously Sennett's claim that it is through the material object— the consumer's *taste* for the well-made thing—that will allow them to "imagine" other categories of "good"? Consider the moment when Hollis Henry puts on a Gabriel Hounds jacket:

> "I haven't tried it on."
>
> "No?" The woman moved behind Hollis, helping her remove her coat. She picked up the jacket and helped her into it.
>
> Hollis saw herself in the mirror. Straightened. Smiled. "That's not bad," she said. She turned up her collar. "I haven't worn one of these for at least twenty years."
>
> Gibson 2010: 32

Let us return to how Benjamin had imagined what had been at the heart of all of Proust's infinite efforts, the desire to create an image that would satisfy his homesickness. The fashioned thing, however beautifully made, might only present back to us our own image of our own subjectivity, which temporarily assuages homesickness, the metaphor of alienation. But if wearing something that is "fucking real, not fashion" could mean anything, it may do so through an appeal to the language of "deeper code" (Gibson 2010: 119, 116). Knowing something in our "limbic brain" extends thinking to include sensations of pleasure, "dreams [...] as well as cognitions that occur in the limbic system, the central nervous system, and the viscera," as N. Katherine Hayles, in her analysis of the functioning of code in *Pattern Recognition*, describes, an extension of human thought into "nonconscious processes" (2006: 139–40). And if it is true that Cayce, by making objects, is writing code, the dissemination of code throughout the network—"coming out," rather than "opting out"—will become "a powerful resource through which new communication channels can be opened between conscious, unconscious, and nonconscious human cognitions," a world made up of both humans and things (140). But whether simply *buying* the well-made thing can provide the leap necessary to make this happen remains uncertain.

References

Benjamin, W. (1968), "On the Image of Proust," in *Illuminations*, New York: Schocken.

Berardi, F. (2009), *The Soul at Work: From Alienation to Autonomy*, Los Angeles: Semiotext(e).

Berlant, L. (2008), "Intuitionists: History and the Affective Event," *American Literary History*, 20.4: 845–60.

Gibson, W. (2003), *Pattern Recognition*, New York: Berkley (Penguin).

Gibson, W. (2010), *Zero History*, New York: Putnam (Penguin).

Hayles, N. K. (2006), "Traumas of Code," *Critical Inquiry*, 33.1: 136–57.

Heise, U. K. (2009), "Virtual Travellers: Cyberspace and Global Networks," in J. Zilcosky (ed.), *Writing Travel: The Poetics and Politics of the Modern Journey*, Toronto: University of Toronto Press.

Lazzarato, M. (1996), "Immaterial Labour," trans. P. Colilli and E. Emory, in P. Virno and M. Hardt (eds), *Radical Thought in Italy*, Minneapolis, MN: University of Minnesota Press.

Marx, J. (2006), "The Feminization of Globalization," *Cultural Critique*, 63: 1–32.

Sennett, R. (2008), *The Craftsman*, New Haven, CT and London: Yale University Press.

Sterling, B. (2010), "Atemporality for the Creative Artist," *Wired*, 25 February, www.wired.com/2010/02/atemporality-for-the-creative-artist/, accessed 8 July 2014.

12

Control and Flow: Winterbottom's Migratory Cinema

Graeme Stout

University of Minnesota, USA

In his essay, "Postscript on the Societies of Control", Gilles Deleuze argues that the disciplinary societies of the eighteenth and the nineteenth centuries were in a process of general decay and that they were slowly being replaced with a new form of power. The institutional society that Michel Foucault and Louis Althusser used as the model of power in the modern age was disappearing at the end of the twentieth century. Regarding this transformation, Deleuze writes:

> It's only a matter of administering their last rites and of keeping people employed until the installation of the new forces knocking at the door. These are the *societies of control*, which are in the process of replacing the disciplinary societies. "Control" is the name Burroughs proposes as a term for the new monster, one that Foucault recognizes as our immediate future. [...] There is no need here to invoke the extraordinary pharmaceutical productions, the molecular engineering, the genetic manipulations, although these are slated to enter into the new process.
>
> Deleuze 1990: 4, emphasis in the original

Deleuze starts with the model of labor and the factory and ends with the image of the transformation of life into information: information to be analyzed and manipulated, and through which the very nature of life itself will be transformed. This economic, social, and cultural shift from a model that produces docile bodies to be turned into productive subjects, to one that regulates and predicts the flow of information and life through a micro-politics of the codes and patterns of biology, exemplifies the new deployments of power in the twenty-first century.

If Deleuze speaks of social, economic, and political transformations in his analysis, he is making a rhetorical appeal to science fiction and dystopian literature in his programmatic and prophetic style. From the perspective of Deleuze, writing in 1990, the evocation of the pharmaceutical, the molecular, and the genetic sounds like something akin to science fiction in its prediction of a "brave new world" being born from within the ruins of the old order. From our own perspective, this same evocation reads as a prescient description of our current moment were he to add (and he does later in the same article) the digital revolutions in communication and surveillance. This conjunction of science fiction with our current political and economic reality allows us an opportunity to think about how popular cultural modes of expression can give us access to the social reality that lies beneath our daily experience of, and interaction with, the world.

Two films by Michael Winterbottom, *In this World* (2002) and *Code 46* (2003), illustrate and critically develop Deleuze's concept of the society of control in a way that allows us to conceptualize the shifts in both economic reality and ideological perception that exemplify our current age of anxiety. An analysis of these two films will help us to understand the transformations of global capital and labor at the beginning of the twenty-first century. As we move from a political and economic system defined by interactions between discrete nation-states to systems increasingly defined by the distinction between global centers of power and wealth to which labor and information flow, and those undifferentiated zones of exception, where surplus labor and creativity reside, cinema offers us a forum in which we can imagine the amorphous and ethereal nature of global capitalism. In Winterbottom's films we will see that capital's expanse extends to the very nature of life, turning Winterbottom's *Code 46* and *In This World* into films that explore economics as an ontological frontier, picking up on Deleuze's predictions in his 'postscript.'

Produced and released within a year of each other, *In This World* (2002) and *Code 46* (2003) offer a series of images that visually explore the global realities of, and anxieties over, migration, geography, and reproduction. Although Winterbottom classifies both films as "road movies," *In This World* and *Code 46* have striking dissimilarities in their use of well-established genres:[1] *In This World* represents the contemporary plight of the refugee in an increasingly destabilized political and economic world through *cinéma vérité* and documentary styles, whereas *Code 46* gives us the image of a future-present dystopia through many of the hallmarks of science fiction cinema. These two films, however, share an interest in the contemporary transformations of power in the twenty-first century and how they are represented by the landscapes through which the characters in both films travel: the Middle East, South Asia, Asia Minor, Europe, and the global cities that increasingly bind these regions together.

These landscapes embody the configuration of power within the societies of control. These are open, fluidic spaces through which bodies, populations, and power move. What Winterbottom's films add to Deleuze's reading of our contemporary moment is an understanding of the way in which power is distributed across the globe—not simply as a general, theoretical schema, but as a concrete series of spatial and geographical examples. In both films we see a world divided between centers of power and prosperity and those open and barren spaces in which the dispossessed, the excluded, exist. In *In This World*, those configurations are well known to us: refugees from the countries of the Middle and Near East in which the proxy wars of the Cold War were fought, juxtaposed with the centers of wealth and power in the European Union with its increasingly exclusionary sense of unity. In *Code 46*, the dispossessed are those who, for political, legal, or genetic reasons, have been cast out of, and denied entry back into, the centers of wealth and technology. Together these two films highlight the new models of travel and the flow of people and power between global centers. Returning briefly to Deleuze, we can think of these two films as adding an important note to his analysis as they serve as reflections upon the ways that these new "modulations" (Deleuze 1990: 4) of power are made manifest in geographical and cartographic terms, for the rise of the nation-state is synonymous with the demarcating and securing of national boundaries which serve to define—legally and semiotically—the very identity of the nation-state. These borders have been abandoned for a series of "modulations" that allow the movement of individuals to be monitored and guided toward particular biopolitical activities. In both films, there is not a radical break between the interior and the exterior. There are, instead, varying degrees to which all within the two worlds of Winterbottom's films are employed to service larger economic, political, and technological systems. As Bruce Bennett[2] argues, Winterbottom's films have consistently challenged the political borders, as they have generic borders, in order to shed light upon the cultural and political realities of our contemporary moment (Bennett 2014: 2). Beyond an analysis of the two films, this essay points to the ways in which our contemporary experiences and understanding of migration, identity, and work are articulated in an age of transnationalism in which the refugee, the alien, is established as an allegorical figure for the human.

Down The Silk Road

In This World tells the story of two teenagers, Jamal and Enayat, who are sent by their families on a desperate voyage from the Shamshatoo refugee camp in Northern Pakistan to London. Both actors were hired for the film once Winterbottom and his team arrived in Pakistan and they were responsible for creating an improvised dialogue that the crew never understood until the post-production process, when subtitles were generated. We are told by the narrative voice-over at the beginning and end of the film that the impetus for this voyage is the deplorable state of life within the refugee camp. Citing the basic level of nutrition for each individual in the camp and weighing this against the total spent to bomb neighboring Afghanistan that same year (2001–2002), a sharp contrast is drawn between the life on the ground in Afghanistan and Pakistan and the technological excess unleashed by the militaries of the 'First World.' As the audience, we are led to the belief that a better life awaits them in London.

The voyage takes them, via truck and foot, across Pakistan, Iran, and Turkey from whence they are smuggled with eight others in a sealed shipping container to Italy. Here, they arrive in Trieste after the forty-hour ordeal that kills all but sixteen-year-old Jamal and a young child. Jamal is now left to fend for himself and travel across Europe where his course leads him to the Sangatte refugee camp on the shores of the English Channel. Escaping detention with another young man, he arrives in England where the diegetic world of the film dissolves into that of the real world of 2002. Jamal the character has transformed into Jamal Udin Torabi the actor who, as with his character, now seeks refugee status in the United Kingdom. We are told that he has been denied recognition as a refugee but has been granted permission to enter the United Kingdom up to his eighteenth birthday, at which point he will be repatriated to Afghanistan: a country he has never known.

These spaces and landscapes, through which these two young men move, re-establish and reinvigorate a Western fascination with the spaces between the centers of power and wealth in the East and the West—China and Western Europe. If these countries are the limits of Alexander's imperial mission and the route of Marco Polo's journeys to another world,[3] they also serve as the site of colonial fantasies within a British imaginary: these are the limits and threats to British power in the nineteenth century; these are the places of the Great Game of imperial competition between Britain and Russia as well as the location of

Kipling's tales of empire and adventure. Now, of course, they are sites of another imperial struggle that is producing its own cultural images of and anxieties over empire. In Winterbottom's film, as Loshitozky argues, the landscape is presented for the consumption of the Western audience, not for the actors who stand in as refugees (and who are themselves refugees) (2006: 753). These are places of open movement and possibility, seemingly without any landmarks or concentrations of people and power: they appear to us as an empty space that compels or impels movement through it. From the European perspective, they appear otherworldly in their bleak sense of desolation or they evoke another form of the sublime—as scriptwriter Tony Grisoni describes them, they are "biblical" (Special Features, *In This World*, 2002). They are presented to us as endless expanses measured only by the rising and setting of the sun and the call to prayer. The only interruptions within these spaces are those offered by the seemingly random and ineffective checkpoints of the state and the transition point from one handler—one who transports people illegally—to another. These spaces force us to go beyond Loshitzky's argument and see them not only as places for Western fascination with the other-worldly, but as confrontations that force the audience to rethink the nature of migration as well as, following Winterbottom, the genre of the road movie, turning it from a cinematic form identified with individuality and adventure, to one that represents the nameless and desperate movements of people in *this* world.

On a cinematic level, the travel narrative is based around the continuous images of driving on the open road that Winterbottom and cinematographer Marcel Zyskind captured on digital video and then wove together in order to represent the monotony of travel as well as the fantasies associated with the Silk Road. The muted palette of digital video adds to the 'authenticity' of Winterbottom's use of documentary techniques and rhetoric. Winterbottom also employs another technique associated with movement and travel in film, the animated map. Interspersed throughout the film are short segments that track the two teenagers' progress from Afghanistan to London. This technique is one borrowed from newsreels and historical documentaries, most often associated with military campaigns and celebrity tours. Tom Conley, in *Cartographic Cinema*, argues that the map has always served as an important cypher or allegory within the history of cinema:

> [T]he perception of a map both in and as the film begs consideration of the rapport of the image to movement and to time. The film moves insofar as the map offers a spatial picture of a shape and duration other than those of

the image in which it is found. Quite often the map locates the history of the film within itself. It has affinities with a *mise-en-abyme*, but while it may duplicate or mirror the surrounding film, the map can reveal why and how it is made and how its ideology is operating. As an "archive," a film sums up a history of its production through contextual citation. As a "diagram" or a model that maps perception and comportment through the image-field, the map is in flux where it shows how the archival aspect of the film might also be its diagram. The fluid and shifting spaces of the film and its cognition become *terrae incognitae* that the viewer explores in different directions and from various angles.

                                                                          Conley 2007: 20–1

The map opens up imaginary worlds as it also serves to locate the film within a series of cultural imaginaries. Here, we return to the specific landscapes through which the teenagers move as well as their destinations. The animated segments within the film each anticipate arrival in a major urban center: Tehran, Istanbul, Trieste. Each of these cities serves as a respite, but they also point to particular elements of the global economy. For instance, when they arrive in Istanbul, Jamal and Enayat are put to work in a makeshift workshop making cutlery for the European market. These cosmopolitan centers are not simply the "stops" on the way to London, but are themselves central nodes within the global systems of commerce, migration, and culture.

Once Jamal reaches Europe, he exists apart from the Italians and the French in whose country he subsists. In Italy, he is a peddler and, eventually, a thief. Having purchased a ticket to Paris, the fourth animated map segment takes Jamal from the Italian border to the Sangatte refugee camp where he—as one of thousands—exists as a liminal being: detained and separated from the rest of French society within the sprawling, makeshift structures near the Pas de Calais and the entrance to the Channel Tunnel.[4] This structure, which both "protects" and shelters while maintaining its inmates within a state of constant fear of deportation, speaks to Giorgio Agamben's description of the camp:

> The soccer stadium in Bari in which the Italian police temporarily herded Albanian illegal immigrants in 1991 before sending them back to their country, the cycle-racing track in which the Vichy authorities rounded up the Jews before handing them over to the Germans, the refugee camp near the Spanish border where Antonio Machado died in 1939, as well as the *zones d'attente* in French international airports in which foreigners requesting refugee status are detained will all have to be considered camps. In all these cases, an apparently anodyne place (such as the Hotel Arcade near the Paris airport) delimits instead a space

in which, for all intents and purposes, the normal rule of law is suspended and in which the fact that atrocities may or may not be committed does not depend on the law but rather on the civility and ethical sense of the police that act temporarily as sovereign.

Agamben 2000: 42

Here the refugee exists in a liminal state, at the mercy of an authority that is not bound by any legal necessity or moral compulsion. The specific case of Sangatte challenges somewhat Agamben's notion of the camp given its openness (mockingly referred to as "sans-gate"). This, however, marks another change in the function and nature of the camp, as escape would only be the escape away from the chance of securing any legal status in Europe. The camp can now function with a minimum of security given the ability and willingness of the security services and general public to track down and deport illegal immigrants. Returning to Deleuze's notion of control, we could see the example of Sangatte, which was renowned for its levels of poverty, violence, and corruption, pointing to a more "free floating" notion of power that is able to better surveil and track the individual than any panoptic space ever could. Sangatte marks a transformation of the refugee camp and its closure the year after *In This World* was filmed there does not mark an end to the incarceration of refugees, but an ability to relocate and redistribute large numbers of those outside the protection and recognition of the law.

Jamal's 'escape' from the camp is not accomplished with daring, nor does it result in reaching any final refuge. His journey to London is accomplished with great danger to his own person as he stows away on the undercarriage of a shipping container truck. Here, he is transported via the "Chunnel" to the United Kingdom where his status as one without rights continues. The journey itself is presented to us as a visual and sonic assault that suggests a repetition of his journey to Italy with Enayat. It also marks the return of another central figure of the global age: the shipping container. If, according to Agamben, the camp is the "*nomos* of the modern," we could certainly think of the intermodal shipping container as, at least, the *oikos* of the global, defining all forms of economic exchange and economic exchange *itself* given its ubiquitous nature and its role as part of a globally tracked system of continuous trade and exchange (Roland 2007: 386–7). In their harrowing trip from Istanbul to Trieste, it is an improvised shipping container that provides the doomed refugees with their mode of entry into Europe. The shipping container can be thought of as an allegorical figure that brings together life (the hope of a new life), death (all die within it), and the economic order (as it is through the shipping container that one can move smoothly across borders undetected).

Upon reaching London, Jamal phones his family in the refugee camp in Pakistan. When asked about the whereabouts of his cousin, Jamal has to explain to his uncle that Enayat is "not in this world." Although this phrase—the negation of the film's title—references Enayat's death in Trieste, we could also understand it in a larger sense to refer to Enayat's lack of status in the contemporary geopolitical order. He is not *within* the West as his very death was the result of the obstacles erected to prohibit this movement into a more (potentially) prosperous life. He is not within the world of the dispossessed, of his family in the refugee camp—this world he left as part of a gamble that—whether he lived or died—would have cut him off from them. Enayat exists in no world as his death goes unnoticed: he cannot be mourned and buried by his family, nor can he be recognized as a statistic within the bureaucracy of the West. As with the others smuggled into Italy, his body—it is implied—will be disposed of by the smugglers whose recklessness lead to his death. Like Enayat, Jamal is also not "in this world," for he is without status, without rights, neither in one place nor the other.

If *In This World* offers us a cinematic text that represents the movement of potential and desperate labor across the open expanses of the Central Asia and Asia Minor into the heart of capitalist liberal democracies, *Code 46* offers us a vision of a future in which unspecified ecological and biological changes have altered the nature of human society. At the same time, this future is one familiar to us as it is visually composed of the physical elements of globalized capitalism, in particular its urban centers. Here, as in *In This World*, the central geographical focus is the space between centers of commerce, industry, and capital. The landscape of the world is what lies outside of the concentration of wealth and architecture made manifest through the landmarks of global cosmopolitanism: the high rise, the airport, and the construction and transportation networks built in the expectation of the future movement of capital into such places as Shanghai and Dubai. The modern lines as well as the emptiness of these spaces—as with the expanses of Pakistan, Iran, and Turkey—suggest movement and the smooth flow of labor, power, and capital into and through these cosmopolitan centers. But, beyond these movements, we see another flow: that of biological information.

Amor fati

Code 46 presents us with a dystopian vision of the future in which the world has been ravaged by ecological disasters which have forced humans to live and work at night in order to avoid the sun. It is also implied in the opening sequence that the human ability to reproduce has been compromised, requiring medical and genetic intervention which has left the human race composed of a limited number of genetic lines, thereby increasing the chance of incest. During this opening sequence the meaning behind "code 46" is explained to the audience, not through a narrative voice, but through 'legal' text. It reads:

code 46
article 1
any human being who shares the same nuclear gene set as another human being is deemed to be genetically identical. the relations of one are the relations of all. due to IVF, DI embryo splitting and cloning techniques it is necessary to prevent any accidental or deliberate genetically incestuous reproduction.
Therefore:

i.   all prospective parents should be genetically screened before conception. if they have 100%, 50% or 25% genetic identity, they are not permitted to conceive
ii.   if the pregnancy is unplanned, the foetus must be screened.
      any pregnancy resulting from 100%, 50%, or 25% genetically related parents must be terminated immediately
iii. if the parents were ignorant of their genetic relationship then further medical intervention is authorised to prevent any further breach of code 46
iv.   if the parents knew they were genetically related prior to conception it is a criminal breach of code 46

The definition and implication of code 46 are presented to us as a set of sanctions designed to prevent the possibility of incest and, in those cases when it does happen, to prescribe a series of measures against it. This prohibition sets up the Oedipal narrative of the film in which William Geld (Tim Robbins) falls in love with his biological mother Maria Gonzales (Samantha Morton), leading to their eventual arrest and punishment—her exile, his memory erased—for their code 46 violation.

The Oedipal drama within the film[5]—although it can produce interesting readings given its presentation as biological control confronting a willful choice

Alien Imaginations

to disobey the incest taboo incest becomes the final act of rebellion—will not be the central focus of this essay. Instead, it is the relationships between bodies and landscapes and what these tell us about the shifting deployment of power in the digital age that provides the most productive reading of the film. Specifically, returning to the notion of the biopolitical, the genetic structure of humans becomes the final object of power and, more specifically, control. As Deleuze argues:

> In the societies of control [...] what is important is no longer either a signature or a number, but a code: the code is a *password* ... the numerical language of control is made of codes that mark access to information, or reject it. We no longer find ourselves dealing with the mass/individual pair. Individuals have become "*dividuals*," and masses, samples, data, markets, or "*banks*".
>
> Deleuze 1990: 6, emphasis in the original

The language here of "codes," "*dividuals*" and "data" offers us a way to read Winterbottom's film as a reflection upon the growing extent of control in a digital and bioinformatic age. In this dystopian projection, individuals are reduced to information and probability. All humans are protected by their password, the *palabra* in the hybridized language of the film. Now, in this precarious world, all human possibilities are determined and guided by the Sphinx: a shadowy corporate entity that decides who has the right to travel and for how long. At first, when we hear of this controlling power, we sense that it is some form of totalitarian institution, but, as the film progresses, we find that the Sphinx is, in reality, able to both predict and protect—those who turn against it die or are expelled into the inter-wastes, the spaces between. In the latter case, they are deemed unworthy or there is a "reason why they cannot get cover" to enter the cosmopolitan centers of the global economy. The Sphinx does not rule based on an absolute authority but, rather, an ability to understand what possibilities will be generated by human activity, and, then, to compensate for them.

The initial 'scrolling through' of the codes during the opening credits suggests not an accretion of law, but a remodulation of it in the face of new circumstances. Unlike code in the legal sense, which suggests an entire, systematic series of laws, here "code" stands in for the deployment of force and control on a genetic and biological level: as with a police code, it is a shorthand that explains fully the situation as well as necessary reaction to it. Unlike a legal code that is normative and prescriptive, here code is simply a description of an inevitable interaction, a statistical probability in a world that is increasingly reduced to a limited number of

. genetic lines and variants. The numerical import of "code 46" is never definitely established in the film. In the open sequence the animated titles quickly scroll from "1" to "46" before the full code is explained to us. Given that the code is also a series of definitions and measures against "unwanted pregnancies," we can read the value of 46 as a combination of the two sets of 23 chromosomes. At the beginning of the twenty-first century, we are also predisposed to see or, more aptly, to hear code as a speaking to the genetic code which, as Eugene Thacker points out in *The Global Genome* (2005: 20), was viewed by Crick and Watson as just that: a code to be broken and from which we can extract useful and malleable data. Thacker observes that the metonymic relationship between DNA as raw biological information and digital information has become one of seemingly absolute identity. We can no longer image/imagine the biological without doing so with, and through, computer graphics. Similarly, we imagine biological information as an object to be controlled through representation and digital manipulation.

Here we can again turn to Agamben's reading of the biopolitical to understand the implications of this implied meaning behind "code." Agamben writes:

> The political system no longer orders forms of life and juridical norms in a determinate space; rather, it contains within itself a *dislocating localization* that exceeds it and in which virtually every form of life and every norm can be captured. The camp intended as a dislocating localization is the hidden matrix of the politics in which we still live, and we must learn to recognize it in all of its metamorphoses.
>
> Agamben 2000: 44, emphasis in the original

In this passage Agamben comes quite close to Deleuze's reading of control as "a *modulation*, like a self-deforming cast that will continuously change from one moment to the other, or like a sieve whose mesh will transmute from point to point" (1990: 4); it is "short-term and of rapid rates of turnover, but also continuous and without limit" (6). For Agamben, the camp is immanent throughout the political order, simply awaiting a reason to "descend" and, in the wake of the institutional society's collapse, to establish a temporary space outside of the juridical order. The adaptability of control to modulate and reform itself marks it as a form of power that is able to cope with the chaos of life by, in the case of *Code 46*, calculating potential outcomes and possibilities in order to inoculate itself against the likelihood of incest being committed in a world with a much reduced genetic diversity. 'Incest' can be read in Winterbottom's film as a shorthand for the control of reproduction itself.

Biology is not simply the object that power seeks to control. Rather, biology or, more specifically, genetics, is the very means or object that controls itself. At the beginning of the narrative, we see a world in which biological essence has been converted into information. This information is then used to control and transform life itself. When we first meet William, he has ingested an empathy virus that allows him, after a short and friendly interrogation, to read people's thoughts through their emotional state. The only defense against this virus is a counter-virus that transforms William's empathy virus into the common cold. Likewise, after each of their two liaisons, either Maria or William has her or his memories altered to erase the memory of the incestuous act. Furthermore, when it becomes known that Maria is pregnant as a result of their first sexual encounter, the pregnancy is terminated according to Subsection ii of code 46.

Here the very act of reproducing life is analyzed and controlled. Throughout the film, when anyone is asked about their birth or their children's birth, we find out that all are created through some form of 'artificial conception' from a limited number of models. The raw material of capitalism (laboring bodies and minds) has now been replaced by the raw material of biology. The ultimate code of *Code 46* is not a legal or political code, but the code that predicts the behavior and development of life. Now the factors and means of production—to interject a more Marxist terminology—have become nothing more than life itself, the most basic sense of production. Here we can read the society of control as an acceleration of the biopolitical order in its ability to not simply produce docile (human) bodies to be disciplined and focused toward productive endeavors as Foucault described it, but to rewrite and restrict the very component codes that generate life. What Winterbottom's films illustrate is the transformation of the function, form, and flow of labor across the globe. They also point to the ways in which this reality, when coupled with a translation of life into information, produces a series of fantasies (and anxieties) about the limited possibilities inherent within this new configuration of power that threatens to turn our codes into the very means of our subjugation.

Bennett argues that the dystopian element of the film is based with the corporate world through which William Geld and Maria Gonzales move. He writes: "*Code 46* imagines a society in which commercial biotechnology is a state apparatus responsible for constructing a docile, self-policing citizenry—the military industrial complex superseded by the biopolitical-biotechnological complex, and the government superseded by the corporation" (2014: 68). It is not that Bennett's analysis of *Code 46* is flawed, only that it does not go far enough in its analysis of the biopolitical. In many ways, Bennett still holds on to an Althusserian notion of the institutional ("apparatic") society which is not really present in Winterbottom's film. The Sphinx, for instance, has some form of corporate body, but its power comes from its ability to predict the actions and delimit the movements of people based on their genetic predispositions. Within the film, the Sphinx is a background reference of which people speak as an ironic article of faith, "the Sphinx knows best." This phrase, always spoken with a mixture of reverance and humor, suggests that the faith in the Sphinx is like the faith in capitalism, a belief that *the* system must be supported as the alternative is death and disaster. The iron-tight control that typifies most dystopian worlds is absent. Instead, the metonymic linkage between the Sphinx and fate points to the "fatalism" that is omnipresent in this world as well as *our* world. What is most important in the film is how this faith works within the diegetic world of the film to seal ideologically the radical juncture between the interior and the exterior ("*al fuera*") which marks all human interactions and movements. The Sphinx serves as a material symbol that both explains and justifies a system based on economic and political exile: it is the very visible hand of the entire economic system. This distinction is only vaguely marked by borders and checkpoints; its true force comes across in the ways that individual bodies are recorded, surveilled and converted to data.

Returning to the opening sequence when the nature and import of code 46 is related to the audience, we can pay particular attention to the use of architecture and aerial cinematography. Although we are quickly informed by the voiceover provided by Maria Gonzales—who, from her narrative vantage point, now looks back upon all the events unfolding—that William is flying into Shanghai, we do not see the signs of Shanghai. Instead, we are presented with aerial shots of expanses of desert landscapes and commercial spaces that are from Dubai. Once in Shanghai, William moves through the blank spaces of airports and hotels and, in the early morning, on the deserted elevated road system. As the narrative unfolds, we realize that the diegetic world of the film is something that we will need to piece together as we go. As disorienting as this strategy is, it also engages the audience in an act of interpreting the "future present" world that we see before us. What we instantly realize is that the dystopian world of the future is made up of the component parts of our own world. Certainly the space of the airplane and its aerial perspective—one that as we fly into Shanghai is an essential element of "airport culture" (Berger 1997: 24)—speaks to the global mobility of money, peoples, and information. The view "from the window"—composed of shots of both William looking out the window from his first-class seat and the aerial view that, we imagine, composes his particular vantage point—also reveals to us multiple signs that help us to read this world. In particular, the barren and seemingly endless landscape points to open lines of movement without the impedance of barriers as they equally suggest poverty. This landscape, when seen from above, is marked as an object of fascination for both William and us. When coupled with the intertitles explaining the relevance of the film's title and the ambient music of the Free Association,[6] these expansive vistas are presented as both spaces across which one moves and flies, and as places with only the basic outlines of civilization: roads, buildings, and the lines of communication. If there is a beauty in these landscapes, as well as a fascination for them, we find ourselves facing a similar dilemma as that which Loshitzky pointed to with *In This World*: we are looking at the outside from a Western perspective and, as such, can only understand this "other" world as an object of fascination which is valued only as such. William's obsession with Maria can also be read as a fascination with someone who has been outside and who places herself outside of the law by forging passes ("*papeles*"). Perhaps, the outside could be read not as a simple negation of the inside, nor as a simple object of spectatorial fascination, but as an alternative: the thought of an outside to a system that determines life and death on the most basic level. Even in the desolate(d) landscapes that Winterbottom uses we can see a possibility of hope and resistance. There is also a level of hope and humor that runs throughout *Code 46* which is made manifest in the resistance to the restrictions placed upon individuals by the Sphinx, even if the Sphinx (as a system that can predict and prevent the possibility of death for each individual) "knows best." Whether it is in the, ultimately fatal, decision of Damien Alekan to seek illegal cover to travel to Mumbai to study the bats that have always fascinated him or the play of the language at work in the film as English, the *lingua franca* of the global age, is seeded with words from multiple languages; there is a playfulness that always breaks through the oppressive certainty that the Sphinx represents. If *Code 46* echoes our own contemporary world, it also does so in its desperate quest for an alternative to the logic of a system that controls all life and death.

Xenotopia

In This World and *Code 46* play with the images that saturate our contemporary media age and its presentation of the global interaction of bodies and spaces. In their reinterpretation of cinematic genres, they force the audience to take an active and, at times, confusing journey through worlds outside of the safety of the cinematic space. They also provide us with two figures that we can use to understand the heterotopic space of the global age: the shipping container and the jet airplane. These "spaces" function to articulate the non-spaces of the global economy: neither are actual places, only modes of transportation. They are, however, the most essential spaces of our current moment as they are the basic building blocks of a global age defined by the flows of people and goods. Michel Foucault, in his lecture "Of Other Spaces," speaks of such figures as heterotopias:

> There are also, probably in every culture, in every civilization, real places—
> places that do exist and that are formed in the very founding of society—which
> are something like counter-sites, a kind of effectively enacted utopia in which
> the real sites, all the other real sites that can be found within the culture, are
> simultaneously represented, contested, and inverted. Places of this kind are
> outside of all places, even though it may be possible to indicate their location
> in reality. Because these places are absolutely different from all the sites that
> they reflect and speak about, I shall call them, by way of contrast to utopias,
> heterotopias. I believe that between utopias and these quite other sites, these
> heterotopias, there might be a sort of mixed, joint experience, which would be
> the mirror. The mirror is, after all, a utopia, since it is a placeless place.
>
> Foucault 1984: 24[7]

Beyond the plane and the shipping container, we could locate another such figure in the human cell, for we see that genetic information becomes the central mode of communicating information in *Code 46* which allows for the human body, as a biological and genetic entity, to become an object of control through pharmaceutical and medical intervention. Together these three "containers"[8] help us to understand the riddle of the global system in which we have placed our faith.

Notes

1 Every study of Winterbottom need make, for obvious reasons, reference to his use of genre and cinematic convention. In his review of *Code 46*, A.O. Scott referred to Winterbottom as "prolific and stylistically promiscuous" (Scott 2004). I would follow Bennett's approach to Winterbottom by looking to the larger thematics that tie films together across generic boundaries and, in doing so, critique genre's hypothesized status in many approaches to film studies.

2 Bennett's monograph *The Cinema of Michael Winterbottom: Borders, Intimacy, Terror* (2014) is the first systemic analysis of Winterbottom's films and presents an equally praiseworthy and challenging examination of a diverse body of work.
3 The original title for the project was "The Silk Road."
4 The tunnel, as both an engineering marvel and a symbol of European unity and technological daring, plays an important part in the film as the point of access for Jamal into London, which is presented as a harrowing descent into the earth. Most recently the "Tunnel" also served as the titular and geographic backdrop to the Sky Atlantic remake of the Danish/Swedish co-production *Bron/Broen* (*The Bridge*) which, amongst other themes, focuses on the economies of migration, smuggling, and European racism and neo-colonialism.
5 For a reading of the Oedipal entanglement in *Code 46* that is both effective and imaginative, see Bennett's analysis (2014: 67).
6 Reminiscent of Brian Eno's *Music for Airports* in its style if not in its instrumentation.
7 For a larger discussion of the heterotopia of the ship in the nineteenth century, see Cesare Casarino's *Modernity at Sea: Melville, Marx, Conrad in Crisis*. I am indebted to Cesare for his help and discussion of the heterotopic figures over the years.
8 The anxieties associated with these three containers are not limited to Winterbottom's films. The plane has now become a cliché in every "pandemic" film, and the shipping container has a prominent place in, as just one example, Christopher Nolan's Batman trilogy, where they serve as the entry point for terror as well as the hideout of the "caped crusader" himself.

References

Agamben, G. (2000), "What is a Camp," in V. Binetti and C. Casarino (trans), *Means Without End: Notes on Politics*, Minneapolis, MN: University of Minnesota Press.
Appelbaum, S. (2002), Interview with Michael Winterbottom, www.bbc.co.uk/films/2003/03/03/michael_winterbottom_in_this_world_interview.shtm, accessed 1 July 2014.
Bennett, B. (2014), *The Cinema of Michael Winterbottom: Borders, Intimacy, Terror*, New York: Wallflower Press.
Berger, P. L. (1997), "Four faces of global culture," *National Interest*, 49 (fall): 23–30.
Conley, T. (2007), *Cartographic Cinema*, Minneapolis, MN: University of Minnesota Press.
Deleuze, G. (1990), "Postscript on the Societies of Control," *OCTOBER*, 59 (winter): 3–7.
Foucault, M. (1984), "Of Other Spaces," J. Miscowiec (trans.), *Diacritics*, 16: 22–7.
Loshitzky, Y. (2006), "Journeys of Hope to Fortress Europe," *Third Text*, 20.6: 745–54.

Roland, A. (2007), "Containers and Causality—*Box Boats: How the Container Ships Changed the World* by Brian J. Cudahy; *The Box That Changed the World: Fifty Years of Container Shipping, an Illustrated History* by Arthur Donovan; Joseph Bonney; *The Box: How the Shipping Container Made the World Smaller and the World Economy Bigger* by Marc Levinson," *Technology and Culture*, 48.2: 386–92.

Scott A. O. (2004), "A Future so Nasty, Because It's So Near," *New York Times*, 6 August, www.nytimes.com/movie/review?res=9C05E3DE123CF935A3575BC0A9629C8B63, accessed 11 August 2008.

Thacker, E. (2005), *The Global Genome: Biotechnology, Politics, and Culture*, Cambridge, MA: The MIT Press.

Filmography

Code 46 (2003), directed by Michael Winterbottom, London: BBC Films, 2004, DVD.

In this World (2002), directed by Michael Winterbottom, London: BBC Films, 2002, DVD.

13

"This is I, Hamlet the Dane!" Hamlet's Migration and Integration in the Dramatic Theater as Cyberspace

Gerrit K. Rößler
University of Virginia, USA

When Hamlet, to the great surprise of his uncle, who thinks him executed in England, appears at Ophelia's grave, he identifies himself to the astonished crowd with the words: "This is I, Hamlet the Dane!" (Shakespeare [1603] 2010: 115).[1] In doing so, he labels himself not only as the current king's stepson but the late king's son. By following the custom of using the name of the realm to refer to the ruler,[2] he also steps forward as the rightful heir to the throne. Moreover, he uses the first-person singular, rather than the royal plural, marking the transition from the medieval to the modern stage and the advent of the modern individual and humanist subjectivity (cf. Benjamin 2011). The definite article before the term that expresses his national allegiance implies that he is not just any Dane, an arbitrary subject, but the embodiment of Danishness per se. Politics, history, psychology, national and cultural identity resonate in this declaration, in the name and, as this essay will show, its performance.

The theatrical event is a complex texture, the components of which create an equally complex environment in which spectators, actors, and characters relate to and interact with one another. The play is more than just its "words, words, words" (Shakespeare 2010: 44) but a plurality of material and immaterial articulations and figurations, which are linked through Hamlet's embodiment on stage. His name, whether it labels the figure on stage or the play itself, simultaneously activates and summarizes its own appearance in whatever written, filmed, performed, orally transmitted, or critically remembered version it has survived through the ages. There is, as of now, no formal vocabulary that adequately and satisfyingly describes and assesses these connections and movements. This essay offers such a vocabulary by approaching the stage through the lens of modern computational information theory.

I argue that Hamlet (I, Hamlet) moves through this web of references, signs, and possible meanings like an avatar (iHamlet) would move through the virtual, computer-generated representation of hypertextual linkages, known as cyberspace. To be clear, I take the link between computational information technology and theater to be integral to the phenomenon of theater, rather than metaphorical. As I hope to show in these pages, theater *is* a type of cyberspace with its own specific cyberculture. As user and product of this technology "Hamlet the Dane" *is* a cyborg. He uses the informational technology of the theater with great virtuosity; the same technology that, through visits to the theater, readings of plays, histories or critical essays, gives access to a vast network to millions of users.

Hamlet is also a migrant. He crosses various geographical and historical boundaries with great transformative effect to the realms in which he appears. He is, at times, met with great suspicion and fear and, at others, welcomed as the bringer of cultural renaissance. While cultural and literary histories are, most likely, best equipped to describe these movements and impacts of migration, they fall short when it comes to describing their place in the actual theatrical experience. I believe that the approach presented in this essay offers a way to think about the theater as a physical place with a particularly high density of information, a node that gives access to these networks of information and communication, and which makes such transcultural movements possible. In cyberspace Hamlet, like his father's ghost, continues to walk the realm between life and death (between 1 and 0, between "to be or not to be") and makes his haunting appearance in the performance. Hamlet, one of the theater's most canonic figures, becomes an existential figure of the digital age.

The pioneer of applying the insights of computational technology to literary analysis, George P. Landow, of course, vehemently disagrees that drama is anything like cyberspace. In addition to Aristotle's two distinctive modes of telling and showing, "[t]he immersive video game, in which we take part as actors, is a third, fundamentally different mode. Saying that video games are like drama seems not much different from saying a cow is like a frog, except that, well, it's bigger, and it's a mammal, and it doesn't live in the water" (Landow 2006: 251). While I agree that such comparisons have to be made with great care, it is my hope that my discussion may alleviate some of his concerns. As I will demonstrate, theater, that is, live performance and not only the written dialogue, has a lot more in common with cybernetic worlds—not just video games, but all worlds created with the aid of information technology—than a frog with a cow. Theater is a lot more than just the choice between telling or showing. It is interactive and collective relations, actions, and information processing in a hybrid space.

I will outline Hamlet's migration through the theatrical cyberspace in two steps. The first and most significant one, which requires the largest leap into science-fictional territory, will be to establish the idea that theater is indeed a kind of cyberspace and to consider what the implications of this discovery are. The next step, provided the first one is successful, will follow easily: how can we think of Hamlet as a type of migrant and a cyborg?

Act I: Theater as cyberspace

Most definitions of cyberspace do not exactly conjure up images of peasants and nobility gathered in the analog reality of the Elizabethan Globe Theatre. Pramod K. Nayar states that "cyberspace describes the worlds and domains generated by digital Information and Communications Technologies (ICTs). It is a set of relations and actions in electronic space" (2010: 1). Such "relations and actions" may take a variety of forms, from online banking and wikis to chat rooms and social media. Likely the first thing that comes to mind when thinking about the theater in terms of computational environments is the concept of virtual reality. Virtual realities go beyond augmenting our experience of the actual world, as, for example, the internet and mobile telephony do. They are computer-generated three-dimensional worlds in their own right, which the user can explore and inhabit and manipulate from within (Ryan 2001: 1). Cyberspace on the other hand "projects not a continuous territory but a relatively loose net made of links and nodes, of routes and destinations, with nothing in between" as Marie-Laure Ryan puts it (73). Ryan emphasizes that virtual reality aims at the bodily experience of travel and exploration, while cyberspace, with its immediate and discontinuous representation of information, makes the user's body disappear (74). It seems that the former lends itself well to our larger discussion of migration. However, beyond the obvious comparison between virtual reality and the diegetic world of a play, I suggest looking at theater as a set of relations and actions that occur in worlds and domains generated by information and communications technology.

The idea that we as postmoderns can, and perhaps should, think about texts and textuality in terms of inter- and hypertextuality is not new. Landow opened that door in the early nineties when he pointed out that "the writings of

Roland Barthes, Jacques Derrida and other critical theorists neither caused the development of hypermedia nor coincided exactly with it. Nonetheless, their approach to textuality remains very helpful in understanding our experience of hypermedia. And vice versa" (Landow 2006: xiv). For these poststructural theorists, texts are not static, monolithic entities but dynamic textures that, as we read, constantly interact with other texts, discourses, and literary traditions. Hypertext, with its ability to directly link a word or a passage to other sources of information, which are again further linked, is, for Landow, intertextuality put in practice.

I argue that, in the case of theater, these relations and connections are much more akin to hypertext than intertext. Theater goes further than the poststructural idea of an associative chain that connects writing to endlessly decentered and interconnected semantic textures. The stage does not only reference or quote other texts, contexts and meanings, but places them directly in front of us. Like the Ghost, these other textualities come to life during the performance (in the form of acting bodies, props, buildings, etc.) as material realities that always also reference themselves. If I choose to ignore the figure of Hamlet during the performance and recognize David Tennant moving about the Shakespearean stage instead (or his most popular role, the Tenth Doctor in *Doctor Who*, appearing at the Globe as he does in the 2007 episode "The Shakespeare Code," Charles Palmer), then I am no longer experiencing intertextuality, but the more disruptive and interactive linkage of hypertextuality.

Epistemological distance

Science fiction author William Gibson is famously credited with coining the term "cyberspace" in 1984 in his seminal novel *Neuromancer*. At one point in the novel, the protagonist watches a television show for children, which explains the term as follows:

> Cyberspace. A consensual hallucination experienced daily by billions of legitimate operators, in every nation, by children being taught mathematical concepts […]. A graphic representation of data abstracted from the banks of every computer in the human system. Unthinkable complexity. Lines of light ranged in the non space [*sic*] of the mind, clusters and constellations of data. Like city lights, receding …
>
> Gibson 1984: 51

Cyberspace, this passage suggests, can only be experienced voluntarily and consensually, with full knowledge of its alternative status. This epistemological twist, the alterity of the experience, is crucial for the definition of cyberspace and virtual reality. Without a sense of difference between the physical world of the user and the immaterial realm of virtual experience, cyberspace would simply be reality; epistemologically no different from the reality we are experiencing normally. We can be immersed into cyberspace, forget that it is an alternative reality, lose ourselves, but, like Gibson's protagonist, we are cruelly reminded when biological needs or technological failure pull us back into the world we have come to think of as our "reality."

Theater operates with the same epistemological distance. No amount of immersion into the world of the play will let us permanently forget that we are, indeed, watching a play. Even the most sophisticated illusion comes to an end when the lights go up and we leave the theater. As Hamlet notes before the Dumb Show begins, we "must be idle" (Shakespeare 2010: 64) during the performance in order to maintain this distance, which makes the hallucination both consensual and voluntary. Of course, he breaks with this requirement when he speaks up, interrupts the players, comments on the action and, in Ophelia's words, becomes "as good as a chorus" (69). As the young prince interacts with the world of the play within the play, he decreases the distance between the world of the audience and the world of that play, as well as the play that bears his name. He furthermore breaks the illusion that the world of the play is an independent and hermetically sealed reality.

Marie-Laure Ryan argues that throughout the history of the institution of the theater there have been very different ideas with regard to whether or not theater should (or can) be an interactive or immersive experience at all (2001: 295–305). An interactive experience is one in which the audience can influence the action on stage and is simultaneously aware of itself as something distinct from the world of the play. An immersive experience is one where the audience loses itself in the world of the play and forgets about the existence of actors or other audience members. The darkened auditorium is an extension of the world on stage, from which we secretly and quietly observe the action. That is, until a noisy candy wrapper, a cough, or the omnipresent cell phone disrupt the immersion and painfully raise our awareness of the other spectators. Historically, as Ryan demonstrates, various eras and traditions have alternatively and impossibly tried to approach absolute immersion or absolute interaction.[3]

Even the most sporadic theater attendees can attest that passive immersion and active interaction remain unattainable extremes. To think about staged events as illusory reality means accepting theatrical customs—such as painted backdrops, objects lowered from wires, ghosts—as part of an alternative reality, with its own laws and conventions. The hallucination of the Ghost is therefore limited to the space of the theater and, to use Gibson's terms, consensual. In contrast to Plato's cave, where the onlookers are prevented from peeking behind the stage and so take the shadow play for the world itself rather than its representation, theater audiences perceive the world of the theater as theater, whilst collectively agreeing on the laws of theatrical presentation. Hamlet, in his role of editor, producer, and director of the pantomime and "The Mousetrap," understands this difference very well. Leading up to his call for idleness, he gives a litany of suggestions to the players. He recommends that actors behave "as 'twere the mirror up to nature" but that they do so in a fashion that is not "overdone or come tardy off" (Shakespeare 2010: 62) but appropriate to the rhetorical conventions of theater. His advocacy of Aristotelian mimesis is particularly peculiar in light of the odd language of Shakespeare's works and, by extension, of Hamlet's own writing. They are highly stylized imitations of language and behavior at court and far from a mirror to nature. Instead, they maintain the conscious distance between the world of the play and the world of the audience. Like the worlds of cyberspace, the theatrical illusion can never be total, or else it becomes like the protagonist's simulated environment in Philip K. Dick's *Time out of Joint* (1959)—just another reality for those who inhabit it.[4]

That the conceptual distance between the stage and the audience, cyberspace and its user, needs to be maintained in order to be recognized as play or cyberspace respectively, does not mean that there is a clear and stable boundary between the two. The characters in Shakespeare's play spend much of their time conceiving plots with the intention to figure out the plots of others. It is precisely because they cannot determine whether Hamlet is legitimately mad or just pretending, that Polonius eavesdrops on the prince. It is precisely because Hamlet cannot know whether his uncle is guilty of the murder of the late king and whether Gertrude was involved in the crime that he stages the play within a play. Hamlet is a user of information technology, a superuser—that is, with privileged access to the network. Hamlet, above all, is in possession of information so secret that it causes the downfall of Denmark and its usurpation by Norway. All of this happens because spectators are unable to tell acting from genuine motivation, simulation from fact. The amount of scholarship that has been spent on the question of Hamlet's madness indicates that audiences still cannot say with certainty.

Experienced theatergoers know what it is like to wonder "is this part of the production or is this real?" The world of the play and the world of the audience bleed into one another frequently and often change the experience of the performance dramatically. Interactive plays such as *Sleep No More*, an immersive production of *Macbeth* by the British Punchdrunk theater company, which continues to draw audiences in London and New York into a world of witches, ghosts, and murder, blur this line even further. Like many cybernetic spaces, from shopping sites to role-playing games and first-person shooters, such performances offer the audience a tremendous amount of involvement and agency.

Suspended materiality of the stage

N. Katherine Hayles points out that the electromagnetic patterns that form the building blocks of cyberspace are concealed from our experience and need to be transformed and represented by computer software in such a way that we can interact with them: "Existing in the nonmaterial space of computer simulation, cyberspace defines a regime of representation within which pattern in the essential reality, presence an optical illusion" (1999: 36). I suggest that Hayles' assessment of cyberspace is essentially true for the theater as well. Let me give two reasons.

First, on a technological level, cybertechnology is just as rooted in its present material and temporal realities as theater. Bert States reminds us of the chance "that an act of sexual congress between two so-called signs [on stage] will produce a real pregnancy" (1983: 373). Intercourse between two virtual bodies, on the other hand, will not. Yet, I do believe it is more complicated than that. In Gibson's aforementioned novel *Neuromancer*, cyber cowboys, hired hackers who operate in the virtual world of cyberspace, are in danger of something called "flatlining": the death of the biological body while the user's consciousness occupies cyberspace. Death in the simulated world, Gibson seems to suggest, may cause death offline. In our world, tabloids frequently report addiction to online games, broken relationships, lost jobs, and financial ruin, all because users did not maintain the social and physical well-being of the bio-component. To my knowledge, such real-life impacts of cyberspace are much more frequent than children being conceived on stage. The point is, the strict separation of the world of the user and the simulated world is itself an illusion, just as the separation between the world of the audience and the world of the stage.

Second, on a semiotic level, the stage dissolves its own materiality in the process of signification and representation in the same way cyber technology does. The building blocks of "reality on stage—the playwright's text, the actor's acting, the stage lighting—all these things in every case stand for other things," as Jindřich Honzl says (1998: 269), Long before the digital age comes into its own, the author seems to suggest that a certain amount of abstraction from the specific material and temporal particulars of the performance is essential in order for it to become theater. Honzl's classic theory is fairly self-evident if we think about the fact that, on stage, Richard Burton does not stand for Richard Burton as much as for Prince Hamlet (and, in turn, Hamlet stands for a whole series of other things). It is a little less clear when we think about props, such as a crown, which does indeed stand for a crown. However, it does not stand for the particular crown presented on stage during a particular performance, but becomes *the* crown, an instance of crown per se, a symbol of monarchy, perhaps its past, present, and future. Imagine a production of *Hamlet* that features a crown, obviously made of cardboard, or other ill-fitting materials, with the intent to expose the mechanisms of theatrical illusion and alienate the audience to assume a critical and reflective distance to the play. Even in such a production, this crown of "shreds and patches" (Shakespeare 2010: 81) would stand not for itself but for the conceptual weight behind it.

It becomes clear that Shakespeare and his audiences indeed thought about the stage as a place of such suspended materiality if we look more closely at the figure of the Ghost—and the Elizabethan stage is full of ghosts. The Ghost is a non-material apparition in the diegetic world of the play. In Act III, when only Hamlet can see the Ghost, while his mother Gertrude cannot, the actress playing Gertrude can certainly see the actor playing the Ghost. Within the world of the play, only Hamlet can interact with the Ghost and decode its data. Of course, so can the audience, but only if they enter the theatrical cyberspace, where they, like Hamlet, become cyborgs: hybrids of biological body and theatrical technology. As readers or moviegoers, they would have no access to the full spectrum of signification. While the body of the actor playing the Ghost has a very material presence for the audience, it has to be simultaneously absent. The Ghost speaks to us only if we see beyond the material limits of the actor. Only then is it a "bodiless creation" that "is the very coinage of [one's] brain" (82). The Ghost is haunting the text as material signifier in the printed version of the play, but this basic code needs to be interpreted on the next level in a chain of codes: the stage. Only the performance allows us access to the virtual embodiments of the text.

To be sure, I am not advocating a simple equation between the object on stage and its intended or unintended referent. The relationship between the signifier on stage and its signified is not one-to-one. The stage is not an analog medium that reproduces its referent in the way a typewriter does, but rather a digital one, like a computer. A single keystroke on a typewriter produces an imprint of a single letter on the paper. A stronger keystroke produces a darker letter, etc. The written text is a direct analog result of my manual labor. With digital computational technology, however, this direct link is broken (Kittler 1999). The multisensory text of the theater is not produced by one single technology nor by a single mind. Like film, it is the interplay of various technologies and sign systems, but unlike film, there is no apparatus like a camera to arrest this interplay and turn it into a singular reproducible artifact. Instead, like digital media, the totality of the play is made of discrete units (narrative and material) that can (for example, in rehearsal) be broken down into and stored as discontinuous data that is related to, but not directly analogous to, the performance. Props, print editions, even admission tickets, are digitized representations of the play, which are then processed into more or less continuous information by the cybernetic machine that is the theater.

Hive-mind theater

The passage from Gibson's novel quoted above implies that, in order to be experienced at all, cyberspace depends on the active contribution of its users and "billions of legitimate operators" (Gibson 1984: 51). For Hayles this collective agency is one of cyberspace's defining characteristics: "Network users collaborate in creating the richly textured landscape of cyberspace" (1999: 36). Without a central entry point or origin, cyberspace gives equal agency to its users. It is extremely malleable and dynamic, which allows for highly individual and unique experiences that are, for the most part, impossible to repeat in exactly the same way. The stage, too, operates as a "multicoded, multidimensional, and pluralistic new textual system" (Carlson 1990: 96). Marvin Carlson's description of the complex semiotic texture of the theatrical spectacle highlights the fact that every event that occurs in the theater becomes part of the overall spectacle, while at the same time breaking the spectacle up into what he calls a "psychic polyphony" (103). Like cyberspace, the theater signifies on a—potentially infinite—number of code systems (props, clothes, sound, movement, written signs, music, projections, etc.).

Theater allows its audiences a great deal of autonomy when it comes to deciding where to direct one's attention. This includes the performers, who also observe the action from their respective vantage points. Do I watch Hamlet or do I inspect Polonius hiding behind the arras? Do I look at the Ghost or do I peek at the stage machinery that creates the illusion of a king rising from the grave? Moreover, whose inner self do I choose to imagine? Whose psyche is expressed at a given moment? Is Hamlet a kind of avatar for the actor's (or actress') own personality, or is he a kind of "Idoru" with its own artificial intelligence and agency, brought to life by the technology of the theater?[5] The idea of psychic polyphony refers precisely to our inability to make that distinction, which makes each spectator's experience of the play radically unique and non-communicable to other spectators. Cyberspace, the experiential environment created by computational technology, is just such a psychically polyphonic realm.

All these distinct but interconnected minds and objects at work in the theater possess the processing power of numerous biological and high-capacity RAM (random-access memory) units, networked into a complex machine that stores and accesses large amounts of cultural memory. For Marvin Carlson, the stage is literally a "memory machine" that recycles its own materialities (props, costumes, buildings, special effects, sounds, etc.) and is haunted by ghosts of productions past (actresses, actors, directors, writers, audiences, etc.).

Each of these production elements are also, to a striking degree, composed of material "that we have seen before," and the memory of that recycled material as it moves through new and different productions contributes in no small measure to the richness and density of the operations of theater in general as a site of memory, both personal and cultural (3).

Users of cyberspace access these memory banks, whenever they activate the building blocks of Gibson's "consensual hallucination" in performance. Hamlet is aware that the Ghost, that is, the dead king who haunts the performance of his substitutes Hamlet and Claudius, will only be remembered as long as "memory holds a place in this distracted globe" (Shakespeare 2010: 30). "Globe," in this context, alludes to Hamlet's skull, the world as a whole, and the Globe Theatre, where the Ghost appears on stage night after night. It is, in other words, essential to the very idea of theater that it functions as an access point to various types of memory. It is the foundation of its operation as a cybernetic network.

Theater and cyberspace, in other words, are profoundly collective cultural phenomena. As such they fundamentally challenge the notion of autonomous human subjectivity and agency. In Gibson's novel the users' biological bodies are hooked up to electronic consoles or implanted with digital enhancements. Only as such hybrids can they experience digital worlds. Even now, cybernetic technology is fundamentally integrated into our present biological existence, blurring the lines between "natural" and "artificial." Hayles suggests that we, as self-aware subjects, have always existed in a state she calls posthumanity (1999). The posthuman is characterized by its hybrid existence, cognizing the world with the aid of technological and artificial enhancements, of which, I suggest, the theater is one. Rather than seated in an autonomous mind in control of a more or less altered and enhanced body, subjectivity is a byproduct of various cognitive processes, which occur not just in the brain but throughout our biological and technological extensions. Hayles calls this process "distributed cognition" (4). In her view, cognition and thinking always involve human and nonhuman actors.

We find the concept of distributed cognition already seeded in Gibson. The experience of cyberspace, does not happen "*in* the computer" or even "*on* the television" but in the "non space of the mind." Cyberspace is not a material object external to the human body, nor is it internal to a single autonomous subjectivity. It involves data from "every computer in the human system," which includes both technological and biological embodiments of distributed cognitive processing power. As a product of this distributed cognition and biotechnological hybridity, Hamlet is less example of the autonomous Cartesian subject, touted by humanist readings of the play, but an example of the posthuman.

Hamletmachine

Psychic polyphony and haunting memory in the theater hinge on the fact that I cannot have theater without at least one person observing another person acting. This acting person, of course, is always also observing. The knowledge that at least one person or object takes on a role that goes beyond themselves is implied, even guaranteed, by the institution of the theater. The theater is, like cyberspace, a radically collective practice that involves semiotic conventions, which are specific to this practice and limited to the space in which it takes place. From this, Benjamin Bennett develops the idea that dramatic theater is

> an agent of collective thinking with relation to structures in culture that must be regarded as products of continuing human thought, but thought of a type that cannot be adequately enacted in an individual mind: structures ranging from mass-psychological phenomena, such as fads, to culturally definitive pursuits, such as "poetry," and on up to the phenomena of religion.
>
> Bennett 2011: 22

The argument here is not that we cannot think about these radically social phenomena as individuals. Instead, like Carlson, Bennett suggests that the theater functions as a "thinking machine" (2011: 9). In Bennett's case, it is not a machine for memory storage and access, but one in which the audience thinks these "unthinkable" phenomena, collectively and deeply rooted in the present moment, without any of the nominalist and prescriptive tendencies of other types of cultural analysis. This is possible simply because the experience of the analyst does not stand in for that of another but is merely one in a multitude of simultaneous experiences that, in the material immediacy of the theater, form a network of distributed cognition.

In the case of our Danish prince, the machine thinks the problem of fate. Hamlet, in Bennett's reading, appears to understand that he is doomed to die. As a consequence, he neither tries to escape his fate, which would of course render the knowledge of his allegedly certain future false, nor does he passively give in to it. Instead, he lives the interim—between the Ghost's appearance that affords him a glimpse into his impending doom and his eventual death at the hands of Laertes—by filling it with a series of inconsequential actions that have no effect on the inevitable outcome of his life within the five acts of the play. For Bennett, it is precisely in these inconsequential actions that the audience can collectively think the cultural concept of fate: "Hamlet affords us the indirect view of a thinking that neither he nor the actor who plays him, nor we in the auditorium, can ever experience directly as individuals, but which is still constantly carried out by the institution in which all of us participate, the theater as thinking machine" (2011: 14). If we take Bennett and Carlson seriously in their assessment that theater is a kind of machine, then we must think of Hamlet, Horatio, and Ophelia as cyborgs: hybrid constructs of biological bodies and artificial technology.

Bennett argues elsewhere that whenever characters announce their interiority, for example, in Shakespearian soliloquies, the theater reveals interiority as a problem, insofar as it is understood as a positive and communicable presence. The dramatic stage reveals "the truth that the individual human self is not a naturally given unit but rather an artificial composite, cobbled together out of gestures that are developed in the course of theatrical tradition" (Bennett 2005: 166). As audience, we may be under the illusion that we can see beyond this performative surface of gestures and "words, words, words." These words and gestures are in a way the computational source code, processed by the theatrical machine. After all, the world on the stage is codified by words, not by autonomous subjectivities, a lesson Rosencrantz and Guildenstern learn the hard way when "words, words, words" cause their execution. Interiority is not a presence we can observe or that can be communicated to us. Rather, it is produced by cognitive processes, distributed in the hive-mind theater. Hamlet's cyborg body brings to our attention that we have no access to other interiorities, or even proof of their existence, except via the theater as collective and thus radically decentered machine. Hamlet (text, performance, body) is what Hayles calls the "progeny of the fascinating and troubling coupling of language and machine" (1999: 32).

When Hamlet identifies himself as "the Dane," he does not and cannot express or communicate a positive identity that may relate to a kind of internal presence of "Danishness." Like subjectivity in Hayles' concept of distributed cognition and interiority in Bennett's concept of interiority in the theater, identity is an effect, a byproduct of posthuman interaction. The figure of the Danish prince is but one instance where these concepts are revealed as such. Hamlet's self-labeling remains a hollow and unsuccessful attempt at securing a claim to a stable and communicable identity. He is, after all, not the only one who claims to be the Dane, or Denmark. The Ghost is also identified in this manner, when Hamlet first encounters him: "I'll call thee Hamlet, King, father, royal Dane" (Shakespeare 2010: 26). As is Claudius, for example, when Hamlet calls him "incestuous, damned Dane" (127). Polonius is ever so briefly identified as the King of Denmark, after he gains unauthorized access to the Queen's chambers, exercising a right that only the King should have. Identity is not a matter of interiority or even name-label: "I *am* the Dane!" Instead, identity is, as Judith Butler (1990) argues, communicable only in performance: following Butler, "I *act* in a way a Dane is supposed to!" In cyberspace, identity is legible in terms of access-clearance. How you are able to identify yourself to the system has nothing to do with interiority, but with what kind of information (credit card numbers, PINs, passports) you possess. "I pretend to be the Dane and I pass as such!" Polonius' death is as much a matter of mistaken identity as of identity theft. Identity and interiority are effects of reading: of reading bodies in performance.

If we agree that it is possible—and useful—to think about the theater as a kind of cyberspace, then, as promised, the following steps are easy. I will outline a few possible ways of putting the new media approach to use without any claim to completeness. A full description of all the cybernetic links and nodes that the play opens up would by far exceed the scope of this essay. It would also require us to attend an actual production, as the accessible data varies from user to user, from performance to performance.

Act II: Hamlet as migrant and cyborg

"This is I, Hamlet the Dane!" Does it really need saying at the grave of his former lover, in front of the son of the prince's first and all of his future victims? At this point in the play, the audience is well aware of who he is and where he was born. Perhaps he feels it necessary because his journey to England nearly cost him his life. First he is threatened by the forces of Norway, at war with Denmark over a "little patch of ground that hath in it no profit but the name" (Shakespeare 2010: 91), and then by his uncle's plot, in which he tries to have Hamlet killed on foreign soil with the help of a foreign sovereign: "Do it, England" (90). He was supposed to be deleted from the network, an impossibility, of course, as he is restored at each curtain call and his information too vast and stored in too many places to ever be completely erased. Hamlet is Big Data. He escaped deletion only by an act of clever relabeling and rewriting of program code, dispensing of the corrupted files 'Rosencrantz and Guildenstern' in the process. Such adaptiveness is sign of a true, self-enhancing, artificial intelligence. And let us also not forget that it was during his absence in Wittenberg, at the center of reformation in Germany, that his father was killed and the political order at home disrupted. His statement reaffirms his place in the structure (he is back at court in Denmark) and challenges the structure itself (he claims the throne). It references his conflicted identity as it states his autonomy from ("It is I"), and integration into, the system ("the Dane"). The statement encapsulates his status as migrant and cyborg.

Hamlet's transnational and transtemporal migration happens both in cyber-space and in analog space. A brief sketch of his pattern of migration might look something like this. He likely begins his journey in the Mediterranean, haunted by Oedipus the King and Electra the parricidal princess. From there, he migrates via Italy and the Roman stages to Scandinavia, where he becomes Amleth, both national myth and historical figure. Via Thomas Kyd's controversial *Ur-Hamlet*, the prince finds his way to England and finally into the Globe Theatre in Elizabethan London. Initially an immigrant, a foreign body to the London stage, Hamlet becomes a resident alien: Hamlet, the Brit! There, as Carl Schmitt (2008) believes, the Dane poses a thinly veiled allegorical challenge to the legitimacy of both Queen Elizabeth and her rival Mary Stuart. At a time where national iden-tity is not determined so much by territory but the body of the ruler, his very presence at the court of Elsinore, a haunting reminder of the murdered king, brings the Danish nation, as it exists in the virtual space of the theater, to the brink of destruction. From there, he moves on to Germany, where his foreignness is perceived as a perfect challenge to the dominant French court drama and comes to haunt Goethe's *Willhelm Meister* (1795/96) and his attempts at conceiving a national German theater. Walter Benjamin (2011) thought of Hamlet as the modern, alienated human being, Jacques Lacan (1982) read *Hamlet* as a psychoanalytical play of desire, Simon Critchley and Jamieson Webster (2013) as a comment on the paradox of the modern human condition—and there are many more.

Cyborg Hamlet remains the eternal migrant, who haunts and is haunted by various literary traditions, criticism, and philosophy all over the world. For Marvin Carlson, *Hamlet* is an especially haunting and haunted phenomenon:

> Our critical and theoretical memories are haunted by *Hamlet*, as Shakespeare in general and *Hamlet* in particular have occupied a central position in critical thought for the last two centuries, a situation that has not changed at all even with the development of the most recent, most iconoclastic critical approaches, such as feminist theory, queer theory, new historicism and cultural materialism.
>
> Carlson 2001: 79

What the various readings, rewritings, appropriations, and stagings have in common is that they are all users of the theater as cyberspace with "the Dane" as their access point. *Hamlet* (the play, the character, the history) opens up this web of interpretations, readings, variations, and rewritings. It functions as an interface by which we can access this web, move around in it and "log in." Most critical editions of Shakespeare's play provide a snapshot of the vast structure of such textual inter-relations and their genealogies surrounding the figure of Hamlet. Some, like the comprehensive compendium by Robert S. Miola for Norton, also include surveys of literary criticism, cultural histories, performance practices, and extracts of works that inspired or were inspired by the Danish prince. Under the title "Imagining *Hamlet*" Miola provides a concise twenty-two page introduction that constitutes a taxonomy of the intertextual and historical links that show Hamlet (the historical figure and dramatic character, the written drama and the concept of the drama, the totality of performances and particular experiences of the play, etc.) as a complex hypertext and the theater as cyberspace (Miola 2010: xi–xxxiii).

Hamlet travels and migrates across national borders and into national literary and philosophical traditions at a time where these traditions begin to shape the very notion of nationality. For Benedict Anderson (1991) it is the sudden avail-ability of the printed word in the sixteenth century, especially the writings of the Reformation coming out of Wittenberg (Hamlet's place of education!) that accelerated the division of Europe into communities that were bound by a sense of shared cultural identity rather than the political influence of the sovereign alone. Anderson suggests that, for the first time, readers imagined themselves as part of a community with other readers they could not personally know (Anderson 1991). In the process, they created cultural allegiances that were as imaginary as they were real in their social and political impact.

Anderson focuses on the printed word for his argument and remains largely silent about the role of the dramatic stage. Perhaps it is the boundless virtual mobility of the theater and the unpredictable permutations of performance that save Hamlet from being beholden to any particular national identity. While Goethe's Wilhelm Meister aspires to become part of a national literature, safe-guarded by an elusive and secret society of readers, Hamlet is, for the duration of the performance, part of a community of a concrete body of people at a concrete point in space and time. Each audience, each performance, will produce their own Hamlet. As T. S. Eliot suggests, interpreters of Hamlet tend to find them-selves in the play and in the character (1998: 55), furthering his migratory pattern and expanding the cybernetic network through the technology of the theater.

The rest is silence, or is it?

In this essay I focused on the singular example of Shakespeare's *Hamlet*. I do believe, however, that all theater, even very localized one-night-only perform-ances of obscure plays, constitutes this type of information technology and taps into the networks and structures described above. While Hamlet's status as migrating cyborg may be particularly well pronounced, the informational and communicational links that actors, audiences, critics, sets, and buildings create, always make such migration possible. Upon Hamlet's death, Horatio is tasked with telling the story of Hamlet all over again and to continue the data stream from one performance to the next. It appears that, when it's all over and the lights go on in the house, the rest is not silence after all.

Notes

1   All page references refer to the Norton Critical Edition of the play, edited by Robert Miola (2010).

2   With variation the play's characters refer to different sovereigns as Denmark, Norway, England, and Poland.

3   Ryan names, among others, Bertolt Brecht and Antonin Artaud as examples for each end of the spectrum. Brecht's epic theater was designed to create distance from and reflection on the action on stage, while simultaneously making the audience active participants in the theatrical event. Artaud on the other hand created almost ritualistic events aimed at immersing the audience into the action and erasing the lines between performance and spectatorship (2001: 302).

4   The protagonist Ragle Gumm believes he lives in a quiet American suburb in 1959 until he finds out that his familiar environment is an elaborate simulation put on by aliens. The title is obviously a reference to the scene in *Hamlet*, in which Horatio seems to suggest that after the Ghost's revelations it has become impossible to perceive the world as before. The same goes for Gumm after he discovers his alien captors.

5   In William Gibson's novel of the same name, an Idoru is a virtual mega star whose artificial intelligence exists entirely in cyberspace (Gibson 1996).

References

Anderson, B. R. O. (1991), *Imagined Communities: Reflections on the Origin and Spread of Nationalism*, London: Verso.

Benjamin, W. (2011), *Ursprung des deutschen Trauerspiels*, Frankfurt am Main: Suhrkamp.

Bennett, B. (2005), *All Theater is Revolutionary Theater*, Ithaca, NY: Cornell University Press.

Bennett, B. (2011), "The Thinking Machine," *Revue Internationale de Philosophie*, 255.1: 7–26.

Butler, J. (1990), *Gender Trouble: Feminism and the Subversion of Identity*, New York: Routledge.

Carlson, M. A. (1990), *Theater Semiotics: Signs of Life*, Bloomington, IN: Indiana University Press.

Carlson, M. A. (2001), *The Haunted Stage: The Theatre as Memory Machine,* Ann Arbor, MI: University of Michigan Press.

Critchley, S. and Webster, J. (2013), *The Hamlet Doctrine*, London: Verso.

Dick, P. K. ([1959] 2002), *Time out of Joint*, New York: Vintage Books.

Eliot, T. S. (1998), *The Sacred Wood and Major Early Essays*, Mineola, NY: Dover Publications.

Gibson, W. (1984), *Neuromancer,* New York: Ace Books.

Gibson, W. (1996), *Idoru*, New York: Berkley Books.

Hayles, N. K. (1999), *How We Became Posthuman: Virtual Bodies in Cybernetics, Literature, and Informatics*, Chicago: University of Chicago Press.

Honzl, J. (1998), "Dynamics of the sign in the theater," in G. W. Brandt (ed.), *Modern Theories of Drama*, New York: Oxford University Press.

Kittler, F. A. (1999), *Gramophone, Film, Typewriter*, G. Winthrop-Young and M. Wutz (trans), Stanford, CA: Stanford University Press.

Lacan, J. (1982), "Desire and the Interpretation of Desire in *Hamlet*," in S. Felman (ed.), *Literature and Psychoanalysis: The Question of Reading Otherwise*, Baltimore, MD: Johns Hopkins University Press.

Landow, G. P. (2006), *Hypertext 3.0: Critical Theory and New Media in an Era of Globalization*, Baltimore, MD: Johns Hopkins University Press.

Miola, R. S. (2010), "Imagining *Hamlet*," in R. S. Miola (ed.), *Hamlet*, New York: W. W. Norton.

Nayar, P. K. (2010), *The New Media and Cybercultures Anthology*, Chichester: Wiley-Blackwell.

Ryan, M.-L. (2001), *Narrative as Virtual Reality: Immersion and Interactivity in Literature and Electronic Media*, Baltimore, MD: Johns Hopkins University Press.

Schmitt, C. (2008), *Hamlet oder Hekuba: der Einbruch der Zeit in das Spiel*, Stuttgart, Klett-Cotta.

Shakespeare, W. ([1603] 2010), *Hamlet*, R. S. Miola (ed.), New York: W. W. Norton.

States, B. O. (1983), "The Dog on the Stage: Theater as Phenomenon," *New Literary History*, 14.2: 373–88.

Index

The letter n after a number indicates this refers to a note.

Sonnenfeld, Barry
   Men in Black 14
soul, the 43, 45–6, 48, 58, 61, 66, 196–8,
   201–2
Space Race 145
Stephenson, Neal
   Snow Crash 129
Sterling, Bruce 204–6
subculture 174, 199
subject formation 60, 107, 155, 162, 165,
   168, 175, 184
Suvin, Darko 32, 50–1n, 73, 80–1, 96, 122,
   176, 177–8n
Swift, Jonathan 4, 38, 40, 42

Tawada, Yoko 7, 73–88
   Adventures in German Grammar 74
   "Canned Foreign" 77, 80, 83, 85
   "From Mother Tongue to Linguistic
     Mother" 78, 80, 85–7
   Talisman 7, 73–8, 80–4, 87, 89n
   Where Europe Begins 74, 81
technology 19, 39–40, 45, 53n, 84, 147–48,
   177n, 195, 211, 228–9, 232–8, 242
Tennant, David 230
Thacker, Eugene 219
theater 9, 42, 47, 81, 87, 105, 108, 228–42,
   243n
   Noh 166
translation 7, 13–14, 26, 31–2, 42, 73, 83,
   87, 110, 165, 167, 177, 220
transnationalism xiii, 2, 6, 8–10, 31, 73–74,
   82–3, 86, 141, 191, 211, 240
travel literature xii–iii, xv, 2, 4, 6, 8, 31–2,
   38, 74, 76, 81–4, 87–8, 89n, 197, 213,
   241
Trujillo Muñoz, Gabriel 8
   "Cajunia" 130, 133–5

utopia(n) 5, 6, 8, 32–4, 38, 40, 46,
   50–3n, 83, 98–9, 129–31,
   133–9, 144, 177n, 183, 185,
   190, 198
utopianism 122, 201

Van Zon, Gabrielle 33
Vint, Sheryl 163
virtuality 8, 74, 82–6, 142, 147–8,
   198, 228–34, 240, 243n
Voltaire 4
   L'ingénu 75
   Micromégas 38

Waldenfels, Bernhard 4
The War of the Worlds (film)
   Spielberg, 2005 18
Weimar Republic 7, 58, 67
Weller, Archie 182
   "Going Home" 9, 187–93, 193n
Wells, Herbert George 5, 15–26,
   27–8n, 38
   The Time Machine 7, 31, 41–3,
     50n
   The War of the Worlds 7, 14, 51n,
     161, 177n
Wenders, Wim 81–2, 88
   Tokyo- Ga 82, 89n
Wilhelmine Empire 7, 58, 68, 70n
Winterbottom, Michael 9, 209–3,
   224n
   In this World 210–16, 222–3
   Code 46 210–11, 216–23

Zamyatin, Yevgeny 7, 44–5
   We 32, 46–9, 129
Zionism 24, 67, 70n
Zipes, Jack 59–67, 70n